Manifest Ambition

MANIFEST AMBITION

James K. Polk and Civil-Military Relations during the Mexican War

JOHN C. PINHEIRO

In War and in Peace: U.S. Civil-Military Relations
David S. Heidler and Jeanne T. Heidler, General Editors

Praeger Security International
Westport, Connecticut · London

Library of Congress Cataloging-in-Publication Data

Pinheiro, John C.
    Manifest ambition: James K. Polk and civil-military relations during the Mexican War /
John C. Pinheiro.
        p. cm.—(In war and in peace: U.S. civil-military relations, ISSN 1556–8504)
    Includes bibliographical references and index.
    ISBN 0–275–98409–5 (alk. paper)
1. Polk, James K. (James Knox), 1795–1849—Political and social views. 2. Polk, James K.
(James Knox), 1795–1849—Military leadership. 3. Civil-military relations—United States—
History—19th century. 4. Jackson, Andrew, 1767–1845—Influence. 5. United States—Politics
and government—1845–1849. 6. Mexican War, 1846–1848—Causes. 7. Mexican War,
1846–1848—Social aspects. 8. United States. Army—History—Mexican War, 1846–1848.
9. Soldiers—United States—History—19th century. 10. Presidents—United States—Biography.
I. Title.
E417.P56 2007
973.6'1092—dc22   2006038814

British Library Cataloguing in Publication Data is available.

Library of Congress Catalog Card Number: 2006038814
ISBN-10: 0–275–98409–5
ISBN-13: 978–0–275–98409–0
ISSN: 1556–8504

First published in 2007

Praeger Security International, 88 Post Road West, Westport, CT 06881
An imprint of Greenwood Publishing Group, Inc.
www.praeger.com

Printed in the United States of America

The paper used in this book complies with the
Permanent Paper Standard issued by the National
Information Standards Organization (Z39.48–1984).

10 9 8 7 6 5 4 3 2 1

For Anthony Drath,
a great teacher

Contents

Series Foreword

No other aspect of a nation's political health is as important as the relationship between its government and military. At the most basic level, the necessity of protecting the country from external and internal threats must be balanced by the obligation to preserve fundamental civil liberties. The United States is unique among nations, for it has successfully maintained civilian control of its military establishment, doing so from a fundamental principle institutionalized in its Constitution and embraced by its citizens. The United States has thus avoided the military coup that elsewhere has always meant the end of representative government and the extinguishing of individual freedom. The American military is the servant of citizens, not their master.

This series presents the work of eminent scholars to explain as well as assess civil-military relations in U.S. history. The American tradition of a military controlled by civilians is venerable—George Washington established it when he accepted his commission from the Continental Congress in 1775—but we will see how military leaders have not always been sanguine about abdicating important decisions to those they regard as inexperienced amateurs. And while disagreements between the government and the military become more likely during wars, there is more to this subject than the institutional arrangements of subordination and obedience that mark the relationship of government authorities and the uniformed services. The public's evolving perception of the military is also a central part of this story. In these volumes we will see explored the fine line between dissent and loyalty in war and peace and how the government and the armed forces have balanced civil liberties against national security. From the years of the American Revolution to the present, the resort to military justice has always been an option for safeguarding domestic welfare, but it has always been legally controversial and generally unpopular.

The United States relies on civilians to serve as most of its warriors during major conflicts, and civilian appreciation of things military understandably changes during such episodes. Opinions about the armed services transform accordingly, usually from casual indifference to acute concern. And through it all, military and civilian efforts to sustain popular support for the armed forces and mobilize enthusiasm for its operations have been imperative, especially when the military has been placed in the vague role of peacekeeper far from home for extended periods. The changing threats that America has confronted throughout its history have tested its revered traditions of civil-military relations, yet Americans have met even the most calamitous challenges without damaging those traditions. The most successful representative democracy in the world has defended itself without losing its way. We are hopeful that the volumes in this series will not only explain why but will also help to ensure that those vital traditions Americans rightly celebrate will endure.

David S. Heidler and Jeanne T. Heidler,
General Editors

Acknowledgments

I began writing this book while I was assistant editor of the *Papers of George Washington* at the University of Virginia and finished it as assistant professor of history at Aquinas College. During my journey between these two institutions, many people contributed to my writing of this book. They did so in a variety of ways, and I gratefully acknowledge them here: Jason Duncan, Chad Gunnoe, James Guba, Frank Grizzard, Jr., Kris Ray, Paul Bergeron, Wayne Cutler, Dan Feller, Kurt Piehler, Philip C. Davis, Jr., John D. Fowler, Ben Severance, Mark Williams, Jeanne Heidler, David Heidler, Heather Staines, Adam Kane, Jack S. Lewis, and SBM.

I would like to thank Aquinas College for awarding me two successive faculty development grants to help fund my travel and research. I am grateful also to the kind, helpful staffs at the Huntington Library in Pasadena, California; the Special Collections Library at the University of Texas at Arlington; the Tennessee State Library and Archives in Nashville, Tennessee; Alderman Library at the University of Virginia; the University of Tennessee Special Collections Library; the Filson Historical Society in Louisville, Kentucky; the Wisconsin Historical Society Library at the University of Wisconsin-Madison; the National Archives and Records Administration; and Asman Photo Service in Washington, D.C.

Finally, I wish to thank my wife, Cassandra, for her love, support, and especially for her not-so-subtle encouragements to finish this book on time.

Introduction

In 1835 the French aristocrat Alexis de Tocqueville, having toured the United States a few years earlier to assess its democracy and explain its longevity and prosperity, argued in *Democracy in America* that "in the midst of a great war" either liberty or the American Union would crumble beneath the weight of the "absurd and destructive doctrines," codified in federal and state constitutions and in law, that governed relations among the U.S. Army, the U.S. government, state governments, and the militia. But all was not lost, however, for America's saving grace, according to Tocqueville, would be its isolation "from the rest of the world" and from equally powerful nations "as if it were surrounded by water on all sides....The great good fortune of the United States is therefore not to have hit upon a federal constitution that enables it to endure a great war," Tocqueville concluded, "but rather to be so situated that it need not fear such a war." Still, at some point in the distant future when "the Union comes into contact with the empire of Mexico...great wars will probably come from that quarter."[1] What might happen then to liberty and the Union, he did not say.

A mere 10 years after Tocqueville wrote these words, the United States annexed Texas, and the following year, 1846, it declared war on Mexico following a skirmish between American and Mexican soldiers in disputed territory along the north bank of the Rio Grande. Rather than present another chronological retelling of the Mexican War of 1846–1848, *Manifest Ambition: James K. Polk and Civil-Military Relations during the Mexican War* examines civil-military relations during this war in light of Jacksonian politics and doctrines, American beliefs about how best to preserve liberty, and the citizen soldier tradition. The impact of Jacksonian democracy, with its populism, "spoils system," inherent emphasis on territorial expansion, and doctrine of majority rule, plays a defining role in this book's interpretation of the actions of the main players, particularly Polk, Henry Clay,

Gideon J. Pillow, Zachary Taylor, Winfield Scott, and John C. Frémont. Among the war's key commanders, only Stephen Watts Kearny seems to have risen cleanly (though not unscathed) above the politics of his day while fulfilling his military mission. The quest by Whigs and Democrats to control the executive branch, the army, or both, complicated perennial issues like military obeisance to civilian authority and the preservation of the chain of command.

Tocqueville's normally uncanny insight failed him when he asserted that "of all the armies the ones that desire war most ardently are the democratic ones, while the most peace-loving of peoples are also the democratic ones."[2] In the case of the Mexican War, which antiwar critics and Whigs labeled "Mr. Polk's War" at its outset, just the opposite was true. Democrats like Polk claimed they did not want war with Mexico or Great Britain, but their territorial objectives and the policies they instituted to pursue them belie these protestations. Yet those who elected them, who in turn flooded recruiting stations in the spring of 1846 to join the army to fight as volunteers, clearly desired war more than did their elected representatives. Most importantly, their *rage militaire* far surpassed that of the regular army's upper echelon, including Zachary Taylor and Winfield Scott—two men who knew from personal experience the inglorious reality of actual combat.

This book argues that Jacksonian attitudes, partisan politics, Americans' traditional aversion to professional armies, atrocities committed against Mexicans, and the unprecedented requirements of conquest and occupation posed a significant risk to U.S. military victory and to the James K. Polk administration's limited objectives for the Mexican War. Although Polk's own political ambitions and controlling personality at times threatened troop morale or victory, in the end it was his ability to overcome his strong partisan leanings and his careful management of Congress, the War Department, and his own cabinet that resulted in a victory that met his primary goal: the annexation of California. Any political damage done to the Whig Party in the process or to its presidential contenders was, for Polk, merely icing on the cake.

Historians elsewhere have connected the Mexican War to distinctive elements of Jacksonian democracy, especially the partisanship it fomented in the 1830s and 1840s and its "Manifest Destiny" rhetoric. Taking as broad a view as possible of what Frederick Merk calls a sense of "mission" embedded in expansionist sentiment, Sean Wilentz agrees that "there was a deeply idealistic side" to what he admits "can look like the most arrogant form of imperial bullying." "Manifest Destiny," writes Wilentz, in an attempt to understand the Mexican War's causes in international terms while simultaneously seeking to explain how democracy and Democrats could produce such unabashed conquest, "was rooted in its proponents' allegiance to the beleaguered forces of democracy outside the United States." Thomas R. Hietala is more straightforward and much less apologetic:

"For two decades fundamental Jacksonian preoccupations and principles found expression in territorial expansion."[3]

In terms of partisanship, Justin H. Smith briefly describes "The War in American Politics" in his monumental, two-volume study of the war. Other scholars have more specifically tried to get at the root of Polk's tumultuous relationships with Scott and Taylor, alternately blaming a collision of personalities or politics. John S.D. Eisenhower argues that "the disharmony" came from neither, really, but instead stemmed from the fact that in the 1840s the "respective roles of the president and the generals [were] not yet clearly delineated" and "military professionalism...had not yet come of age." But using such hindsight does little to explain the concrete source (or, rather, sources) of the quarrels, which involved real people with ideologies and personalities and character flaws who were more than just developmental points on an inevitably progressive time line of military and political history. In any case, President Theodore Roosevelt's much later row with General Nelson A. Miles occurred during a period of nascent presidential power and military professionalism, and one cannot imagine without a Herculean effort that Roosevelt's vigorous personality played but a small part in it. President Harry S Truman's dispute with General Douglas MacArthur during the Korean War came along near the height of cold war era military professionalism *and* presidential power.[4]

Looking beyond politicians and generals, including their character traits, we come to the volunteers, who formed the core of the army in wartime prior to the Civil War. That American volunteers during the Mexican War saw themselves as part of a long republican tradition of virtuous patriots defending their country is not disputed, but the source and significance of this sentiment is. Paul Foos argues that the grand rhetoric of this "republican tradition" actually masked unhappiness among regulars and volunteers with their respective military establishments, which Foos identifies as belonging to "the labor system of antebellum America." In spite of all the principled talk about virtue and liberty, soldiers were just another class of waged laborers and war was their work, according to Foos. The harsh discipline meted out by their officers, or bosses, especially in the regular army which practiced "archaic forced labor conditions," led soldiers to seek their payment instead in the form of loot and atrocity.[5]

Richard Bruce Winders discounts the tidy, prefabricated Marxian categories used by Foos and instead stresses commonalities among the volunteers that they themselves would have understood. He emphasizes that volunteers during the Mexican War were a "product of Jacksonian America" in that regardless of their individual political persuasion, "all held republican notions common during Jackson's day." These notions included a belief in American exceptionalism, unwavering confidence in their ability to elect virtuous men, a derision of regulars that contradictorily viewed them as elites and servile automatons, and a belief in their racial and cultural superiority as

Anglo-Saxon Protestants. This army, which Winders appropriately terms "Jacksonians at War," marched triumphantly as it "carried its view of democracy to the land of the Montezumas."[6]

The intent of *Manifest Ambition* is to explore the above themes at length by looking at some of the Mexican War's well-known events as well as many of its less studied but more instructive episodes. Chapter 1 briefly recounts the war after investigating the American love affair with militia and presenting a social, economic, and political overview of the 1820s–1840s. This democratic age, named after its patron saint, Andrew Jackson, is indelibly linked with the war it spawned, and understanding this connection is invaluable if one is to grasp the political animal that was James K. Polk. Succeeding chapters explore particular themes outside of a strictly chronological format, expanding on events or trends introduced in the first. While these sometimes treat the same incident, such as the controversial armistice granted by Taylor at Monterrey, they do so from different angles and for different purposes.

The democratization of politics that began in the decades after the War of 1812 deepened the citizen soldier tradition and invigorated the republican principles underlying the faith Americans placed in volunteers and in their militia system. By 1846 these traditional republican attitudes, reinforced by increased civic engagement and a charged political atmosphere, stood as guideposts inside of which President Polk, congressmen, and state governors acted. Chapter 2 takes this into account in order to understand why Polk and Congress tackled war preparations and the buildup of the army in the way that they did.

Chapter 3 explores the political and military effect of Jacksonian doctrines, personality conflicts, and political machinations on the relationship between Polk and his generals. Zachary Taylor and Winfield Scott were Whigs with presidential ambitions, and Polk endeavored to balance his partisan urge to undermine them with the realization that, especially in the latter's case, he needed them to win the war. Polk tried in different ways, legislatively and through surrogates in the army, to weaken their political prospects. For example, he attempted to revive the rank of lieutenant general so that he could appoint a Democrat to occupy the army's highest post. Just in case that did not work, he loosed his friend Gideon J. Pillow on Scott. Polk also sought to pack the officer corps, at least for the duration of the war with Mexico, with Democrats, even as state governors intervened in the process and Congress whittled away at the number of new vacancies or put restrictions on those that remained.

For all the planning and management that politicians can bring to bear, once troops are in the field the best laid plans can easily come to naught. The Mexican War proved no exception to this rule. Because the Polk administration wanted a conflict of short duration resulting in a limited territorial concession, it gave strict orders to respect private property, to buy supplies, and to honor in the most conspicuous manner possible the Mexicans' beloved Roman Catholic Church. Looting and atrocities committed by American soldiers, mostly volunteers, threatened to enrage Mexicans to the point where the United States feared becoming mired down in a bloody and costly occupation. Chapter 4 explores the sources of discontent among the American soldiery, the connection between this discontent and the criminal activities troops engaged in during the Mexican War, and the uneven response by all grades of officers to these crimes and to lesser forms of disobedience.

Chapter 5 analyzes the military governments in areas occupied or conquered by the U.S. Army, particularly in those places to which the United States laid permanent claim early in the war—California and New Mexico. Because of their unprecedented nature, these governments resulted in substantial but not unforeseen dangers to civilian authority. The manner of their establishment also instigated a political fight in Washington. The Polk administration and the Democratic Party defended the civil and military governments of New Mexico and California, arguing that those territories had been conquered in a declared war under the law of nations. Whigs asserted that no such right existed under the Constitution and raised the specter of the Roman Republic's decline into empire at the hands of glory-hungry generals.

Chapter 6 examines James K. Polk's leadership style and personality, measuring the effects these had on the war and on Polk's capacity to deal with Congress, keep his own cabinet in check, and respond to Americans who either protested the war as unjust or complained that Polk's idea of territorial conquest was too small. Polk's leadership as commander in chief was critical to American efficiency and victory in the Mexican War.

The final chapter places the Mexican War within American civil-military relations since the War of 1812, in order better to assess its consequences in terms of four recurrent themes: the growing recognition that a larger, commercial America demanded a new type of professional military with a well-educated officer corps; the evolution of American voluntarism and the citizen soldier tradition; the growth of presidential power on the grounds of military practicality; and quarrels between presidents and generals.

The story of civil-military relations during the Mexican War is largely one of politically explosive measures taken or supported by Polk and the response to them by his political or ideological enemies and U.S. military personnel. Jacksonian politics and doctrines interacted with traditional American attitudes and republican principles to impact how Americans went to war in 1846. This occurred in the field, in state houses, in the U.S. Capitol, and, above all, in the Executive Mansion of James K. Polk.

Map of Mexican War (David Heidler).

1

Jacksonian America and the Coming of the Mexican War

During the French and Indian War in 1756, George Washington had this to say of the Virginia militia:

> The difficulty of collecting them upon any emergency whatever, I have often spoken of as grevious; and I appeal to sad experience...how great a disadvantage it is....They are obstinate, self-willed, perverse, of little or no service to the people, and very burthensome to the country. Every *mean* individual has his own crude notions of things, and must undertake to direct. If his advice is neglected, he thinks him self slighted, abased, and injured; and, to redress his wrongs, will depart for his home. These, Sir, are literally matters of fact... chiefly from my own observations.

Two decades later, events during the first three years of the Revolutionary War did nothing to alter Washington's low opinion of militia and temporary civilians-turned-soldiers. He ridiculed the inordinate confidence Americans placed in "Motives of public virtue," which they believed would keep the flames of liberty lit and make Americans free of British rule. Washington agreed that for a short time virtue and lofty principles like liberty could prompt men to fight, but ultimately, he concluded, "Interest is the greatest governing principle....Few men are capable of making a continual sacrifice of all views of private interest, or advantage, to the common good." Washington applied this judgment to officers, too, whom he noted by 1778 had "abated in their ardor" due to the hardship of war.[1]

Tracing the views of Americans in the 1840s about their military to the period of the American Revolution reveals much about the constancy of the citizen soldier ethic in American history. In 1775 Americans believed that in order to preserve liberty, they must be worthy defenders of it. What made one worthy was virtue, ultimately defined as one's willingness to sacrifice life and property for the common good. Thus, "a well-regulated militia" and the willingness of citizen volunteers to form an army and fight for hearth, home, and principle, would always be necessary if Americans' liberties were to be protected and allowed to flourish.

THE REVOLUTIONARY WAR

This belief in the binding relationship between virtue and the maintenance of freedom, however, conflicted during the Revolutionary War with the obvious need, as voiced by Washington, for professional fighting men in an extended fight against the world's best trained army. From experience Americans knew that professional, or regular, armies more often than not stifled soldiers' liberty with arbitrary rules and burdensome regulations, created an elite officer corps akin to an aristocracy, and especially in peacetime threatened the freedoms of the people they were supposed to guard. Thus, Americans in the 13 rebelling colonies who went to war as militiamen commonly sneered at those who joined the Continental Army. In so doing, they reflected the thinking of the second Massachusetts provincial congress, which could not have disagreed more strongly with the conclusions Washington drew from his experiences in the 1750s with the colonial militia:

> and having great confidence in the honor and public virtue of the inhabitants of this colony that they will readily obey the officers chosen by themselves, and will cheerfully do their duty when known, without any such severe articles and rules (except in capital cases), and cruel punishments as are usually practised in standing armies; and will submit to all such rules and regulations as are founded in reason, honor, and virtue.

In the words of historian Charles Royster, "The war against the greatest power in the world was fought in the belief that virtue gave strength."[2]

Despite this citizen soldier ethic, after patriotic voluntarism crested in 1776, the Continental Army under the leadership of General Washington carried the war effort almost alone between 1777 and 1780. Congress, in the name of protecting liberty, refused to authorize enlistments longer than one year, and Washington complained bitterly that this was barely enough time to train an army, let alone sustain one for what surely would be a long, difficult war. He distrusted militiamen because he thought they carried over their democratic mores from civilian life into the army, and as such, could not be trusted to behave in camp or to perform adequately on the field of battle. Washington's experiences with militia in Virginia convinced him that only a well-disciplined, professional army could defeat the British Army, the greatest military force in the world. Until 1780 the general faced immense difficulties in getting arms, men, and supplies from both the states and from

Congress, but he criticized "the evils brought upon us by short enlistments" the most, calling it "pernicious beyond description."[3]

Glenn A. Phelps describes Washington's predicament succinctly: "As commander-in-chief he was subject to the authority of a curious array of departments, committees, secretaries, and boards at the national level, while simultaneously having to assuage the local concerns of thirteen very in-dependent, very different constitutional republics." With Congress ignoring his complaints, states balking at sending supplies for want of remuneration for previous expenditures, and few men willing to join the army for so little (or no) pay, Washington could have led his troops on Congress or on state capitals and forced the issue. Instead, he admirably muddled through as commander of an undermanned and poorly supplied army, without threatening rebellion and even periodically squashing the talk of such things among his officers. This explains why the young marquis de Lafayette praised Washington during the long winter at Valley Forge in 1777–1778, telling him that "if You were lost for America, there is no Body who Could keep the army and the Revolution for Six months." Washington's impor-tance, noted Lafayette, lay in his steadfast leadership in the face of "Open dissentions in Congress, parties who Hate one an other as much as the Common ennemy, Stupid men who without knowing a Single word about war undertake to judge You." Washington agreed there was "much truth" in Lafayette's observations, and referring to the initial revolutionary fever that had gripped the newly independent states from 1775 to 1776 he "lamented that things are not now as they formerly were." Washington apparently had forgotten that even in 1775 and 1776, although innumerable men were willing to fight the British, supplies, funds, and long-term war planning were not easily won from Congress or from the states.[4]

LIBERTY, VIRTUE, AND IDEOLOGY

Despite these facts, by 1783 Americans nevertheless convinced themselves that the war had been a concerted effort fought in the name of liberty by incorruptible volunteers and crack militias, not professional Continental soldiers drawn from the lower orders of society who, with the exception of Washington, fought for pay. As any lover of liberty could have predicted, Providence had favored the virtue of good republicans over the vice of monarchical European soldiers. Thus, "a whole generation" could "claim that their strength had been proven by the standard of 1775," even if after that year the Continental Army had done most of the fighting.[5] After the victory at Yorktown in 1781, the Continental Army disbanded, and posterity came to see the fight for independence as one great passionate fight for liberty lasting from 1775 to 1783. This firmly planted among Americans the belief that their militia system constituted the superior means of guarding the republic. Americans, based on this belief system that could better be described as an ideology, asserted that in a true federal union the rights of the states and the people were best protected when each state had a citizen militia and when the central government possessed only a small, token force of regulars.[6]

Neither the fear of a standing army nor Americans' trust in their own virtue and reliance on wartime voluntarism had lessened by the early 1800s. Americans continued to maintain a high opinion of themselves and a corresponding fear or low opinion of professional rank-and-file soldiers. Historian Marshall Smelser sums up the reasons for this continued adoration of militia: "Some ...loved the militia because of antimilitarism, others because it was cheap."[7] "Cheap" as county militias were to maintain, they were often poorly led, inadequately trained, and armed literally for bear (or rabbit), not battle. What they did offer, however, was a tangible reminder that virtuous common men stood ready to defend the republic from within and without—from within by negating the need for a large standing army of regulars and its attendant threat to liberty, and from without, because of the citizens' moral superiority to savage Indians and monocratic Europeans.

An ideologue is one who continues to advocate a system of beliefs in the face of clear evidence to the contrary and against all experience. He or she acts thusly because his or her conception of this world or how to devise the world of the future rises and falls not so much on traditions or practical experience but on a set of political or economic beliefs that promise to create and sustain the perfect society, perfection in this case being a republic protected by virtuous citizens ever vigilant of their liberties. Ideas falling outside of those beliefs that might in fact strengthen such a society are *a priori* deemed fanatical and downright dangerous. As Russell Kirk wrote, "The ideologue will accept no deviation from the Absolute Truth of his secular revelation."[8]

The advent of political parties in the mid-1790s intensified this ideological debate over the nature, necessity, and role in American society of the U.S. Army, as well as its relationship to government. The first two political parties in the United States coalesced during disputes over what ought to be the American policy toward the worsening situation in France following the French Revolution, which began in 1789 and quickly degraded into a frenzied bloodbath and European-wide war by early 1793. Thomas Jefferson, Washington's first secretary of state, engineered the creation of the first party, the Republican Party, with the help of James Madison and others. The second party was the Federalist Party, to which Alexander Hamilton, Washington's first secretary of the treasury, belonged. Although Hamilton did not mastermind the creation of the Federalist Party and, in fact, found himself by 1800 a member of its smaller (and more aristocratic) faction, his name became attached to its ideals even as Jefferson's became attached to the Republicans'.

The Jeffersonian Republicans retained the view that the United States was a compact of independent states rather than a federal union similar to a nation state, even after the U.S. Constitution replaced the Articles of Confederation. Consequently, to preserve individual liberty, the Jeffersonians argued that state power had to be hedged against the power of the U.S. government. Although they would not have used the later astronomical term, "black hole," this was indeed how the Jeffersonians viewed the federal government: once it acquired for itself any one power from the states or from the people, it would never, in fact, *could* never, relinquish it. Instead, it would grow into a tyrannical behemoth as had the British government. To ensure, therefore, that the central government remained weak, the states and the people had to guard their liberties jealously. If they did so successfully, they and their republic would prosper.

The other feature of Jeffersonian doctrine involved the country's yeoman farmers, whom Jefferson idealized. Yeomen were agrarians who farmed their own, small tracts of land. These self-sufficient, noncommercial farmers, in Jefferson's opinion, constituted the most virtuous segment of the population, because of their independence and eschewal of Yankee acquisitiveness. Not beholden to an employer or indebted to a bank, they could freely cast their vote on principle in order to guide the republic. This does not mean that Jefferson believed yeoman farmers should hold high, elective office; that, indeed, was for the landed gentry and educated men of means, like Jefferson himself. But it does mean that liberty was safest in the hands of the yeomen, whose virtue all but predetermined they would elect equally virtuous people to office (or, in the case of the president and senators, elect the electors). The radicalism and egalitarian rhetoric of the French Revolution charmed the Jeffersonians, who supported the French fight against many of the countries of Europe, most notably Great Britain, even after hearing of events like the bloody 1794 Reign of Terror.

The Hamiltonians in the Federalist Party also sought to protect liberty, but to do so they favored a centralized commercial society modeled after Great Britain rather than a loose agrarian confederation tied to a pro-French policy. This wedded them to support for their former enemy in its war with France, for men like Hamilton knew all too well how important the British were to the current and future American economy. Hamiltonians argued that only a strong national government (though infinitesimally small by post–Civil War standards), with a central bank and other mechanisms designed to encourage commercial development, could assure prosperity, and only prosperity could forge a nation strong enough to defend itself from European encroachment. The Hamiltonians saw the United States as a federal nation in which the states, rather than being sovereign entities belonging to a loose compact, were clearly subservient to the national government. Only a centralized nation such as this could maintain the order needed for the proper exercise of liberties.

The chaos that ensued in France during the French Revolution convinced Federalists of this all the more.

As president, Washington typically played the role of referee between Hamilton and Jefferson. In April 1793, however, with Federalist support he declared the United States neutral in the war between France and Great Britain, Spain, and the Netherlands. Republicans criticized this neutrality, since the size of the British navy and France's sorry economic state made American neutrality effectively pro-British. Republicans accused Washington of ruling like a dictator, since he had proclaimed neutrality without congressional authorization or approval.

Unlike Jefferson, who only claimed to despise partisanship, Washington, in spite of his Federalist sympathies, truly viewed all political parties with contempt. To him, parties positioned themselves between the people and the state primarily to perpetuate their own influence or their leaders' power. As such, parties benefited neither the people nor the state. Regional parties were the most dangerous, Washington argued, because within them lay the promise of not merely partisans spread equally throughout the states, which was bad enough, but sections divided by ideology and party lines. Sectionalism and partisanship, if melded together, could sink the country into ruin and possibly civil war.

When John Adams succeeded Washington as president in 1797, he did so as a member of the Federalist Party. The dispute among Americans over the situation in Europe continued to worsen, and by 1798 the United States was involved in what historians refer to as the Quasi-War with France, a conflict fought mostly by privateers and navies on the high seas. So vociferous was Republican opposition to Adams's foreign policy that he signed into law the Alien and Sedition Acts, to the Federalists' everlasting chagrin. Three of these four laws placed restrictions on the political activities of foreigners and restricted naturalization in order to stop the creation of more Republicans out of French refugees, but the fourth outlawed as sedition criticism by American citizens of the president and U.S. government. In response, Jefferson and Madison—anonymously—authored the Kentucky and Virginia resolutions, each of which to varying degrees toyed with the idea of whether states could nullify federal laws within their own borders, if they deemed those laws unconstitutional.

To John Adams's credit, he successfully headed off a full-blown war with France, dooming him with his own party. This, and the widespread perception that Federalists had threatened Americans' liberties, helped make Adams the first one-term president. In 1800 the Republican Party swept into power, and in 1801, with a Republican majority in Congress, Jefferson began his first of two terms as president. His primary goals as president were to decrease U.S. government power over the states, weaken the Federalist hold over the judiciary and U.S. Army, and to accelerate the formation of a lasting agrarian republic. Jefferson confidently believed this latter goal would be assured when in 1803 he approved the purchase of the enormous expanse of Louisiana. The goal of the Louisiana Purchase was to provide land for his beloved yeoman farmers for at least one hundred years to come.

The judiciary and the army were tougher nuts to crack, both having been packed with Federalists by Adams in the twilight of his presidency. James Madison, Jefferson's secretary of state, tried to thwart Adams's attempt to stack the judiciary by refusing to commission his "midnight appointments." One of these, William Marbury, sued in an attempt to make the U.S. Supreme Court issue a *mandamus* requiring Madison to present his commission. Jefferson assumed the court, dominated by Federalists, would do just that, and so he planned to use the opportunity to showcase the court's ideology and thereby diminish its influence. But the court surprisingly ruled against Marbury in *Marbury v. Madison*. In so doing, however, Chief Justice John Marshall used the decision to establish the precedent of the U.S. Supreme Court's judicial review of federal laws, a power not expressly stated in the U.S. Constitution. After achieving mixed results in his attempts to unseat Federalist judges through impeachment, Jefferson turned to military reform.

THE FOUNDING OF THE U.S. MILITARY ACADEMY

"When Jefferson took office in 1801," Theodore J. Crackel writes in *Mr. Jefferson's Army*, "he inherited an army filled with Federalist officers." Reforming the army was "just as vital" to Republicans as the Republicanization of the judiciary. The election of 1800, which Jefferson called a "revolution" wherein the reins of government had reverted to the people, convinced Republicans that as long as the army remained Federalist in composition, it "would constitute an illegitimate opposition." The army, according to Jefferson, was "openly hostile to Republican political aims, if not to republican values themselves."[9]

This opinion of the army explains why Jefferson founded the U.S. Military Academy at West Point, New York, an institution long desired by Washington but stymied by Republicans, including Jefferson, during the 1790s. By the time Jefferson left office in 1809, the army was nearing 9,000 soldiers and had begun efforts to modernize. More importantly, at least to Jefferson, its officer corps had become better trained and more Republican, thanks mostly to West Point. Even the U.S. Navy, which Jefferson valued over the army, was using the academy to train its officers. As Crackel explains, West Point by 1809 was "a source of the rudimentary instruction for Republican youth, circumventing the Federalist monopoly of education and overcoming their monopoly of office." Americans still mistrusted standing armies and career military professionals, but they mistrusted a Republican army and officer corps less.[10]

The partisan acrimony during Jefferson's administration between Republicans and Federalists thus goes a long way toward explaining why a

Republican, traditionally opposed like most Americans to a standing army, would proceed to increase the army's size and found a military academy. But why did Jefferson, a Republican's republican, not turn instead to the militia, which better embodied republican principles and inevitably had to be peopled by virtuous citizens ready to defend their liberties? First, he recognized just how ineffective the militia could be in certain situations, but like presidents before and after him, his attempted reforms of the militia went nowhere in the face of an already entrenched citizen soldier tradition and militia ethic. Likewise, politician that he was, Jefferson realized that any substantive reorganization of the militia would lessen the need, not to mention the courage, of congressmen to reform the U.S. Army along Republican lines.[11]

Second, Jefferson was well aware of the partisan complexion of militia companies, which was evident long before the Jacksonian era when the rugged partisanship of that period encouraged the use of companies in campaigns and to persuade people, in not so gentle ways, to vote. The militia, due to Federalist domination of local politics in states like Virginia, was officered by Federalists, even in predominantly Republican counties. For these reasons, Crackel concludes, Jefferson "preferred the idea of volunteers—but not militia."[12]

Jefferson was not the only president who tried and failed to reform the militia system, nor is it accurate to say that all Americans accepted without question the contention that the militia stood ready and able to fight. But Congress and state governments, composed of so many pro-militia ideologues, ignored critical organizational problems and the lack of arms and equipment. Instead, they continued to operate on what they had convinced themselves was the historical precedent set by the Revolutionary War, namely, that in time of need the United States really had hundreds of thousands of well-trained citizen soldiers prepared to take the field.[13] This proved foolhardy when the United States, led by President James Madison, Jefferson's protégé, went to war against Great Britain in 1812.

THE WAR OF 1812

During the War of 1812, the militia, which composed the bulk of American troops, proved itself "no match for professional soldiers."[14] Militia did prove relatively effective when defending familiar regions in their home states. However, they were unreliable and ineffective when attacking British regulars, and at times refused to enter Canada or to cross state lines in order to attack or pursue the enemy. Logistical problems, poor planning, and desertion often offset American victories.[15] Moreover, because of a short-term enlistment policy, itself based on a libertarian mentality which viewed long enlistments with suspicion, the United States never amassed more than 8,000 militiamen for a fight at any one time. Meanwhile, sectionalism and feuds between congressional Republicans and Federalists prevented a timely culling of the herd of inept U.S. officers until very late in the war. Madison seemed helpless to shape events. Overcoming what C. Edward Skeen calls "the militia myth" proved insurmountable for congressmen who sought to use the war as an opportunity to remedy the ailing American military system.[16]

The most famous exception to this rule of dismal militia performance was Andrew Jackson's remarkable victory at the Battle of New Orleans in January 1815. As Skeen writes, the same pragmatic congressmen who months earlier had dragged their feet and avoided a militia call-up in favor of enhancing the U.S. Army with regulars "shifted to accolades for the citizen soldier and to refurbishing the militia myth" after Jackson's success—a success entirely dependent on militia. In the minds of militia supporters, the exception of New Orleans offered proof to support continued reliance on a system that during most of the war had actually proved ineffective. Indeed, most Americans had come to agree with the Jeffersonian argument that there was no better way to protect an agrarian republic than to have the yeoman farmers rise up to defend their own communities not for payment but out of virtuous, patriotic zeal.[17]

Historians have, explains Smelser, traditionally assessed the War of 1812 in the harshest terms possible, as an event in which "an incapable president mismanaged an unnecessary war."[18] Two contributing factors to Madison's mismanagement, however, were Federalist resistance in Congress and the withholding of critical funds and troops by New England's Federalist governors. This latter problem was not entirely ideological or political, for the spiraling costs to states inherent in the militia system forced on them unpopular tax schemes to pay for a war much of their citizenry called "Mr. Madison's." Even states with Republican majorities where the war was popular practiced extra-Constitutional methods to contain costs or to fill War Department quotas of militiamen, such as the formation of actual state armies. Although arising in this case from pro-war sentiment, these actions similarly demonstrated a lack of consensus over the respective roles of the states and the War Department. Serious disagreement existed over whether governors or state legislators could restrict the president's Constitutional authority to call out the militia. In 1827 the U.S. Supreme Court, in *Martin v. Mott*, answered this question in the negative, but the behavior of several governors during the Mexican War later showed that Americans remained unconvinced. Meanwhile, costs incurred by Massachusetts during the War of 1812 were not reimbursed by the U.S. government until the middle of the Civil War.[19]

Although Gordon S. Wood does not deny Madison's inability to organize a force capable of defeating the British in the face of the militia myth and Federalist resistance, he provides a different perspective on the precedent set by President Madison's performance as commander in chief. Wood argues that Madison's most important achievement was the deliberate attention he paid to protecting the Bill of Rights, proving that the American republic could fight a major war without sacrificing civil liberties. Unlike John Adams, who resorted to the infamous Alien and Sedition Acts, Madison did no such thing.[20]

Federalist opposition to the War of 1812 placed their party on the path to extinction. In late 1814, members of the Federalist Party gathered at Hartford, Connecticut. Already primarily sectional in nature with a power base in northeastern states, the Federalists came together to propose Constitutional amendments designed to protect New England interests and to limit presidential power. They also threatened secession, but only implicitly, if their amendments were not approved. The Hartford Convention was the last attempt by the Federalist Party to protect its own interests and its region's interests—the two things now being one and the same. After the war, Americans remembered the whole affair as traitorous because of its proximity in time to Jackson's victory at New Orleans and to news of the signing of the unexpectedly favorable Treaty of Ghent. Thus, the convention at Hartford became a warning to future opposition political parties that to survive they must engage in dissent only in a measured, careful manner that could not be interpreted as undermining a president or the nation during time of war.

The War of 1812 also provided Americans with several valuable lessons for organizing their military in future conflicts. First, the militia proved relatively effective in defensive operations but ineffective when attacking the professional British army. Second, although nearly 300,000 American troops served during the war, never did more than about 8,000 fight in any one battle. The reason for this was a short-term enlistment policy that saw troops coming and going with disturbing regularity. Third, by the time the army had weeded out and replaced inept officers, a task fraught with sectional and political implications, the war had all but ended. The question to be answered by the outbreak of the Mexican War in 1846 was whether Americans had learned from their near defeat at British hands the need of a well-trained militia, the importance of a long-term enlistment policy, and the absolute necessity of a professional officer corps.[21]

THE MARKET REVOLUTION

The war's end in 1815 brought vast changes to the lives of many Americans. Republicans felt freer to adopt the mostly defunct Federalist Party's formerly controversial economic programs, and in 1816 Madison approved the creation of a second Bank of the United States (B.U.S.), Hamilton's brainchild and an institution traditionally viewed by Republicans as the tool of Anglophile Federalist merchants and bankers. But the biggest transformation of the era occurred outside the realm of politics, strictly considered, for the prevailing agrarian society in America based on fatalism, barter, and community cooperation was changing. Rapid commercial development and an expanding market substantially affected all areas of American society and culture. As capitalism spread from urban areas, so did an economy increasingly based on market forces, waged labor, and radical individualism. Whereas traditional rural values typically reflected a person's inability to control the natural environment and required a dependence on God's mercy and on the local community, the ideology of the emerging capitalist elite reflected self-confidence and a thorough individualism that trusted neither God nor neighbor. This radical individualism that shaped the world view of the urban elites was far different than the ideal of independence envisioned by yeoman farmers, for it was based more on an acquisitive commercialism than any desire for self-sufficient living.[22]

After his brief visit to the United States in 1831, an astonished Alexis de Tocqueville remarked, "The entire society is on the move." "When a certain way of thinking or feeling is the product of a particular state of humanity, and that state happens to change," Tocqueville wrote a few years later in *Democracy in America*, "nothing remains."[23] This was indeed an accurate appraisal of circumstances in the United States during this period, for so quickly did Americans find their world altered and buffeted by market forces that many historians refer to the time period between 1815 and the late 1840s as the era of the market revolution. Technological advances in transportation, communication, and manufacturing, along with the success of capitalism, operated in symbiotic relationship with this revolution, being both facilitated and spurred by it.

The market revolution did not affect all areas or populations of the United States equally. As people in the Northeast came to accept market capitalism as the natural outgrowth of their commercial and maritime spirit, Southerners began to see the free labor system inherent in the market economy as a threat to the institution of slavery and, therefore, to their reigning social system. While some Americans embraced market capitalism, the depression known as the Panic of 1819—a consequence of speculation, bank fraud, and a reliance on distant, domestic markets and overseas trade—convinced many others that social problems could only be addressed in the political arena. The panic awoke Americans to the rigors of the market, laying the foundation for intense social and political conflict. This newfound diversity led, by the mid-1820s, to the distillation of two main factions within the only remaining national party, each based on the Jeffersonian and Hamiltonian paradigm.

THE JACKSONIAN ERA

The Jacksonian era, roughly the years 1824 through 1848, falls under the umbrella of the market revolution, and for good reason. So-called Jacksonian democracy rose partly in response to the anxieties and changes wrought by the market revolution, or, as Tocqueville described it, the fearful realization that very soon nothing worth preserving might remain of the old world. By the mid-1820s, white males in most states had won the right to protect their interests through suffrage, regardless of how much property they owned or their level of education. Meanwhile, Martin Van Buren of New York worked tirelessly to pioneer a new form of systematic, robust, and popular campaigning. He successfully struggled to create a political party—uniting northern, southern, and western interests—with South Carolinian John C. Calhoun and Missourian Thomas Hart Benton to be its regional anchors in the South and West, respectively.

After the War of 1812, leading Republicans like Henry Clay came to be called National-Republicans because they favored a strong central government and institutions like the Bank of the United States. National-Republicans also supported a high protective tariff to help American industries like textile manufacturers compete with European companies. The other faction, calling themselves Democratic-Republicans, thought that Clay's National-Republicans had sold their soul to the ghost of Hamilton and, as such, were just Federalists by another name. Democratic-Republicans took the Jeffersonian view and argued that the United States, as a result of the market revolution, was involved in the age-old conflict between the liberty insured by an agrarian society composed of virtuous yeoman farmers or small slaveholders and the power of concentrated wealth which leads to tyranny.

When Democratic-Republican Andrew Jackson won the popular vote in the presidential contest of 1824 but nevertheless lost the election to National-Republican John Quincy Adams, the public persona of what one historian calls "the symbol for an age" was born.[24] Jackson, labeled "Old Hickory" for his resolute toughness, went on to win the presidency in 1828 and 1832 and became the face of the Democratic Party, also called the Democracy. Van Buren, Jackson's vice president, won in 1836. Jackson's protégé, James K. Polk, called "Young Hickory" by some and also a Tennessean like his mentor, later placed his own mark on what came to be known as the Jacksonian era through his expansionist policies and the Mexican War.

With Jackson's election, suddenly the word "democracy" no longer implied mob rule but instead promised to protect the majority and to give them whatever they wanted in the name of liberty. The word "Republican" was even dropped from the name of the party, and the saying, *vox populi vox dei* ("the voice of the people is the voice of God") best sums up the political philosophy of Democrats during this period. In the name of the people, presidential power steadily grew under Jackson. To Jackson, democracy above all meant majority rule in the harshest possible terms, and as the only political leader elected by all the people, he proceeded to overrule the Supreme Court. Using questionable treaties and the U.S. Army, he removed

Indians westward in order to make more room for white farmers, ignoring Supreme Court decisions he deemed undemocratic and, as he reportedly reminded Chief Justice John Marshall, unenforceable. Expansion would always be necessary if the United States was to remain a largely agrarian republic along Jeffersonian lines, with one whole region of the country supported by a slave-based, plantation economy. When Marshall died in 1835, Jackson replaced him with Roger Taney, who is best known as the primary author of the infamous *Dred Scott v. Sanford* decision.

Jackson also made it policy to lower tariffs, which Southerners, especially slaveholders, believed punished them in order to serve New England commercial interests. When Congress attempted to use federal money to build the Maysville Road through Kentucky, he vetoed the bill, the first veto cast by a president not on Constitutional grounds but purely for political reasons. Democrats believed the funding of internal improvements, such as roads or canals, was best left to states lest the U.S. government become too influential in consequence of its ability to dole out money. In the early 1830s Jackson also helped stop early renewal of the B.U.S. in a major political fight called the Bank War. But halting renewal was not enough for Jackson, who then effectively killed the bank four years prior to its intended expiration by removing all federal deposits and placing them in private banks in various states. This resulted in wild speculation leading to a depression in 1837 worse than the Panic of 1819. No wonder, then, that Winfield Scott, hero of the War of 1812 and various Indian wars, lamented in ideological language that, "Early in the times of Jacksonism...demagogues broke the Constitution."[25] Despite all this, Jackson was strongly in favor of the Union and nearly went to war with South Carolina when, based on rationale taken from the Virginia and Kentucky resolutions, it threatened to nullify the federal tariff within its borders.

Organized opposition to the Democracy coalesced during the Bank War in the form of the Whig Party, and the Second Party System was born. Jackson's opponents, led by former National-Republican, Henry Clay, formed the nucleus of the Whig Party. The Whigs took their name from the traditional opponents of the English monarchy, implying of course that Jackson was behaving more like a king than a president. But the name also showed that, above all else, opposition to Jackson and Jacksonian democracy—what Scott called "Jacksonism"—held Whigs together. Jacksonism contained not merely a cult of personality but also the specter of executive tyranny in the name of the majority—two things noticeably absent from its Jeffersonian predecessor.

The Whig Party, with Clay as its recurrent presidential candidate, proposed a platform called the "American System," which supported having a national bank, federally funded internal improvements, and high tariffs designed to protect young American industries. Democrats opposed the American System as overly favorable to New England and ruinous to small farmers and urban craftsmen who found themselves increasingly having to work for wages. Some southern elites (Clay himself was a Kentucky planter) gravitated toward the Whig Party, but its supporters came mainly from the merchants and moneyed men of New England and the Northeast, the center of U.S. manufacturing and former home to the bulk of the now defunct Federalist Party.

The moral, class, and sectional differences fostered or exacerbated by the market revolution helped shape the policies of each party. Both even represented divergent religious interests. The ideological underpinnings of the Federalists and Whigs were much the same as those of the Republicans and Democrats, except for the latter's more radical support of democracy. Slaveholders, small farmers, Irish-Catholic immigrants (who saw in Whigs shades of their former English oppressors), and urban workers supported the Democratic Party. Thus, the Whig Party emerged as the more starkly sectional of the two parties, which made it difficult for it to win the presidency even though the House and Senate remained roughly divided in equal numbers between Whigs and Democrats throughout most of the 1830s and 1840s.[26]

The Democratic political juggernaut built by Van Buren took a brief hiatus in the presidential election of 1840, in which Whigs mobilized voters and employed democratic tactics like catchy slogans and populist rhetoric to elect William Henry Harrison, who had edged out General Winfield Scott for the nomination. Hero of the Battle of Tippecanoe in 1811, Harrison had helped clear the way for white settlement of the Indiana Territory. When Harrison died within days of taking office, Vice President John Tyler stepped in to fill his shoes. Although a member of the Whig Party, Tyler disappointed his partisans by vetoing bills based on the American System. Nevertheless, the Whig electoral victory and campaign of 1840 demonstrated that what Sean Wilentz calls "the demagogic arts" now dominated American politics.[27]

By the early 1840s, then, the Second Party System was firmly entrenched, and it reflected great political divisions among Americans. In 1846 the Mexican War, with its prospect of a massive territorial acquisition, was to further these divisions because it forced Americans to decide immediately how they would use the West: as an area into which slavery could expand or as a region dominated by a free labor system and the capitalist market. After 1803 Americans had moved westward in great numbers into the Louisiana Purchase, and after the War of 1812 they increasingly came to realize that the futures of the North and the South, and of farmers and merchants and craftsmen, depended on whether new states in the West would be slave or free. The question was could the democratic process and the nations' two leading political parties chart a path out of this predicament without rupturing the Union? The eventual answer turned out to be "no," but the Missouri Compromise of 1819–1821 and a compromise in the early

1830s over the protective tariff averted disunion and civil war. Thus, the Union limped along, guided by the Whig and Democratic Parties and seemingly containing enough room for yeoman and small slaveholder, planter and entrepreneur, slave and wage earner.

At the same time Americans willingly or unwillingly adjusted to their changing social and economic world, they clung stingily to their old values, ideals, and attitudes, even in the cities. Indeed, the party of Jackson found as many supporters inside cities as outside them. Democrats like Jackson and Van Buren portrayed Whigs as Anglophile elitists who endangered individual liberty in their rush to broaden the powers of the federal government and establish centralized banking in order to bring about an industrial, capitalist nation. Whigs, said Democrats, profited from debt and other negative consequences of the new economy. Whigs, on the other hand, viewed Democrats as, at best, a regressive and unruly mob given to demagoguery and, at worst, as tools of southern slave owners, corrupt urban bosses, and militant expansionists. Whigs saw themselves as Hamiltonians and Democrats prided themselves as neo-Jeffersonians, but in truth the principles of each, though descended from Hamilton and Jefferson, had been molded and then tempered in the furnace of the market.

The one American attitude that evolved little during the Jacksonian era was that of Americans toward their military. Since the Battle of New Orleans the democratic militia system had grown in popularity while declining in effectiveness. Meanwhile, in war volunteer companies of the kind favored by Jefferson were expected to form separately from extant militia companies. Both could be mustered into service in accordance with a state's militia laws to fight for the U.S. government. However, Americans placed greater trust in the militia on the assumption that its members were equipped and had regularly trained together as a unit. At the time of the War of 1812 militias commonly mustered six times per year, but by 1830 that number was down to three times per year. By the 1840s musters had dropped to once per year. Moreover, by 1846 most states had abolished mandatory militia involvement in the face of complaints that it wasted time and money. At that time musters occurred so irregularly that in many cases men did not even know to which company they belonged. Nevertheless, militia rolls totaled over two million men nationwide, and companies maintained their ceremonial functions by marching on holidays, sponsoring festivals, or serving as a sort of social club.[28]

In Jacksonian America militia companies, like nearly everything else, took on an increasingly partisan cast, adding voting en masse to their nonmilitary functions. By 1846, this intensified the usual problems associated with the system. In case of war, how would partisanship affect the call-up of the militia? How would officers be chosen? If a state governor was a Whig, would only Whig companies be called to serve? Could a Democrat effectively lead a mostly Whig battalion or vice versa? And what about those militia companies organized by ethnicity or religion, as in the case of Irish-Catholics and Germans who were otherwise unwelcome outside the regular army? In the Jacksonian era, these were important questions indeed. During the Mexican War, they were to prove crucial to military morale and combat effectiveness.

Generally speaking, Whigs and Democrats equally feared the threat to liberty that a large standing army might bring; participated in local militias; and in the case of national emergency, counted on the citizen soldier tradition to produce a force of volunteers. Virtue and a dead aim won battles, not rigorous training and professional officers. Most cited the Revolutionary War and the "victory" in the War of 1812 as proof of the citizen soldier's superiority. Volunteers of incorruptible republican stock, they believed, would always outmatch the soldiery of despotic countries. Naturally, then, when revolutions swept the Spanish colonies of middle and South America beginning in 1808 after Napoleon's conquest of Spain, Americans looked southward with a heady combination of hope and enthusiasm. Would the Little Corporal and aspiring dictator of Europe inadvertently help spread republicanism throughout the Americas? Certainly Americans had a pressing interest in the answer to this question.

U.S. RELATIONS WITH MEXICO

Of more immediate concern than the events taking place in Spanish America at large were circumstances in nearby New Spain, or Mexico, which had been mired in turmoil since 1810 as competing groups struggled to establish power. In 1813 Mexico declared independence from Spain. The next year King Ferdinand VII returned to the throne of Spain, eager to reestablish the *ancien régime* there and strengthen his hold over New Spain. By 1820, however, constitutionalism returned to Spain and the rebellions in Mexico had largely been pacified. In 1821, after a victorious insurgency led by Colonel Agustín de Iturbide, Mexico reasserted its independence. Contrary to American hopes, Iturbide's Mexico was no liberal republic but a monarchical empire stretching from California and Texas southward through Costa Rica. Iturbide ruled as king from 1822 to 1823, at which time he abdicated.[29]

One year after Iturbide's abdication Mexico promulgated a constitution and declared itself a federal republic. Hoping to secure good relations and a restatement of past treaties, in 1825 the United States named Joel R. Poinsett minister to the new Republic of Mexico. What Poinsett found on his arrival in Mexico City, however, was not a fragile but promising republic. He encountered a loosely united country mired in factionalism, regionalism, and racial antagonisms. Making matters worse was that the democratic yearnings of the population remained subject to the autocratic demands of whichever general currently controlled the capital. The greatest tension lay between those who wanted a true confederation and those who wished for a strong central state, albeit a republic, based in Mexico City. Mexican generals-turned-presidents used to their advantage the passions of the masses, especially when it came to their own power struggles with the United States. Indeed, Poinsett became the first in a line of American ministers who discovered that the usual niceties of diplomacy did not apply in Mexico, where coups made and unmade presidents on a regular basis between 1824 and 1846. American diplomats had to take into account the durability of regimes, competing factions, public opinion, and the influence of Mexico's Roman Catholic clergy.

Poinsett's primary mission, according to John Quincy Adams' secretary of state, Henry Clay, was "to lay for the first time the foundations of an intercourse of amity, commerce, navigation, and neighborhood."[30] Yet Poinsett also was to reaffirm the boundary between Mexico and the United States that had been drawn in the Adams-Onís Treaty of 1819, except where Texas was concerned—Poinsett was to purchase Texas outright.

In 1819, when the United States had relinquished its tenuous claim that Texas composed part of the Louisiana Purchase, the two nations set their boundary at the Sabine and Red Rivers. Adams, then President James Monroe's secretary of state, had negotiated the treaty himself. Mexico, fully aware of American designs on California, distrusted Poinsett from the very beginning. In 1829, after a signed treaty confirming the Adams-Onís boundary between Spain and the United States as the border between Mexico and the United States inexplicably met its death at the hands of Mexican legislators, Mexico requested Poinsett's recall. The plant that came to be known popularly in the United States as the "Poinsettia" turned out to be the only success the diplomat brought back with him from Mexico. President Jackson replaced Poinsett with Anthony Butler, who received similar treatment in Mexico (due partly to his own poor negotiating skills). Jackson recalled Butler in 1835. Remarkably, by that time Butler had managed to achieve a treaty of amity and commerce with Mexico and to secure an agreement reaffirming the boundary of 1819.[31]

As diplomats wrangled over border claims, American immigrants to Texas were already gaining by numbers and economic influence what Presidents Adams and Jackson hoped to achieve through negotiation. Riding the complimentary waves of the market revolution and King Cotton, southern farmers and their slaves had begun moving into Texas even before they received permission to do so by the Mexican government in 1824.[32] By 1825, over 3,000 American citizens were living west of the Sabine River. Most willingly swore allegiance to Mexico and even agreed to become Roman Catholic. Under the encouragement of the most important *empresario*, or land agent, Stephen F. Austin, settlers flocked to Texas. Requiring allegiance to Roman Catholicism and forbidding slavery did little to stem the tide of American settlers eager for farmland, wealth, and a fresh start in a foreign land. Mexico's closure of the border in 1830 also failed to restrict further immigration by Americans. In 1834, nearly 18,000 Americans lived in Texas—more than twice the number of Mexicans residing there. Erratic governance in Mexico City helped convince those who had come since the late 1820s to seek independence for Texas.

Relations between the United States and Mexico remained tense but manageable until the outbreak of the Texas Revolution. Austin had helped Mexican authorities quell rebel disturbances in the past, but when an army under the command of General Antonio López de Santa Anna entered Texas in 1835, the Texan sided not only with Mexicans in the several Mexican states rebelling against Santa Anna's autocratic rule, but also with the newer American settlers in Texas who favored total independence. Austin's patience with the unstable Mexican government had reached an end. President Jackson declared the United States neutral in the civil war, but adventure-seeking Americans like former congressman David Crockett of Tennessee crossed the border to take up arms beside the Texans. Mexicans could little doubt the result Americans hoped for in the contest.

More than did all the diplomatic posturing of the 1820s and early 1830s, two events during the Texas Revolution helped to create among Americans an enduring image of Mexicans as brutal and treacherous. The first occurred just outside San Antonio at a mission known as the Alamo. In February and March of 1836 around 200 men, including Crockett, fortified the mission and from within fought off a 3,000-man Mexican army, led by Santa Anna. When the remaining Texans finally succumbed on March 6, Santa Anna ordered all of the wounded men to be put to death and their bodies burned. The second event critical in shaping American public opinion also involved the execution of prisoners, and occurred less than a month after the battle at the Alamo. Over three hundred Texans surrendered at Goliad to an encircling Mexican army, which initially treated them as prisoners of war. On learning of their capture, however, Santa Anna ordered the men to be shot to death.

The defenders of the Alamo quickly became heroes in Texas and in the United States, and "Remember the Alamo!" served as the revolutionaries' rallying cry when they soundly defeated Santa Anna's army one month later at the Battle of San Jacinto. In that battle, Texans killed surrendering Mexican soldiers in revenge for the massacre at Goliad. Led by Samuel Houston, the Texans' biggest prize was the capture of Santa Anna, who secured his own release by signing a treaty recognizing the independent Republic of Texas. The fact that the Mexican government never ratified the treaty, however, proved to be the key sticking point when the United States later sought to annex the "independent" republic. In the meantime, Texans set about running their own political affairs and Americans soon lost interest.

THE ELECTION OF 1844

After a bungled attempt by President Tyler in early 1844 to annex Texas, Americans entered the election of 1844 assuming that Henry Clay, not Tyler, would be the Whig nominee and that former president Martin Van Buren would represent the Democrats. A vote for Clay would mean a vote for the American System, a program Tyler, although a Whig, had inexplicably vetoed. No one was sure what a vote for Van Buren meant, including Michigan Senator Lewis Cass, who challenged the Democratic heir apparent for the nomination. To avoid splitting their respective parties, Clay and Van Buren each equivocated on their Texas annexation stance—their positions were by no means clear. But when Cass and Van Buren cancelled out each other's votes at the Democratic convention, James K. Polk, a surprise "dark horse" candidate from Tennessee, emerged the winner (with Jackson's help), and so the election pitted Polk against Clay.

There was no doubt where Polk stood on the issue of Texas, for he spoke of "the reannexation of Texas to our Union."[33] Clay, afraid of alienating the southern wing of his party, continued to refine and massage his annexation stance. Although Polk lost his home state due to divisions among Democrats and Whig strength there (Tennessee had gone to Harrison in 1840), he won the national contest by about 38,000 votes out of over 2.6 million ballots cast. Just a few thousand votes in New York alone would have swung the electoral college over to Clay. Yet, interpreting Polk's election as a referendum in favor of Texas annexation, Congress quickly formulated a resolution to annex the republic. On March 1, three days before Polk took office, Tyler signed the resolution, which with Texan acceptance would add Texas to the Union. Texans, however, were less sure about annexation than some Americans, particularly because they claimed the Rio Grande as the Texas-Mexico border. Even if Mexico agreed to honor Texas's independence, Mexicans believed the Nueces River, farther north, stood as the border. What did the Polk administration believe, Texans wondered?

In November 1845 President Polk dispatched Louisiana congressman John Slidell to Mexico, ostensibly to discuss the border issue. Polk enthusiastically supported the Texans' claims and aimed to secure recognition of the Rio Grande boundary. Polk also secretly ordered Slidell to purchase California, for no sooner had Texas joined the Union than buoyant Democrats predicted that before long California would assert its "natural right of self-government," followed by annexation.[34] Mexican officials first welcomed Slidell but then, as the weak regime of José Herrera stood at the mercy of General Mariano Paredes, refused to accredit him as a minister plenipotentiary of the United States. In December Slidell despondently admitted to Polk that "a war would probably be the best mode of settling our affairs with Mexico."[35]

As the new year opened, however, Polk's primary diplomatic entanglement involved not assuaging Mexico's fears over Texas annexation or convincing the Mexican government to sell California to the United States but wrangling with Great Britain over the future of the Oregon Territory. If a war was to result from territorial expansion, most Americans expected it to come from that quarter, not south of the border. Employing just the right mix of bluster and brinkmanship, in early April Polk successfully settled the Oregon border dispute. Despite the popular Democratic slogan of "54°40' or Fight," Polk wisely agreed to a British-American border at the forty-ninth parallel. This gave Americans access to the port of Puget Sound and virtual control of the Columbia River. All that was left to guarantee decisive American control of the West Coast was to annex California.

THE MEXICAN WAR

Scarcely had the ink on the Oregon treaty dried when fighting broke out on April 25 between American and Mexican soldiers in a disputed area along the Rio Grande. The genesis of the clash lay in Polk's orders, given to Colonel Zachary Taylor one month prior, to take his army south across the Nueces River and fortify positions along the Rio Grande. By placing troops in disputed territory, Polk exerted American control all the way to the Texan-defined borders of the newly annexed state, virtually assuring military confrontation.

News of the clash did not reach Washington City until May 9, at which time Congress and the American public were still celebrating the peaceful resolution of the Oregon issue. Rapidly, they shifted their attention from the northern border with British Columbia to the southern border with Mexico. Polk, however, already was focused on Mexico. Indeed, prior to receiving news of the attack he already had drafted a message to Congress, justifying war on the grounds that Mexico had refused to pay reparations to Americans and had shabbily treated Slidell.

Actual hostilities now all but assured a declaration of war. The Goliad and Alamo massacres psychologically had given Americans a stake in the struggle over Texas. The fact that Texas had been independent of Mexico for 10 years now convinced Americans that although annexing Texas may have led to war with Mexico, adding Texas to the Union was nevertheless a legal agreement between two sovereign nations. The real question remained: the border of the Republic of Texas—was it the Rio Nueces or the Rio Grande? In 1844 Mexico had warned the United States that annexation meant war, but until Taylor's troops marched into the disputed strip of territory beyond the Nueces there had been no bloodshed. In his May 11 war message to Congress, Polk confidently asserted that the United States and Mexico were already in a state of undeclared war, because Mexicans had "shed the blood of our fellow-citizens on our own soil."[36] Therefore, said Polk, a declaration of war merely recognized what already existed in fact. Congress, backed into a corner, engaged in a short but intense debate. Then on May 13 it declared war on Mexico.

Taking into consideration the events immediately leading up to the Mexican War, the election of 1840 was not the full flowering of the myriad implications of Jacksonian democracy, with its doctrine that the executive branch, more so than Congress, was more profoundly democratic because the president represented the majority, not compact or regional constituencies. Neither was Jacksonian democracy's real offspring simply an amorphous potential for "executive tyranny" as Whigs alleged.[37] Rather, it was an incessant drive for territorial expansion that had now resulted in a conflict engineered by a president largely to secure his contemporaries' hopes for a more egalitarian republic predicated on the agrarian vision of Jefferson. At least in Polk's mind, this democratic vision included a concomitant commercial orientation that demanded a United States stretching from coast to coast. "Executive tyranny" this perhaps was, but the Mexican War, to paraphrase a later statement by one of its strongest critics, had been entered into in the name of the people, for the people, and would now be fought by the people.

Specific incidents during the war, such as clashes involving Polk, Congress, the U.S. military establishment, and state governors will be explored at length in later chapters of this book. Let us now turn to a brief summary of the course of the war, to provide the context in which to view broader trends and singular vignettes.

The initial American strategy devised by President Polk was to secure northern Mexico in the hopes that Mexico would capitulate, recognize Texas annexation, and sell California, making an invasion of central Mexico unnecessary. If Mexico did not sue for peace—and there was good reason for Polk to think that it would not—then the United States would be in a strong defensive posture strung across the north of Mexico and the Rio Grande from which it could pursue further military operations. Polk also realized that control of northern Mexico, including New Mexico, would make acquiring California, his primary goal, a near certainty. As he told his cabinet within days of the declaration of war,

> If the war should be protracted for any considerable time, it would in my judgment be very important that the United States should hold military possession of California at the time peace was made, and...to acquire for the United States, California, New Mexico, and perhaps some of the Northern Provinces of Mexico whenever peace was made.[38]

After all, Polk reminded them, he had given Slidell secret instructions to that effect just a few months earlier.

In Colonel Taylor's opinion, invading central Mexico from the north would be doomed from the start by the great distances involved. But the army's job, from the colonel's perspective, was not to look ahead but simply to set up a line along the south bank of the Rio Grande. Taylor felt confident that victories in northern Mexico would create conditions favorable to peace. After defeating Mexican forces at the Battles of Palo Alto and Resaca de la Palma in early May, Taylor's army crossed the Rio Grande into Mexico. On May 17 Americans laid siege to Matamoras, where Mexican forces under General Mariano Arista were entrenched. As Taylor negotiated with Arista, Mexican soldiers filtered out of the city, taking with them arms and artillery. The next day Taylor's troops occupied Matamoras without firing a shot. Taylor's reward for this action was a brevet commission as major general.

The main objective of now-General Taylor's campaign was not Matamoras but the strategically located and heavily fortified city of Monterrey. Domination of northern Mexico depended on control of Monterrey. In July, Taylor's army occupied Camargo, a small town north of Monterrey, just across the Rio Grande from Texas. Using Camargo as a base of operations, Taylor waited for reinforcements while establishing garrisons at nearby towns. By September he was ready to move, although he harbored strong doubts about the volunteers that by then had arrived to supplement his army. After four days of deadly fighting in which General William Worth proved himself a more capable tactician than Taylor, General Pedro Ampudia, Arista's replacement, requested an armistice. Against orders from Washington, on September 24 Taylor signed an armistice that permitted the surrendering Mexican army to depart the city. His army thus captured the prize, the victory boosted troop morale, and Taylor and Worth became heroes back home and to their troops. The armistice angered Polk, however, and so the Battle of Monterrey marked the beginning of rapidly deteriorating relations and increased suspicions between the president and Taylor.

As Polk continued to lose confidence in Taylor and Taylor began to suspect the president of trying to thwart his future in politics, the general continued to execute the strategy of occupying northern Mexico. In November, American troops led by Worth occupied Saltillo, and Taylor soon established his personal headquarters nearby. Taylor undertook these actions despite having received orders to maintain defensive operations only and not to advance south of Monterrey. Meanwhile, since a Mexican peace did not seem forthcoming, that same month Polk named General Scott to lead personally an invasion of central Mexico. Although a Whig with proven political ambitions, Scott was the best man for the job and Polk knew it.

Taylor held a dim view of Scott from the very beginning, not, as some historians argue, as a consequence of misunderstandings that occurred between the two men while in Mexico. Scott procrastinated through much of 1846, offering a variety of excuses for why he was still in Washington and why the United States could not embark on a major campaign until, apparently, the following year. Taylor criticized his superior for "hesitating and throwing obstacles in the way" of his coming to Mexico immediately to take command. In his apparent stalling, which Scott defended as methodical planning, the general in chief had "disgusted the Secretary of War as well as Mr. Polk." By the end of the summer of 1846 Taylor blamed Scott's aspirations to the presidency, an office Taylor claimed he would decline if ever it were offered to him, for getting in the way of the war.[39]

Taylor also disliked General Scott's vanity and penchant for unintentionally making silly or damaging statements, a habit that made Scott's nickname of "Old Fuss and Feathers" seem very fitting. Scott, said Taylor, "writes and speaks with great flippancy and frequently without due reflections." This was a reference to Scott's infamous statement, made when he responded to Secretary of War William Marcy's letter in late May 1846 informing him that Taylor had won battles along the Rio Grande and that he, Scott, could remain in Washington City for the time being. In his reply, Scott complained matter-of-factly that he had just sat down to eat "a hasty plate of soup" when the arrival of Marcy's letter interrupted him. As historian John S. D. Eisenhower describes the incident, "The public laughed at the spectacle of a pompous general simpering at not getting what he wanted." Scott defended the comical statement by blaming Marcy, a New York Democratic operative, for taking the "private note" and "maliciously" publishing it in the partisan press just to embarrass him—which is, in fact, exactly what happened.[40]

Taylor and Polk were both right about one thing: Scott was reflecting seriously on how leading the command in Mexico with James K. Polk as president might impact his political future. As Scott himself told Marcy in the most explicit terms, going to Mexico would place him in "the most perilous of all positions: A fire upon my rear, from Washington, and fire, in front, from the Mexicans." This self-fulfilling prophecy only made Polk and Marcy more suspicious of Scott, primarily because they now knew just how politically aware the general was.[41]

By early 1847 Scott's planning for the invasion of central Mexico was proceeding apace. The American invasion force, taken partly from Taylor's troops, was to land at Veracruz and proceed overland to the capital, Mexico City. Taylor now wished Scott had stayed in Washington after all, for he chafed at having to sit still in a defensive posture at Monterrey and he bristled under the poaching of his troops. Nevertheless, Taylor followed orders and tried to deal amicably with Scott. When communication problems between the two men resulted in Taylor being gone when Scott arrived to take some of his troops, however, relations between the two men eroded further. In early February 1847, Taylor, tired of sitting still and feeling sure General Santa Anna would not attack, decided on his own to move his mostly volunteer army of 4,594 troops south of Saltillo. The result of this dangerous action proved opportune for Taylor, politically delicate for Polk, and led to the most famous clash of the war, the Battle of Buena Vista.

Santa Anna was determined to finish off Taylor's army. Acting on intelligence, he advanced with some 15,000 soldiers against the much smaller American force. Skirmishes ensued near Hacienda San Juan de la Buena Vista at the base of the Sierra Madre mountains on February 22. Mexican soldiers battled the American army throughout the next day. Taylor's only choice was to fight a defensive battle against the larger Mexican force. Still holding the battlefield at sunset, Taylor's men hunkered down and waited for dawn. Yet Mexican morale had been so shattered by their inability to break the American lines that Santa Anna's army quietly retreated during the night and was gone from the battlefield by morning. The resounding American victory, strategic as it was in preserving the American defensive line across northern Mexico and securing the northern approaches to Mexico City in advance of Scott's invasion, was even more important to Taylor politically—the remarkable victory earned him the fame he needed for a presidential run in 1848.

Taylor's men had not been the only American army active in northern Mexico. By the time of the Battle of Buena Vista, American troops already occupied the port of Tampico in the state of Tamaulipas on Mexico's east coast and had conquered California and New Mexico. Polk viewed New Mexico as little more than a useful territorial connection between Texas and California, although trade on the Santa Fe Trail was relatively lucrative for Americans. New Mexico fell quickly and virtually unopposed to American forces, though later uprisings showed that holding New Mexico was not quite as easy as indicated by the initial taking of Santa Fe. Colonel Stephen W. Kearny, commander of the American forces, rapidly instituted a controversial legal code for the territory, earning promotion to brigadier general in the process. Confident that New Mexico was safely in American hands, he departed for California on news of a revolt there against American forces.

The invasion and occupation of California by Americans proceeded from land and sea, as well as from within the state itself. Commodore John D. Sloat possessed standing orders to occupy important port cities in California if hostilities commenced between Mexico and the United States. On July 7, 1846, he seized Monterey, California. Three days prior a small band of American settlers in Sonoma had declared the independent Bear Flag Republic, supported after the fact by Captain John C. Frémont and the few U.S. troops under his command then encamped in northern California. Frémont left straightaway to join the Americans coming in from the coast. In early August 1846, Robert F. Stockton relieved Sloat as commodore, and sailors under his command occupied Los Angeles later that same month. Frémont technically maintained control of the land forces. General Kearny arrived in December, just in time to help quell an uprising. Confusion over who now commanded the occupation forces in California and who by right could negotiate treaties soon led Stockton, Kearny, and Frémont headlong into a politically explosive dispute that proved one of the great tests of civil-military relations during the war.

Colonel Alexander Doniphan's Missouri volunteers occupied Chihuahua on March 1, 1847, giving the United States a firm grip on all northern Mexico—the defensive line envisioned by Polk was complete. Protected from any attack out of the north, General Winfield Scott's unprecedented amphibious landing at Vera Cruz and planned march to Mexico City now commenced. With landing craft already built, the American fleet left for the Mexican coast on March 2. After four days at sea, the fleet rendezvoused just south of Vera Cruz and prepared for the assault. On March 9 American forces waded ashore with surprisingly little opposition from Mexican forces. Instead, Mexicans had chosen to fortify the city of Vera Cruz, which by late March Scott's army began to bombard with artillery. On March 29 the city of Vera Cruz surrendered, giving the Americans a base in central Mexico with open supply lines via the sea back to the United States. The operation's success was due partly to American planning and partly to weak Mexican resistance.

Scott's march inland began on April 8 and ended with the occupation of Mexico City on September 14. The first major contest between American and Mexican forces in central Mexico occurred on April 18 at a mountain pass held by General Santa Anna's men. To follow the National Road to the capital, the pass and a nearby town, both called Cerro Gordo, had to be taken. Leading the Americans to victory were volunteer divisions commanded by regulars Colonel David Twiggs and General William Worth (both formerly of Taylor's command), and later a brigade led by volunteer general Gideon Pillow, Polk's old friend and political ally from Tennessee, whom Scott believed possessed secret orders from Polk to undermine him. Later in the war Scott arrested Pillow and Worth on charges of insubordination, setting in motion a series of events that ended with his own recall from Mexico by the president. From Cerro Gordo Scott pressed on, occupying the sprawling city of Puebla on May 15.

At Puebla, however, the American advance stalled. The cause of the delay was the policy of limited duration enlistment. Scott, left dangerously short-handed as a sizeable number of troops headed home, waited deep inside Mexican territory for new recruits to arrive. Morale declined, troops grew unruly, but in August a reinforced and reorganized American army, now composed of four divisions led by volunteers Pillow and John Quitman and regulars Worth and Twiggs, set out for the capital. Of the possible approaches to Mexico City, Scott chose to march from the southwest. By mid-August a large portion of the American army encamped at San Augustin, barely nine miles short of their ultimate goal.

The path to Mexico City now was even more heavily guarded than before, and though Scott stood just a few miles from the capital, Santa Anna's army still effectively blocked the National Road. One option for the Americans was to send a division to flank the Mexican army at Churubusco by marching across treacherous lava beds, taking the small village of Contreras, and attacking from the rear. This would split the Mexican forces. On August 19 an American division marched across the lava beds, and, though weary from their march, attacked Mexican positions early in the morning of August 20 at Contreras. In under 20 minutes the surprise attack devastated the Mexican army. The Battle of Churubusco, fought later that same day, turned into one of the bloodiest of the war. Scott's army was now just three miles outside of Mexico City.

Rather than advance on the capital, however, Scott offered an armistice to Santa Anna. The U.S. plenipotentiary and peace negotiator, Nicholas Trist, had been in Mexico City since May. Scott apparently hoped that under threat of having their capital occupied by a foreign army, the Mexicans might negotiate a peace with Trist, making the final battle for Mexico City unnecessary. Thus, Trist embarked on his first round of serious negotiations. Santa Anna, meanwhile, used the lull in hostilities to strengthen his positions, having lost cannon, munitions, and one-third of his army at Churubusco.

Negotiations broke down completely in early September, and hostilities again ensued. As Scott's army advanced toward Mexico City it received intelligence that fortifications at nearby Molino del Rey contained a weapons foundry, munitions, and cannon—potentially enough to rearm Santa Anna's entire army or keep any resulting insurgency in arms for many months to come. Scott therefore concluded that he could not yet risk attacking the capital, in case the rumors were true. The Americans won a short but terribly bloody battle on September 8, suffering over 700 casualties, after which Scott discovered there were no munitions or cannon after all. It turns out Santa Anna had hoped to delay Scott's approach to the capital by convincing him that the Mexican army still possessed impressive military capabilities.

Scott turned his eyes toward Mexico City. He announced after extensive consultations with his officers that Chapultepec, a castle-like palace overlooking Mexico City, would have to be taken before Americans could safely enter the capital. After a daylong fight on September 13, Americans took the palace. As Santa Anna fled, Scott's army marched triumphantly into Mexico City the next day and hoisted the Stars and Stripes over the National Palace of Mexico. After some looting on the part of American troops, mostly volunteers, the occupation of Mexico City began.

Besides fighting the Mexican army in several hard won battles, Scott faced the task of dealing with ill-disciplined volunteers, political appointees like Pillow, atrocities or looting by American soldiers, officers' criticism of Polk's conciliation policy toward the Catholic Church in Mexico, and his own worsening relations with President Polk. Scott's ego also collided with the equally vain Nicholas Trist, with whom Polk was so weary by late 1847 that he revoked his plenipotentiary powers. Polk's suspicions of Scott's political aspirations eventually led the president to relieve him of duty on January 13, 1848. The general left for the United States but the army he had led to victory stayed behind until after ratifications of the Treaty of Guadalupe Hidalgo, signed on February 2, 1848, had been exchanged by the two countries. The treaty, negotiated by Trist after his recall by President Polk, netted the United States California, New Mexico, and recognition of Texas's annexation with a border at the Rio Grande. In return, the United States paid Mexico $15 million.

The Mexican War of 1846–1848 was America's first major foreign and offensive war. American soldiers invaded Mexico by land and sea, capturing its major cities, including the capital. This unprecedented military undertaking challenged a dependence on volunteer soldiers and a pro-militia mentality rooted in long-standing American prejudice against a large, standing army. The professional military still was in the early stages of its evolution, and West Point training had yet to prove its effectiveness.

Clashes between the civilian government and the military during the Mexican War were more the rule than the exception, although they never got out of hand. Indeed, the war turned out to be a tremendous military success. Yet victory came in spite of policy conflicts, funding disputes, procedural disagreements, fights over command, and unhappiness among the rank and file with particular Polk administration policies. Though all of the U.S. Army's leading soldiers ultimately deferred to their civilian bosses, such deference did not always come easily. Impulsive military leaders, contrary to the plans of the U.S. government in Washington City, proclaimed their own laws, engaged in unauthorized diplomacy, disobeyed orders, and unilaterally negotiated armistices with the enemy.

Substantial threats to civilian authority, and therefore to Polk, were few, mostly inadvertent, and seldom planned. The largest potential threat came from officers-turned-military governors in New Mexico, California, and the cities of central Mexico. These occupation governments had no precedent in American history, and their stories make for some of the most interesting civil-military developments to come out of the war. Intense partisanship between Whigs and Democrats complicated civil-military relations every step of the way, as the two dominant parties of the Jacksonian era that had formed amid the mixed blessings of the market revolution battled for control of the army and to make the U.S. military victory serve their own political purposes.

The disputes between military and civilian authorities during the Mexican War may have grown out of the anxieties and political tensions of the market revolution, but they were rooted in older republican ideals—personal liberty, a quasi-religious belief in the superiority of the citizen soldier, a tradition of limited duration enlistment, and a concurrent fear of a well-trained, standing army led by a professional officer corps. Yet as the war was to prove, professional officers and West Point graduates provided invaluable leadership and service, setting a precedent for the eventual rise in importance of the U.S. Military Academy.

President Polk's betrothal to Jacksonian doctrines like majority rule and the necessity of territorial expansion for the good of the people goes a long way toward explaining his dominance of war planning and strategy, his unabashed partisanship in organizing a fighting force, and his disputes with generals, governors, and Congress. Indeed, the story of civil-military relations in the Mexican War is largely one of politically explosive measures taken or supported by Polk and the response to them by Whigs, other political enemies, or U.S. military personnel.

In a nation predisposed against an organized and professional army, the events of the war bolstered those who argued for the type of military Americans instinctively abhorred. Volunteer units were organized according to the militia laws of each state, and governors—jealous of their own powers—complicated already strained relations among President Polk, Congress, and the U.S. Army. The challenge for Polk was to devise policies that honored the citizen soldier tradition and respected the roles of Congress and the several states in procuring an army—all the while maintaining morale and military effectiveness in the field. For Polk, a strict partisan with real and perceived enemies and a detail-oriented, micromanager by nature, this proved no easy task. His behavior during the war established the precedent, sometimes followed, sometimes not, of the drive by presidents to expand their executive powers during wartime and to use wars for partisan gain. The attempt by Polk to translate Jacksonian attitudes toward the military into workable federal policy will be explored in the next chapter.

2

"State Feuds and Factious Jealousy"

In late April 1846 most Americans agreed with George Bancroft, Secretary of the Navy, who told President James K. Polk that although the United States ought to seek "redress of the wrongs and injuries" perpetrated by Mexico, war should be declared only "if any act of hostility should be committed by the Mexican forces." Yet except for Bancroft, Polk's cabinet to a man urged the president to declare war before news even arrived in Washington City that Mexicans had attacked Zachary Taylor's army. This attitude, that the United States ought only act in self-defense or to defend its honor, went hand in hand with mythologization of the militia and the belief that large standing armies and long-term enlistment threatened liberty as much as if not more than invasion.[1]

To understand federal policy during the Mexican War we must first examine what Americans believed about how a republic conducts a war, and inquire as to what Americans expected of their elected representatives. Only then can we ascertain to what extent Whig opponents of the war fought on partisan grounds and to what degree they functioned from principled motives or operated within the citizen soldier tradition. In the 1790s George Washington had admonished Americans to be wary of political parties. As parties seek to perpetuate their power, principle inexorably loses out to self-serving partisanship. The most dangerous parties, believed Washington, were ones with distinctly regional constituencies. This is exactly the reason why Washington, like most of the other founders, favored limited suffrage and multistage elections to prevent the development of popular but unprincipled parties. In the opinion of most Americans during the Jacksonian era, be they Whigs or Democrats, partisanship and principle did not have to be mutually exclusive.

Although nearly all Americans regardless of political affiliation accepted without question the superiority of the citizen soldier, especially militiamen, a number of factors shaped American attitudes toward the military. Increasing democratization in politics between 1815 and the 1840s had only deepened the citizen soldier tradition, and by 1846 it varied by region and political affiliation. These traditional American attitudes, spurred on by a newfound civic engagement that inevitably shoehorned all issues into a rabidly partisan context, helped shape the manner in which President Polk approached relations with Congress and state governors and illuminate how he tackled federal policy toward the military during the Mexican War.

To most Americans, "democracy" by the time of the Mexican War no longer carried with it fears of demagoguery and images of mob rule. Rather, it implied a positive collaboration between governor and governed aimed at better securing the God-given liberties guaranteed by the Constitution and American custom. The 1840s came on the tail end of the Jacksonian era, a period marked by expanding male suffrage and a growth of citizen involvement in society and politics. Improved transportation and communication made political involvement easier. So, too, did an expanded postal system and the penny press. All of these together enabled voluntary societies and political parties to spread their word cheaply, efficiently, and quickly. In 1846, federal and state officials recognized that more than ever before they had to measure the public mood closely before formulating policy.

United States congressmen sought to please their national political parties while remaining responsive to the will of their increasingly active constituents. Senators, as appointees of state legislatures, could more freely push policies that lacked support among the citizens of their respective states. President Polk, styling himself along the lines of Andrew Jackson as the only elected official who represented all citizens, proved intensely partisan. Politics figured into every choice Polk made about the war, from the methods he and his party used to pass war appropriations in Congress to his choice of army officers, especially generals.

THE POLITICS OF EXPANSION

Regional differences were not a prime determinant in adherence to the citizen soldier tradition but sectional considerations did make a marked difference in popular support for the war. Generally speaking, Southerners championed the war because of closer familial ties to Texans and their geographical proximity to Mexico. Not a few hoped to expand their "peculiar institution" southward and westward. The Missouri Compromise forbade slavery in new states created north of the 36°30' line (the southern border of Missouri), but potentially all of Mexico lay before them. Some even dreamed of extending the Union into the Caribbean and Central America.

For reasons unrelated to slavery, Westerners also supported territorial expansion. The Mexican War found ready support in the states of Ohio, Indiana, Illinois, Kentucky, and states west of the Mississippi River, including the two territories that achieved statehood during or shortly after the war (Iowa, in December 1846, and Wisconsin, in May 1848). Citizens of these states saw themselves as living proof of the United States's "Manifest Destiny" to bring all of North America under the Anglo-Saxon, Protestant, republican rule of the United States. On a less theoretical level, Westerners faced a tangible and very real Indian threat (except in Kentucky), and so the citizen soldier tradition was more alive and the militia more active in the West than anywhere else in the country.

New Englanders by long habit opposed westward expansion as one way of protecting their diminishing importance on the national political scene and stopping the spread of slavery. But few commercially minded New Englanders could ignore the clear advantages of American ports on the California coast, and so even in the Whig heartland considerable support existed for a tightly regulated expansion aimed at securing Pacific ports in the name of maritime trade. For a few vocal evangelical Protestants, still in the midst of what some historians call the Second Great Awakening, the promise of spreading Christianity to Asia provided further reason to populate the West Coast with Americans. Abolitionists already were addressing slavery as a moral question by the 1840s, but regardless of slavery's evils, northern businessmen and laborers agreed about slavery's detrimental effects on yeoman farmers and waged workers in a free market economy. Obviously, the fact that the Mexican War was a questionable conflict waged under a Democratic commander in chief enhanced the position of the already dominant Whig Party in New England. Employing deftly the Jacksonian rhetoric of their opponents, Whigs lamented "the criminal short-sightedness which prompted our rulers rashly to engage in a war without consulting the great council of the nation." They warned that territories annexed as a result of the war would unleash "chaos" and permanently poison relations between the North and the South. At the same time, however, New England Whigs took great pains to praise the citizen soldier as "the gallant soldier who goes forth to battle to uphold the flag of his country."[2]

New Yorkers, Pennsylvanians, and inhabitants of the middle states commonly supported the war. They demonstrated this by turning out in large numbers to fill the ranks of the armies that invaded California and central Mexico. New York City's confidence in a virtuous citizenry's ability to defend liberty filled Central Park on a recruitment day in May 1846 with over 50,000 men, the total possible for all the states under the requisition. Over 20,000 gathered in Philadelphia expressing their desire to serve.[3]

THE POLITICS OF WAR

According to the U.S. Constitution, the task of "organizing, arming, and disciplining the Militia, and for governing such Part of them as may be employed in the Service of the United States" fell to Congress. Commanding them was the responsibility of the president as commander in chief. Yet to the states the Constitution reserved "the Appointment of the Officers, and the Authority of training the Militia," as laid out according to subsequent acts of Congress. What this amounted to after many years of legislation was that the president called on the militia in times of national emergency, governors selected the companies that would serve, and militiamen elected their own officers up through the rank of colonel—the president appointed generals and staff officers. However, the president typically could only keep militia in the field for three months at a time. This is why volunteers were so important, because three months might be enough time to engage in defensive action but little else could be accomplished in the event of an offensive war.

Fighting for their place in this mix of competing power blocs and interests in 1846 were the state governors. Since volunteer units were organized according to the militia laws of each state, governors potentially could play as important a role in army formation as Polk, Congress, and the War Department, not to mention the U.S. Army itself. Ideally, the militia was designed to respond quickly and efficiently to local disturbances or to defend one's state in the event of invasion. In Jacksonian America, however, national politics and party affiliation, not local concerns, usually determined the actions of governors, especially Whigs who governed states like Ohio and Kentucky where the war was popular. Yet in their rhetoric Whig governors carefully cited local concerns or refused to dispatch militia on Constitutional grounds, saying that there had been no "invasion" or "insurrection." Polk knew, as had Jefferson before him, that these were the sorts of reasons to rely on volunteers and not militia in time of war.

Even before the official request for volunteers by the U.S. government, Americans responded to news of the clash on the Rio Grande with appeals to defend American honor against Mexican aggression. Many uttered jingoistic slogans like, "Our Country, Right or Wrong" as they lined up for recruiters even as they acknowledged the murkiness of Polk's explanation for the immediate cause of the war. Critics demeaned this as "grogshop patriotism," but volunteer companies formed and militia mustered, all hoping to get a chance to go fight the Mexicans.[4]

The needs of the regular army at the time Congress declared war should have been obvious to all observers. Only around 5,500 regulars were in uniform in May 1846, and many of these were ill prepared. Taylor's troops were apparently safe for the time being but ultimately outmanned, and all knew the regular army could be enlarged only so much without exacerbating Americans' customary aversion to professional armies. But Taylor needed to be reinforced and a strategy put in place either to bring Mexico to peace or to conquer it.

Even those who opposed the war declaration (mostly Whigs) on the grounds that a state of war did not exist between the two nations acknowledged that there could be no delay in reinforcing Taylor. Acting on standing orders, Taylor already had requested 5,000 militia from Louisiana and Texas, but their arrival would take time. In any case, as militia they could only serve for three months. Mexico's army reputedly numbered upwards of 40,000 soldiers. Even if every regular from every state and territory of the United States immediately supplemented Taylor, along with these militia his force would have increased only to around 12,000.[5] The question was not so much whether the army sent to fight Mexico should be composed of volunteer and regular forces. That was a given. Rather, the debate concerned the extent to which the regular army should be enlarged, for how long, and how big of a role volunteers would play. Moreover, should the volunteers be drawn from existing militia companies or should each state embark on recruitment days to meet their quota? Indeed, should the state militia itself be mustered at all? Nearly everyone promised to maintain the volunteers' personal liberty and prevent the permanent augmentation of the regular army. To those who already considered Polk a tyrant who had initiated a war for popularity and to serve slaveholders and Democrats, giving him any kind of permanent, regular army would be foolhardy.

Polk was not without the requisite political experience needed to guide war legislation through Congress. Nor did he lack intimate knowledge of the inner workings of government at the state level. In 1823 Polk had combined his expertise as a lawyer, brief experience as a clerk in the Tennessee state senate, and Jeffersonian political philosophy into a successful run for the state legislature. While there, he emerged as one of Andrew Jackson's most reliable supporters. When Jackson lost the election of 1824, Polk determined to run for Congress, and the next year won his first of seven terms. As historian Paul H. Bergeron points out, Polk, now a strong Jacksonian democrat, seemed to find himself "in the center of the controversies over the national bank, the tariff, and internal improvements." As chairman of the Ways and Means Committee, Polk played an instrumental role in ensuring Democratic support for Jackson's veto of the Maysville Road and for his attack on the Bank of the United States. In 1835 Polk embarked on his first of four straight years as Speaker of the House. In 1839 he left Congress and, in Whig-dominated Tennessee, still managed to win the governorship. Yet what he really wanted was the presidency, and for that post Congress and the governorship were mere stepping stones. In 1840, however, Polk's political fortunes suffered a setback when he failed to earn the Democratic Party's vice presidential nomination. This was not to be Polk's last disappointment in the realm of politics, for he lost his reelection bid in 1841 in the face of a resurgent Whiggery still riding high from the election of "Tippecanoe and Tyler, too" in 1840. In 1843, after losing another gubernatorial race, Polk returned to his law practice. Amazingly enough, the next year he became the first "dark horse" candidate for president in American history and won the election.[6]

James K. Polk during his presidency (National Archives).

What Polk possessed in political experience and ambition he lacked in military training. When General Winfield Scott suggested to him that at a minimum 20,000 volunteers would be necessary as an immediate call-up, and then further plans could be made, Polk reluctantly agreed. Still, he "did not think so many as 20,000 volunteers" were necessary. Establishing the pattern he followed throughout the war, Polk second guessed his general in chief, and not entirely for tactical reasons. The Tennessean was decidedly

unimpressed with Scott "as a military man," but feared the political consequences if Mexico defeated the United States due to overwhelming numerical
superiority. Corollary to this was that Polk already suspected Scott, accurately, as it turned out, of renewed presidential aspirations. Polk did not wish
to hand a political issue to the opposition so easily, but neither did he desire
to make Scott appear more militarily competent than himself.

This meeting with Scott promptly launched Polk on an autodidactic effort
at military education that never wavered until the Senate approved the
Treaty of Guadalupe Hidalgo in 1848. As the war was to prove, in spite of
his initial underestimation of needed troop numbers, Polk possessed an
instinctive grasp for the kind of war needed to acquire California and force
a pro-U.S. settlement of the Texas border issue while heading off a Mexican
insurgency on the one hand, and excessive jingoistic fervor by Americans on
the other. The only thing that ever threatened to get in the way of this was
Polk's other, stronger instinct: politics.[7]

If permitted by Congress, the 20,000 volunteers requested by Polk, per
Scott's suggestion, would be drawn from the states of Alabama, Mississippi,
Arkansas, Missouri, Georgia, Illinois, Ohio, Indiana, Kentucky, Tennessee,
and Texas. Publicly, the president argued that these states were closest to
Mexico.[8] True enough, but Polk considered more than just these states'
proximity to Mexico when he issued the initial call for volunteers. He well
knew that the war was popular in the West and the South even as it was
unpopular in the Whig stronghold of New England. With the volunteers as
with other matters, politics figured prominently into Polk's calculation.

Beginning on May 11, the day Polk sent his war message to the Capitol
and two days before the official declaration of war, Congress set out to create
an army capable of defeating Mexico. A couple of bills meant to enlarge
the army, originally written for the abortive war against Great Britain
over Oregon, helped accelerate this process. Polk now urged congressional
Democrats to push war measures through the House in less than one day.

BUILDING AN ARMY

The most immediate problem facing Congress was how to overcome the
American army's small size without permanently creating too large of a
regular army—something Congress had been debating since March. The
"Act to authorize an Increase of the Rank and File of the Army of the United
States," signed by Polk on May 13, accomplished this in part by augmenting
the regular army, also known as the Old Establishment. Without adding a
new regiment, this act more than doubled the number of privates in existing
artillery, infantry, and dragoon companies, from 42, 42, and 50, respectively, to 100 for each. In spite of Missouri senator Thomas Hart Benton's
promise that these companies could be reduced when "the exigencies of the
country did not require the additional force," some Whigs protested that

the act permanently doubled the standing army. However, by not creating a new regiment and only adding privates, no new officers were needed—officers that Whigs knew would be appointed by Polk or promoted by his appointees. Based on this compromise the bill passed overwhelmingly. The few who voted against the bill were Whigs from New England, New York, and Ohio.[9]

The nature of the opposition to another bill, calling for the creation of Company A of the U.S. Engineers, shows that more than simple partisanship or antislavery sentiment animated the Whigs who opposed the Mexican War. This bill received little debate when introduced on May 12, save for a speech by Ohio congressman and Whig, Joshua Giddings. Giddings, a well-known antislavery advocate, opposed creating Company A but claimed to care little whether the war expanded free labor, and thus helped the North, or spread the institution of slavery, thereby boosting the southern economy. Instead, Giddings rested his stance solidly within the citizen soldier tradition. He pointed with no small amount of pride to the fact that he "had at all times opposed every increase of the standing army," and suggested a conspiracy was afoot to exploit the current crisis with Mexico and enlarge the standing army of the United States. The U.S. Army, said Giddings, stripped capable men of their liberty and autonomy, leaving them able only to obey or to command—two qualities that henceforth made them "unfit for the duties of civil life." More still, by becoming accustomed to being on the public payroll, on discharge former regulars lacked the will to go into business for themselves. To support this bold claim he argued that "citizens...possess the inherent power at all times of defending our nation," and so he heaped hyperbolic praise on the militia's performance in the Revolutionary War and the War of 1812. Authorizing 50,000 volunteers ought to be sufficient, Giddings thought, and he urged his colleagues not to give in to the delusion that more regulars were necessary. Of course, Giddings did not favor sending volunteers, regulars, *or* militia to fight in Mexico, for he called the war immoral, unwise, and refused "to participate in the crime of subverting the Government of Mexico." Giddings's colleagues knew this and one derided his speech as irrelevant. In the end, the bill easily passed with only nine "nays," and Polk, whom Giddings saw as the grand conspirator, signed it on May 15.[10]

A few days later Congress again expanded the regular army, this time by voting to form an entirely new regiment of mounted riflemen. The bill in question had been lingering since January, but events in Mexico finally forced Congress's hand. As Senator Benton explained, the regiment would "constitute a portion of the permanent peace establishment" and was not a temporary addition for the war with Mexico. Indeed, the riflemen, according to the title of the act as signed by Polk on May 19, were to guard "the route to Oregon," not fight in Mexico (which they did anyway, before taking up their designated post). Of course, even if deployed on the paths to Oregon, the mounted riflemen's presence there could not but relieve the strain on U.S. forces caused by the war. In this sense, the riflemen were most emphatically *not* simply a part of the "permanent peace establishment," and Whigs knew it. Moreover, the bill as originally written granted Polk the opportunity to appoint Democrat officers to the army. The question facing Whigs, then, was the same one to which Federalists during the War of 1812 had responded so badly: how does one oppose war measures boosting the army's chances in battle and still retain the mantle of patriotism.[11]

Kentucky senator John Crittenden answered the above question by shrewdly proposing that new officers be chosen by merit from the existing officer corps of the army. To other Whig critics of the bill, like Senator William Archer, not doing so could only mean officers would come from "the ranks of executive favoritism." He tried unsuccessfully to restrict the president's power of appointment. Likewise, Crittenden warned the bill would render President Polk's power "arbitrary, absolute, and unregulated." These Whigs claimed their motive was to ensure the army possessed well-trained officers, and this was no doubt partly true. But they also knew, as did everyone, that the army's current officer corps contained more Whigs than Democrats. They rightly smelled a Democratic plan to alter this fact under the guise of a wartime measure that, in the end, also would have the unpalatable effect of increasing the peacetime standing army. The Senate's vote on the Whigs' executive-curtailing amendment was a tie. Polk's vice president, George Dallas, cast the tie-breaking vote to kill it—Polk would freely appoint the officers commissioned for the new regiment. After some additional but minor changes to the bill, it passed both houses and Polk signed it on May 19. Yet, unlike the vote on the Company A bill, this one broke down almost entirely along party lines. A slightly larger standing army was something a Whig apparently could live with; a Democratic president empowered to appoint cronies to high officer positions was not—thus, politics won out over the citizen soldier tradition in the confrontation over the mounted riflemen.[12]

MILITIA OR VOLUNTEERS?

Even with these additions to the army, which brought the number of regulars on paper to 15,540, the United States still lacked an army matching the size of Mexico's. The "Act providing for the Prosecution of the existing War between the United States and the Republic of Mexico" authorized Polk to call up as many as 50,000 volunteer soldiers from the several states, a number far in excess of Scott's initial target of 20,000. The volunteers could serve for up to 12 months, and presumably none but the most adamant antiwar Whigs had reservations about supporting short-term enlistees. The truth is, however, that many viewed the 12-month volunteers as *long termers*. The act did not call out militia troops, although it did authorize Polk to do so if necessary for terms "not exceeding six months" in any given year.[13]

The Democratic Party proved no less guilty than the Whigs in using the war for political advantage and posturing. To trap the Whigs politically, Democrats attached to the prosecutorial bill language blaming Mexico for "the existing war." This was a reference to Polk's argument that since war already existed following the clash of American and Mexican troops in southern Texas, Congress need only recognize it with a declaration. Whigs ridiculed this rationale as casuistry. Objecting to the bill's language, Kentuckian Garrett Davis acknowledged the Whigs' difficult dilemma: "Their purpose was to make the Whigs vote against, or force them to aid in throwing a shelter over" Polk. Like most Whigs, who feared going the way of the Federalists following that now defunct party's opposition to "Mr. Madison's War," Davis ended up voting for the bill.[14]

The lack of a militia call-up in the "Act providing for the Prosecution of the existing War between the United States and the Republic of Mexico" is more significant than it might appear at first glance. While the militia's lack of readiness and inadequacy as an organized fighting force could remain hidden or be ignored in peacetime for political reasons, such was not the case in wartime. For example, on paper the Mississippi militia all by itself could nearly have fielded enough volunteers for the entire war effort, but in reality those numbers were meaningless. In other states, the militia did not even exist on paper. This state of unreadiness, and the fact that militia could not serve for any length of time to be of practical value to an army meant to invade Mexico, made them a poor choice indeed.[15]

One reason in the first place for leaving the choice between militia and volunteers to the president's discretion was that knowledgeable congressmen and state governors were acquainted with the poor condition of their own state's militia. Despite privately conceding the shortcomings of the militia system as it was constituted in the 1840s, politicians everywhere did recognize its political importance, whether this meant the volunteer companies containing educated, politically active men of better means or the regular companies that technically included all adult males in their ranks. The volunteer militia, beyond its dubious military purpose, represented a critical network of supporters for state and federal office holders. One, therefore, had to be very careful at least to pay lip service to the citizen soldier ethic sustaining the militia's existence.

To what degree did Congress's choice to raise a volunteer army rather than muster the militia represent an admission of the militia's poor performance in offensive operations in the War of 1812? Very little, for in their minds volunteers were every bit the citizen soldier as were militia troops, but with two added benefits: they could serve for longer periods of time and do so with fewer restrictions on who must lead them. Moreover, volunteers still honored the same republican spirit behind the concept of the militia; that is, citizens in time of national peril taking up arms to fight their country's enemies. Besides, the customary three-month time limit on militia service, increased to six months in the prosecutorial act of May 13, rightly worried the militarily educated who realized six months (let alone three months) was barely long enough even to gather soldiers, let alone properly arm, supply, and transport them to Mexico.

The principal question to ask is *not*, Why not the militia? but, Why did American politicians so heavily emphasize raw volunteers in the first place, who could be expected to perform little better in offensive operations than had their militia counterparts in the War of 1812? During the Mexican War Americans transformed the rhetoric previously reserved for militia into adulatory praise of volunteers. The motivations of Polk and Congress were complex, but one major reason was that they knew augmenting the regular army by 50,000 men would be impossible both politically and in terms of finding recruits. The volunteer ethic of the citizen soldier forbade it, Whigs were already voicing their displeasure at any substantial or permanent increase in the regular army, and the romantic admiration Americans had for the 1812 militia and their reminiscences of the Revolutionary War made it unseemly. As it were, immediately after the clash along the Rio Grande in April, Taylor had requested 5,000 troops from Louisiana and Texas. These men enlisted for the presumed maximum of six months, a sure sign to Mexico that the United States planned to fight nothing more serious than a defensive border war. More confusing still, under the new law officers were to be chosen according to the laws of the several states. This meant anything from governmental appointment to volunteers electing their own officers; usually, the latter. Field, staff, and general officers were left to President Polk to appoint, as were all the new positions that would be required to quarter, outfit, and feed such a large army.

The lack of a militia muster did not keep existing militia companies from lining up to be accepted as volunteer units. Indeed, not until mid-1847 did the army admit individual volunteers as replacement personnel—prior to that one had to enter as part of a volunteer company complete with officers and, in the case of cavalry, extensive equipment. Nevertheless, most of the men who answered Polk's call for 50,000 volunteers in May 1846 did not come from militia companies.[16] In fact, militia made up only 12 percent of the total force in the Mexican War, as opposed to 88 percent in the War of 1812.[17] Nearly all volunteers belonged to new companies formed during the spring and summer of 1846. These new companies named their own officers, with qualifications ranging from militia experience and local wealth or renown, to promises of plunder and the amount of liquor one could afford to dole out. Companies adopted names based on county, region, or religion, such as the Protestant Invincibles, Hickory Blues, and Bowery B'Hoys. Most designed and paid for their own uniforms, hoping for reimbursement by the U.S. government on their acceptance under the terms spelled out by the act of May 13.

Statistics on the actual numbers of volunteers and regulars can be misleading in determining the size and composition of the American army that went to war in Mexico. Volunteers, who numbered 73,000 by the end of the war, made up the bulk of the American invasion and occupation force. Eventually, 27,000 regulars fought in Mexico, although nearly half were former volunteers who swore a new oath in Mexico when their initial term of service expired. The May 13 war bill authorized a call-up of 50,000 volunteers from every state, although the first volunteers came from the states closest to Mexico, Texas and Louisiana. Southern and Western volunteers, approximately 20,000 men, went immediately to Mexico. Those from the Northeast were to be held in reserve for later action.

Partisanship among volunteer companies played a significant role in the tug of war between states and the federal government, and within states, over officer selection in those units to be incorporated into the U.S. Army. In most states volunteers elected their own officers, all the way up the chain of command to colonel, and these elections were hard fought. Historian Richard Bruce Winders is correct when he argues that "the system guaranteed that the issue of politics would enter the selection process." State governors usually appointed officers above the rank of colonel, but even in these cases, of course, political calculations were not absent. While trust in one's officers is fundamental to *esprit de corps* and good military order, in the highly politicized age of Jackson solidly partisan companies could conceivably end up being led by men from the opposing party.[18]

Most soldiers praised the electioneering by prospective officers, at least at the company and regimental levels, as a democratic practice "sanctioned by the people themselves." Heroism and partisanship could coexist, but politicization of the war itself, openly and in a crass manner for obvious partisan advantage or personal power, was another matter entirely. For example, Taylor's men reacted angrily to the impassioned political rhetoric in the debates over the war bills. They objected to Whig criticism of what they believed to be a gallant affair of arms. Worse, by labeling the conflict "Mr. Polk's War," and blaming it on a suspected southern slaveocracy, critics implicitly accused soldiers of being dupes in a conspiracy. This rhetoric offended soldiers already in Mexico and those lining up to join them there, who accused Whigs of opposing the war simply to spite the northern wing of the Democracy.[19]

The disparity in attitudes between politicians and the citizenry they represented was most apparent in the western states and in South Carolina. Expansionist-minded Westerners and proslavery Southerners by and large supported the war. Discounting for a moment the fear that adding territory to the Union would weaken the political influence of the entire eastern seaboard, a great number of Americans simply interpreted the war as their generation's chance to prove their republican virtue and show themselves worthy of citizenship. They spoke with praise of their fathers' bravery in the War of 1812, conjured up stylized images of the Revolutionary War, and predicted they would prove equal to the task and worthy of past American sacrifices in the name of honor and liberty. Lost in this effusive patriotic shuffle and republican efflorescence were the contestable events surrounding the war's origins.

OPPOSITION: PRINCIPLES AND POLITICS

Political debates in Kentucky, home to two of the most prominent Whigs, Henry Clay and John Crittenden, provide another telling example of how partisanship affected the formation and composition of the army that fought in Mexico, again by taking the form of citizen soldier rhetoric. Politicians often balked while their citizenry rushed down the path to war. Senators Clay and Crittenden served the Kentucky legislature that appointed them but differed with most Kentuckians about the war. Along with Governor William Owsley, also a Whig, they opposed what they derisively referred to as "Mr. Polk's War." Clay and his fellow Kentucky Whigs were proslavery, but this did not mean they favored granting the chief executive the authority to incite a war and then having Congress approve it after the fact. The senators opposed Polk in Congress while Owsley dragged his feet in May as Secretary of War Marcy called for Kentucky volunteers. Clay and Crittenden may have acted the part of senators immune to the passionate excesses of the *demos*, whose task it was to protect the long-term interests of their state, but in the age of Jacksonian democracy they could not openly censure the people, however wrong headed they believed them to be. This explains why nowhere in their dissent did they explicitly attack or try to dissuade the young men who swarmed Kentucky's recruiting stations.

There was recent precedent for the lack of response on the part of Kentucky's government to a militia call-up. In late 1845, trying to strengthen border security in the new state of Texas, Marcy had requested Kentucky militia be used to bolster then-Colonel Taylor's small number of troops. Governor Owsley all but refused; Kentucky, after all, shared no border with Texas. Kentuckians flocked to Taylor's banner anyway, a repeat of choices made 10 years earlier during the Texas Revolution.[20]

Owsley's behavior in 1845 helps explain why in May 1846 excited postal workers opened the secretary of war's letter to their governor and spread the news of a volunteer muster before Owsley had a chance to react. Kentuckians stood ready to rally to the flag, even if their Whig governor and senators did not. Militia companies mobilized and new ones formed before Frankfort publicly requisitioned troops. An entire volunteer regiment was already in place by the time Owlsey called for troops on May 22, and so the First Kentucky simply departed southward. Meanwhile, other regiments took longer to form, organize, and train and did not leave until midsummer.[21]

Henry Clay became a leading voice in the Senate not so much against the war itself, and certainly not against its soldiers, but rather against Polk's conduct of it. The war, said Clay, "was begun without any necessity, and in folly, and is conducted without wisdom." Clay never ceased to praise Taylor, however, whom he personally had concerns about but considered a possible 1848 presidential nominee for the Whig Party. In fact, Clay's son, Henry, Jr., volunteered and eventually served on Taylor's staff before dying at the Battle of Buena Vista in February 1847. Writing prior to his son's death about the pride he felt for him, Clay summed up the delicate Whig position that tried to balance criticism of the war and Polk with admiration for the volunteers: "We cannot but admire and approve the patriotic and gallant spirit which animates our Country men, altho' we might wish that the cause in which they have stept forth was more reconcilable with the dictates of conscience."[22]

The war's popularity in Ohio was tremendous, though state politics seemed topsy turvy when compared to the usual Whig-Democrat divide. Governor William Bebb, a thoroughgoing Whig, commanded a Whig majority in the Ohio state assembly and actually hoped to make the Democrats less popular even as he supported the allegedly Polk-induced war. With Whigs backing him in the statehouse, Bebb in June 1846 mobilized and funded two regiments of volunteers. So many men volunteered that the state turned hundreds away. Many of these perhaps later filled the third volunteer regiment created in 1847. Bebb depended on federal reimbursement for Ohio's expenses, since these were volunteer troops and not militia. (As in the case of Massachusetts in the War of 1812, the reimbursement proved a long time coming.) Yet in this matter of financing, where Bebb could have dragged his feet like Owsley, he did not. Even still, while Governor Bebb cultivated pro-war opinion he vociferously attacked Polk. Meanwhile, nativist Democrats (one of the oddities of Ohio politics) attacked him for allowing too many foreigners to enlist in the army.[23]

Ohio's congressmen and senators behaved less like their governor and more like their counterparts directly to the south in Kentucky. That is, they praised volunteers and danced around the war's popularity while attempting to use the occasion of it to hammer Polk. Senator Thomas Corwin matched Congressman Giddings's fiery opposition and principled stance. He strongly opposed the war not on partisan grounds, so he said, but because republicanism and liberty should be spread by example, not war. To Corwin, the Democratic program seemed to be one of hubristically rushing Providence in order to accelerate the destiny of the United States as a continental power. Antiwar groups around the country popularized Corwin's speech, reprinting it in pamphlets and in newspapers.[24]

Influential Democrats also opposed the war, most notably John C. Calhoun, the senator from South Carolina whom Polk branded "the most mischievous man in the Senate." Calhoun's opposition was more complex than that of party-driven Whigs like Corwin. Likewise, it was not quite based on personal hatred for the president resulting from his exclusion from the cabinet, although Polk believed this to be the case. Rather, South Carolinians had deep concerns about slavery's expansion westward, as that inevitably would weaken South Carolina's political influence and economic power. More importantly, Calhoun had grown increasingly wary of democracy and executive power ever since the fight over nullification during Jackson's presidency. The executive branch would not always be in Democratic hands friendly to the South and to the institution of slavery. Calhoun intended to defend South Carolina's autonomy and oppose the further concentration of power in Washington City against "Young Hickory" even as he had against "Old Hickory."[25]

Calhoun expressed few qualms about arming and supporting American soldiers already in the field, but during the debate over whether to declare war he objected to the imprudence of his colleagues. In Calhoun's opinion, insufficient evidence existed to support Polk's contention that a state of war existed between the United States and Mexico simply because of an ambush along the border. How do we "know that the Government of Mexico would not disavow what had been done?" Calhoun asked. Calhoun's ultimate concern, as a political theorist of the first order, was that hasty approval of Polk's request for a war declaration would permanently undermine Congress's Constitutional power to declare war, in practice making Congress a body capable only of rubber stamping the actions of an authoritarian executive.[26]

One other factor shaped the argumentation of Clay, Calhoun, and Corwin. Their positions against the war and their criticism of Polk were rooted in a republican love of liberty not dissimilar to the principles that animated the citizen soldier tradition to which the volunteers adhered. Therefore, they sought to shape federal policy accordingly, not just for their party's good but for the good of their respective states and for the good of the Union as a whole. The volunteers praised citizen soldiers as distinctive, virtuous republicans who fought for their country and liberty and honor, not for a paycheck like regulars or mercenaries. To Clay and Calhoun, a president who instigated wars of conquest was dangerous to the republic, to the several states, and to individual liberty, even without possessing a large, standing army. Unfortunately, these usually went hand in hand, and the latter promised to follow if American patriots did not keep a watchful eye on Polk. The threat existed to liberty regardless of whether newly annexed lands became slave or free. The slavery issue might stir the masses, Calhoun realized, but it only represented the surface of the true fight, which involved a contest over the incipient expansion of power at the federal level in the hands of the executive. A powerful presidency would diminish

Congress while becoming a sharp-edged weapon with which the U.S. government could cut away at the sovereignty of the states. No responsible politician, then, could utter a jingoistic phrase like "our country, right or wrong" and remain intellectually honest.

Soldiers in Mexico, whether regulars or volunteers, cared little for nuanced positions, honest fears of tyrannical presidents, and the employment of lofty republican arguments against a war in which they might any day be killed or wounded. They considered the senators' behavior traitorous and accused them of placing American soldiers in danger. Lieutenant Daniel Harvey Hill sarcastically reported that the Philanthropic Society of Mexico had publicly thanked Clay and Calhoun "for their warm defence of Mexican interests." Ohio's volunteers, in "a unanimous movement of both regiments," burned Corwin in effigy—a nonpartisan celebration, to be sure. Overall, soldiers assessed the principles laid out by some members of Congress as having been cobbled together flimsily only to oppose Polk or appease their parties.[27]

Outside the realm of political theorists and professional politicians, those Americans who stood ready psychologically to go to war and to conquer vast stretches of territory were, in consequence of their adherence to the citizen soldier tradition, still as yet unwilling to meet the ugly necessities of being an imperial power. The citizen soldier tradition, as interpreted and massaged by pro- and antiwar Americans alike, was the main culprit behind the revolving door of the U.S. Army during the war. One important lesson of the War of 1812 was that an army with soldiers regularly coming and going could not train sufficiently, develop adequate unit cohesion, or engage in sustained offensive operations. This lesson, unable even to crack American prejudices against long-term enlistment, went unheeded by policy makers and soldiers during the Mexican War.

Few out of the first group of volunteers, who signed up for six-month enlistments as part of Taylor's emergency call-up, ever saw battle. What is more, most of the 12-month volunteers chose not to reenlist when their terms expired. Instead, they left for home believing they had fulfilled their duty as citizen soldiers. Most were all too happy to leave, having discovered the discipline and regimentation of military life to be dull and illiberal. They claimed not to mind battle so much; it was the repetitive, numbing drudgery of camp and the constant fight against diseases like the *vomito* that soured their quest for martial glory. To liberty-loving Westerners especially, life in the U.S. Army was something less than egalitarian and nothing like the rowdy pageantry of a traditional militia muster.

Probably the most dangerous consequence of limited duration enlistment occurred during the occupation of Puebla, which began in May 1847. At Puebla, the galloping American advance stalled. The cause of the delay was neither tactical nor strategic—it was the result of the enshrinement in law of an overly egalitarian citizen soldier ethic under the guise of an unrealistic and foolhardy enlistment policy. Scott was left dangerously shorthanded as a sizeable number of his volunteers headed back to the United States. The general had enough men to advance or to hold Puebla and guard his rear, but not both. Forced to wait deep in Mexican territory for new recruits to arrive, he watched as morale declined and troops grew bored, then unruly—reinforcements did not arrive for three more months. European observers commented that Scott's army was doomed. It is no wonder, then, that some of the worst American atrocities and instances of looting occurred during that three-month waiting game in Puebla.

Resistance to more practical terms of enlistment for volunteers was rooted in the same principles that hampered the much needed increase in the size of the regular army. While attempts were made to increase the army throughout the war, manpower shortages usually were filled by eleventh-hour compromises following dangerous delays and much politicking. This was the case with the Ten Regiment Bill, submitted to Congress six months prior to the near debacle at Puebla.

THE TEN REGIMENT BILL

In early December 1846 Secretary Marcy reported to Congress that the American army, despite the recent requisition of additional volunteers, was still undermanned to the tune of about 7,000 soldiers. Marcy requested that 10 more regiments be added immediately. Scott stood ready to depart. The general in chief already would be forced to poach troops from Taylor. The central Mexico campaign alone promised to gobble up significant numbers of troops for garrison duty in the cities and towns along the National Road leading to the capital.[28] Despite this obvious need for more soldiers, action was not forthcoming from the House Committee on Military Affairs until late in the month. Finally, on December 29 Hugh Haralson reported the Ten Regiment Bill to the House. The bill called for adding 10 regiments to the New Establishment—importantly, it called for regulars, not volunteers.

The debate over the Ten Regiment Bill put the political goals and deepest anxieties of Democrats and Whigs on display. The opposition to permanent enlargement of the regular U.S. Army; the excessive trust in the militia; the seemingly blind rhetorical support for volunteers in spite of news of their ill discipline and atrocities committed from New Orleans to central Mexico; the fear of expanded executive power; territorial ambitions; concerns about the expansion of slavery—all of these fall under the wider belief in America's Manifest Destiny as an exceptional republic providentially favored to consume the continent and enlighten the monarchical or barbaric regions of the world. Republican rhetoric and swooning admiration for the citizen soldier dominated the debate over the Ten Regiment Bill.

The House of Representatives set aside January 4 for extended discussion of the Ten Regiment Bill, but the debate dragged on much longer. Whigs suspected Polk, for strictly political reasons, was seeking to increase his control over the military and to expand his powers of patronage, thereby endangering the war effort and threatening the whole citizen soldier tradition. Whigs employed citizen soldier rhetoric and uttered traditional derogations about standing armies, but these masked their primary motivation, which was every bit as political as the president's: to stop Polk from increasing his powers of patronage. Thus the majority of proposed amendments dealt with changing the regiments from regulars to volunteers or somehow altering the manner in which officers in the new regiments would be chosen. Indeed, Whigs were most concerned with how the regiments would be officered, for in its original form the bill promised to give Polk the unprecedented power to appoint officers even at the company level.

Whigs attacked Polk using two arguments. First, they implied that the request for so many regulars showed that Polk doubted the "bravery," "patriotism," and "military spirit" of the volunteers. At the same time, Whigs readily acknowledged that "the present deficiency of the army" in terms of recruits boded ill for its future prospects. This latter claim presaged the Whigs' second angle of attack—they hinted at a conspiracy by Polk to abuse the state of war to increase his patronage by "four or five hundred commissions, of all grades." Why else, asked Robert Toombs of Georgia, would he request nearly 10,000 additional regulars when he "well knew that those regiments could not be filled now?" Since all six brigadier generals appointed by Polk came from "his own particular party...from the past conduct of the President...he will officer the regiments with a set of political adventurers whom the soldiers would not elect." "The battles of the republic," declared Toombs, "ought to be fought by its citizen soldiery."[29]

Antislavery Democrats in the House also sought to amend the Ten Regiment Bill, but as part of a Jeffersonian attempt to keep the central government weak and state governments strong. This produced the anomaly, in this case, of Americans using the doctrine of states' rights to oppose rather than support slavery. The key point, however, is that they pursued their antislavery cause largely by praising the volunteers' virtue as citizen soldiers and by walking a fine line between denigrating regulars in general and praising the U.S. Army's successes thus far in Mexico. The position of antislavery Democrats could best be summed up as supporting additional volunteers, not regulars; opposing the "unnecessary extension of executive privilege"; letting volunteers democratically elect their own officers in true Jacksonian fashion; and ensuring that when the new regiments disbanded at the war's end the officers appointed by Polk would be dismissed as well.[30]

Hannibal Hamlin, who later entered the Senate and governed Maine as a Republican before serving as Abraham Lincoln's first vice president during the Civil War, laid out this Democratic argument in a pragmatic but principled way. First, said Hamlin, the last regular requisition had failed by 2,500 soldiers to meet its quota. Even if all the new positions were filled, it made more sense to call forth additional volunteers. Volunteers could be mustered, organized, and sent to Mexico more quickly and for just about the same expense as regulars. Consequently, Hamlin requested the bill be changed to 10 regiments of volunteers. He intimated that calling for regulars and not volunteers in the first place had already impugned the bravery and fortitude of those volunteers now in the field. Second, "Individuality would be swallowed up, and all State lines obliterated" in 10 regiments of regulars. Why not accede to "the great and glorious doctrine of State rights, State pride, State duty," Hamlin asked. This could mean either volunteers commanded by officers of their choice or a reorganization of the militia. In any case, increasing the "standing army," thundered Hamlin, was neither "justifiable" nor "absolutely necessary at the present time." To knit his argument together into a seamless whole, he pointed out that "there was no necessity for placing the appointment of four hundred officers in the hands of the Executive." This last might be Hamlin's own principled stand against executive power, but it also endeared him to Whigs.[31]

The vast majority of Democrats defended the Ten Regiment Bill's call for regulars. While acknowledging the veracity of their colleagues' patronage concerns, they cited the difficulties Constitutional restrictions posed on raising volunteers and tried to turn the Whigs' logic on its head by praising the fact that volunteers did not blindly join the army to fight for years at a time because they were respectable and productive members of society. Traditionally, regular soldiers were not, and in this case the U.S. Army needed long-term enlistments of at least five years or for the duration of the war. Volunteers might make better soldiers overall, Democrats admitted, but the very things that made them brave and virtuous precluded their enlisting for the extensive period of time needed to prosecute the war against Mexico.

Democrats claimed that the most rational choice in the interest of speed and long-term stability would be to create 10 regiments of regulars and let Polk appoint the officers. But they never strayed from extolling citizen soldiers despite the intimation that in this case all of the *good* things about citizen soldiers made them poor choices for the current moment. Jacob Thompson of Mississippi so effusively praised volunteers that he equated them with militia simply because both were citizen soldiers. Yet he claimed the Constitution's requirement that the president "first...make a demand upon the Executives of the several States" before obtaining volunteers "requires time and causes much delay and expense." With American forces in Mexico undermanned, despite his personal preference for citizen soldiers, Thompson supported regulars in this case. Thompson argued that the only plausible argument against the bill could be "the patronage conferred by it upon the President upon the appointment of the officers."[32]

A looming Congressional recess added a special intensity to the Senate's debate over the Ten Regiment Bill. As Jabez Huntington, a Whig senator from Connecticut, pointed out, the end of the second session promised to "vest in the President the power, in the recess, to appoint officers of the army." Regardless of whether the Senate consented to Polk's choices, Whigs despondently realized that the Senate's hands would be tied, for no senator would request the return of an officer once he had begun leading soldiers in Mexico. In the Senate at least, the patronage issue was tied as much to the Senate's defense of its Constitutional prerogative to advise and consent to executive appointees as it was to partisanship and Whig contempt for Polk.

One of the most vocal Whigs in the Senate who opposed the bill was Spencer Jarnagin. Jarnagin, in his use of citizen soldier rhetoric to oppose the bill, went so far as to call regulars "mere machines" who needed to be bribed with land and money just to enlist. He trotted out the Battle of New Orleans and other volunteer or militia victories from the past. Volunteers stood at the ready, said Jarnagin, and yet Polk called for regulars. No senators and no generals, Jarnagin claimed, had demanded a fresh force of regulars. The bill, therefore, was nothing more than a power grab by Polk.[33]

Senators defending the bill against patronage accusations resorted to identifying recent presidential appointees in the army by political party. Democrats like Sidney Breese of Illinois claimed that over one-third of all officers in the newly created rifle regiment were Whigs. Yet Breese thought it only reasonable that "the head of the army in the field should have the same views on policy as the President." Breese denied that only Democratic generals could see eye-to-eye with Polk on strategy, but his words clearly did not bode well for the future of Whig commanders already in the field, especially Taylor and Scott.[34]

Like the House, the Senate contained its own maverick Democrats, although unlike Hamlin they were not antislavery advocates. Sam Houston deftly joined populist, democratic rhetoric to the economic promise of the expanding American market, and pulled no punches when he called for amending the bill in order to resolve the regular vs. volunteer and officer issues. "The raw volunteer," Houston claimed, "was equal to the raw regular," and the mere fact of calling for regulars implied volunteers were "not worthy of the confidence of the Government." Besides, noted Houston, even if regular regiments could be filled, which he doubted, they could not be fielded before the summer of 1847—just in time for "the sickly season" of the *vomito*. Add to that the expense of outfitting regulars as opposed to volunteers, who "required no clothing...made no charge for quarters... and were always ready for service," and the choice of regulars made no sense. As for the officer issue, Houston pointed out that since states appointed officers in volunteer regiments, and officers could have only one commission, there would be no need for presidential commissions if the 10 regiments were composed of volunteers. Houston reminded his fellow senators that a regular army was "inconsistent with the genius of our institutions," because men ceased to be functional citizens once they became dependents of the army. A volunteer, on the other hand, "returned home to be a producer.... Ceasing to be a citizen-soldier," after wartime the volunteer became "a citizen-producer."[35]

The Senate's bill differed from the House in that it did not allow the president to make recess appointments to the army. Lewis Cass complained that this provision effectively killed the bill, because how could the "law be properly executed" if the president had to wait months to appoint officers while enlisted men gathered and the army sat in Mexico undermanned and outgunned? The conference report struck out this anti-recess appointment provision. The power of recess appointment, argued Cass, was "a temporary trust" and fully Constitutional. Senator Calhoun rejoined that he now would vote against the bill because he believed it to be an unconstitutional impingement on the Senate's right to advise and consent. On February 8 a bipartisan majority in the Senate, on Constitutional grounds, voted down the first conference report and returned it to the conference committee.[36]

The principle of separation of powers had trumped partisanship, and Polk was furious. He blamed the Senate's "Federal Party," by which he meant Whigs, and "Mr. Calhoun and his peculiar friends." Polk now without a doubt considered Calhoun an enemy "in opposition to my administration." He incorrectly but typically blamed Calhoun's opposition to the bill on presidential aspirations and the fact that Polk had not named the South Carolinian to his cabinet. Meanwhile, the *Washington Daily Union*, the organ of the Polk administration edited by Polk's friend and Democratic stalwart, Thomas Ritchie, published an editorial censuring the Senate for rejecting the bill. It accused senators of endangering American lives in Mexico out of pettiness and, ironically, partisanship. Under this public pressure and in the interest of expediency, the Senate approved a slightly altered conference bill on February 10. Polk signed it the next day. But the story did not stop there, for a few days later the Senate got its revenge on Polk when it expelled Ritchie from his seat in the Senate gallery.[37]

What really spurred final approval of the Ten Regiment Bill was not so much the power of Ritchie's pen but the arrival of news from Mexico that American forces, encamped at Saltillo, were in grave danger and outnumbered by Mexican troops. The resulting compromise bill balanced fears of a large professional army with immediate battlefield necessities, the undeniable needs of a possibly long occupation, and apprehension about being labeled unpatriotic. The 10 regiments (one of riflemen, one of dragoons, and eight of infantry), part of the New Establishment because they were created after the outbreak of war, were to be disbanded at war's end. By this time, too many American men had heard of the disease, death, or drudgery that awaited them in Mexico, and so the bill also promised enlistees a bounty of either $100 or 100 acres of land. With the addition of these soldiers, the U.S. Army (on paper, at least) approached 30,000 men and nearly 1,400 officers. So many men flooded into Washington seeking appointments that Polk felt under siege and complained of being surrounded by liars.[38]

The arguments used for and against the Ten Regiment Bill reveal that the debate was much more than a seminal moment in civil-military relations during the war with Mexico, in which troops sat stranded in enemy territory awaiting reinforcements while so many Neros fiddled. The debate also was more than an exercise in Americans' traditional disdain for standing armies or an exposé in how cleverly to use rhetoric amenable to the public (in this case, that of the citizen soldier) while endeavoring to do something averse to the foundational principles on which that very rhetoric rested (i.e., enlarging the regular army). This was a battle between two of the three branches of the federal government over Constitutional roles and over power, fought during a war many believed had been started by an overweening executive in the first place. The question, then, is why did the eventual compromise grant President Polk the power of appointment? The best explanation is that all involved expected a long occupation in Mexico and found themselves trapped by the citizenry's likely equation of opposition to Polk and to the bill with unpatriotic dissent. Whigs, ever conscious of the Federalist Party's politically fatal mistakes, could do the former but needed to refrain from doing the latter at all costs. This they did, by agreeing to the conference bill that made the 10 regiments *and* their officers' commissions expire at war's end. Yet not until March did Congress even fund the new regiments. By that time Taylor, with his vastly outnumbered force, already had secured at Buena Vista one of the greatest victories of the war. Scott, however, later encamped at Puebla for the summer while he awaited his much needed reinforcements.

Whigs, and Democrats like Calhoun and his supporters (Calhounites), opposed Polk's policies not simply on partisan grounds, but on principle as well. Yet in either case they employed pro-citizen soldier rhetoric to boost their position. That is not to say this was mere rhetoric only and that many or even most congressmen who utilized it did not believe their own speeches. The fact is that once they realized circumstances called for an augmentation of the regular army, members of both parties struggled to find the best way to sell that realization to the American people, a vital task in an age of wider suffrage and greater political involvement on the part of citizens. Indeed, the ideologues among them first had to sell it to themselves—perhaps a far more difficult undertaking.

The democratization of politics during the Jacksonian era took the traditional American attitude that denigrated regulars and mythologized volunteers or militia and ensconced it squarely within the highly partisan dichotomy of the Second Party System. What complicated matters for Whigs is that they unapologetically opposed the war from the beginning as a Democratic war of conquest and as an act of executive aggression. They certainly did not want to grant Polk additional power by doubling the army and allowing him to appoint even subordinate officers. Indeed, this issue of patronage helped to shape Whig political strategy throughout the war.

Yet neither did Whigs want to weaken their party's national strength just to please their regional base, for they well knew how popular the war was outside of New England. The Whig Party discovered during the early Mexican War debates that one of the ways it might hope to match the Democratic Party's national popularity across sectional lines was to appeal to the Jacksonian doctrines, popular among the Democratic Party's supporters throughout the country, that lionized the people and, thus, the volunteer. This is how Whigs ended up calling for thousands of volunteers in a war they opposed and how a Democratic president and faithful Jacksonian ended up calling for thousands of regulars in the debate over the Ten Regiment Bill. After the dust settled, however, Congress approved the legislation requested by the Polk administration, but only after much delay, debate, and posturing.

Politics and principle clashed also as governors joined the fray over the composition of the army to be sent to Mexico. Since volunteer units were organized according to state militia laws, governors, as executives in their own right, had genuine prerogatives to protect. In Jacksonian America, however, national politics and party affiliation usually overrode local concerns, even in Whig-governed states where the war was popular like Ohio and Kentucky. Governor William Owsley of Kentucky thus followed along with the influential Henry Clay and tried to place obstacles in the way of the execution of "Mr. Polk's War" when the call came from Secretary Marcy for Kentucky volunteers. In his rhetoric, however, Owsley was careful to cite Constitutional principles and mitigating factors distinctive to Kentucky. Meanwhile, even Whigs like Governor Bebb of Ohio who claimed to favor the war wisely cultivated pro-war opinion in their states as another arrow in their quiver which they could fire at Polk and the Democratic Party.

President Polk rightly viewed governors like Owsley and Bebb not as principled defenders of state prerogative but as partisan enemies. Likewise, Polk interpreted Congressional opposition to the various bills between May 1846 and February 1847 seeking to enlarge the army as entirely motivated by politics or, in the case of Calhoun, personality. Bills like the one "to authorize an Increase of the Rank and File of the Army" and those which created the regiment of mounted riflemen and Company A of the U.S. Engineers offered Polk the chance to appoint Democratic officers during a war Whigs opposed. The Ten Regiment Bill granted him this prospect in spades. Polk's critics called this unseemly patronage and a dangerous increase in presidential power, and they were right on both counts. The Calhounites tried to protect the Senate from encroachment by the president. But neither of these stances negated the need, obvious in Polk's opinion, to expand the army in order adequately to prosecute the war against Mexico and, by early 1847, to reinforce the troops already in the country. Nor did they mean that the rapidly enlarged army was not in dire need of additional quartermasters and staff and field officers.

Like most politicians of the 1840s (and, perhaps, beyond), James K. Polk truly convinced himself that what was good for his party must be good for the country, and so he regarded his own Jeffersonian/Jacksonian principles and rugged partisanship not as potentially clashing and contradictory but as uniquely inseparable and logically consistent. If as the leader of the majority Polk left the presidency stronger than he found it, then, based on the principle of majority rule as Jacksonians understood it, so be it. Polk did not look so kindly on his opposition in Congress and state houses, however, and rarely detected the principles or legitimate concerns at work in their actions or arguments. The relationship between Polk and his commanders, influenced as it was by these same political considerations, especially the issue of patronage that so dogged the passage of the early war bills, is the subject of the next chapter.

3

"All Whigs and violent partisans"

Although James K. Polk claimed that he "had never suffered politics to mingle with the conduct of the war," the evidence suggests just the opposite. Polk's political interpretation of others' actions extended beyond his dealings with Congress and governors to U.S. Army personnel, and it shaped in strikingly conspicuous ways his behavior toward Generals Zachary Taylor and Winfield Scott, whom he assumed must be political animals, though unprincipled ones, like himself. At least in terms of their political acumen, he turned out to be correct. This chapter analyzes the political and military impact of Jacksonian doctrines, personality conflicts, and political machinations on the relationship between Polk and his top commanders.

At the start of the Mexican War all of the generals and most high-ranking officers in the regular army were Whigs. Polk saw no reason why the pursuit of his limited territorial goal of annexing California and possibly New Mexico or Tamaulipas in a quick war could not coincide with attempts to weaken the Whig Party. He also saw nothing to convince him that leading Whigs did not look at the war in exactly the opposite way, as an opportunity to thwart the Democratic Party. Naturally, therefore, Polk was suspicious of his Whig generals: "Several of these officers are politically opposed to the administration and there is reason to apprehend that they would be willing to see the government embarrassed...I shall for the future give more attention to their conduct."[1]

Polk was especially wary of Winfield Scott's political ambitions, but he believed with some degree of confidence (quite accurately, it turned out) that Zachary Taylor also had designs on the Executive Mansion. Meanwhile, there was little love lost between Taylor and Scott, who soon became embroiled in a political melee of their own as each vied to become the leader of the Whig Party. Indeed, politics affected the war effort not only in terms of Polk against the Whigs, but in the disputes between the Whig presidential hopefuls themselves. Thus, even before the official declaration of war outright politics—with "politics" defined as a concern for the perpetuation of one's party over and above the common good—threatened to poison civil-military relations and possibly undermine the war. To achieve his political and expansionist objectives, Polk convinced himself that he needed to bring about the political downfall of Scott and Taylor or in some other way ensure that the Whig Party gained little politically from the war, and he had to do so without unintentionally damaging troop loyalty and morale or decreasing American chances for military victory.

In order to ensure the army would remain loyal to him and serve his political interests, Polk employed a tripartite strategy. First, he tried in different ways to weaken the political prospects of Scott and Taylor to keep the Whig Party from capitalizing on its new war heroes' popularity. The trick was to do this without endangering the U.S. Army on the battlefield—much the same as he assumed his Whig officers were trying to do to his administration. Politically, Whigs and Democrats both desired victory, although for different reasons. Second, Polk attempted to revive the rank of lieutenant general in an effort to place a trustworthy Democrat over Scott, the current general in chief. Third, Polk sought to transform the command structure of the army, at least for the duration of the war with Mexico, by appointing a solid Democratic cadre of volunteer generals. This included trying to fill old and newly created officer vacancies with Democrats, even as state governors intervened in the process and Congress whittled away at the number of new vacancies during legislative battles or put restrictions on those that remained.

As far as politics is concerned, Polk had good reason to distrust his generals. In 1839 Scott had garnered a respectable number of votes for president at the Whig Party convention, so Polk had no doubts about the general in chief's political aspirations or where his party loyalties lay. Taylor, on the other hand, responded early on to queries about his presidential aspirations with such a dazzling blend of evasiveness and humility that Whig kingmaker Henry Clay regarded him with contempt. Taylor's humble equivocation should have been Polk's first clue about the general, who went on to be elected president as a Whig in 1848, but it was not. Instead, fearing Scott was the greater political opponent, Polk relied on Taylor as long as possible, before admitting that military necessity demanded the sending of the more talented General Scott to the theater of operations to ride at the head of the central Mexico campaign.

Zachary Taylor, a Southerner and plantation owner, was a career army officer, having received his first commission in 1808. Since the War of 1812, most of the enemies Taylor had faced had been Indians on the frontier. Still technically on the frontier after Polk's orders to cross the Nueces River into disputed territory along the Rio Grande in January 1846, Taylor now faced the presumably well-trained Mexican army.

Zachary Taylor during the time of the Mexican War (National Archives).

Nicknamed "Ol' Rough and Ready," Taylor proved more than up to the task, winning victory after victory and establishing a strong defensive line across northern Mexico. These successes culminated at Buena Vista in February 1847.

Normally a long series of victories would charm any commander in chief. Not so with Polk. From the beginning of the war Polk thought Taylor "brave" but too inept to mastermind and coordinate a complex offensive like the one required to take Mexico City. Polk similarly lamented Taylor's unwillingness "to express any opinion or take any responsibility on himself" in planning the war. Taylor, in other words, was exactly the type of overly cautious and unimaginative person that Sam Houston argued the regular army produced. All Taylor could do as someone who had spent his adult life in the U.S. Army, Polk wrote in his diary, was "simply obey orders." Still, Taylor received the brevet rank of major general soon after his bloodless victory at Matamoras in May 1846.[2]

Because he lacked confidence in Taylor, Polk second guessed him even on minor matters. For instance, to anyone who would listen Polk spent considerable time criticizing Taylor's decision to use wagons rather than mules to transport goods and supplies in Mexico. Polk preferred mules, an obvious choice according to the president. Yet even as Polk micromanaged Taylor he blamed the general for failing to provide the administration with sufficient information so that it did not have to engage in such long distance generalship. There were few choices that Taylor could make (or avoid making) that pleased the president. Although Polk did not realize this, Taylor did, and this no doubt helped to create the attitude which Polk saw only as unconscionable hesitation and servile obedience.

THE MONTERREY ARMISTICE

The incident that instigated a precipitous decline in the relationship between Taylor and Polk was the armistice Taylor granted to General Pedro Ampudia at Monterrey. Ironically, the armistice was an example of Taylor engaging in exactly the type of decisiveness Polk claimed he wanted. Polk's negative reaction to the armistice illustrates his precarious position in dealing with Taylor. Americans now considered Taylor their first genuine, national war hero since Andrew Jackson. To act harshly toward the general, Polk realized, would be more foolish than letting the glory-hungry Whig extend his string of victories. Thus, Polk, on his cabinet's advice, decided merely to order Taylor to rescind the armistice. No official reprimand for the general or criticism of his granting the armistice without orders was forthcoming from Polk. Taylor saw through Polk's delicate handling of the incident, and without a second thought he blamed the rescission not on military expediency but on "an intrigue going on against me; the object of which is to deprive me of the command." Only "the want of discression on the part of certain politicians, in connecting my name as a proper candidate for the next presidential election" had turned the president against him, Taylor believed. Taylor even began to suspect Scott, whom he knew possessed presidential aspirations of his own, of taking an active role in "the course...pursued toward me by the authorities in Washington."[3]

The touchy situation with Taylor deepened in November 1846, as the need for an invasion of central Mexico via Vera Cruz or Tampico grew more likely. Polk and Secretary of War William Marcy, along with other cabinet members and Senators Sam Houston and Thomas Hart Benton, discussed who was best suited to lead the expedition. All concluded that, to the public, Taylor seemed the obvious choice. Yet Polk still harbored misgivings, even as he knew that not sending Taylor invariably meant he would have to send Scott. Either way, Whigs might end up with a considerable portion of the credit for the war, and Democrats in 1848 would, as in 1840, face a party led by a war hero.

Despite all his victories and Polk's prejudices, Taylor's logistical miscalculations and battlefield performance would have led even the friendliest of Whig presidents to doubt him. As Taylor biographer K. Jack Bauer explains, "Taylor's inability to foresee his future needs" meant, for example, that as even Polk realized Taylor really should have used mules rather than wagons. Because he did not, Taylor's troops found themselves seriously bogged down in the rain-drenched landscape on the approaches to Monterrey.[4] True, once at Monterrey soldiers led by Taylor and Worth performed admirably, but they had done so only in spite of Taylor's poor planning and unreasonable timidity about night operations and house-to-house fighting. The result had been a much greater loss of American life than there should have been. Luck, the fighting ability of the troops, and Worth's steady hand saved the U.S. Army at Monterrey, not Taylor's leadership.

At Buena Vista Taylor's luck almost ran out. The fact is that Taylor himself placed his outnumbered army in harm's way, against explicit orders from Scott to remain in camp near Monterrey, and despite claiming that "I will not if otherwise instructed from Washington, move against the enemy."[5] Only the refusal by Santa Anna's men to retake the field on February 23 saved Taylor's military career, not to mention the lives of the thousands of volunteers under his command. Remarkably, Taylor eked out a victory from a blunder that could have significantly altered the course of war, since Scott was only about two weeks away from his planned amphibious landing at Vera Cruz. A loss at Buena Vista would have destroyed the northern Mexico defense perimeter established earlier in the war. If ever there was a telling example of the critical role contingency plays in history, it occurred at Buena Vista, for the battle earned Taylor the fame he needed for a presidential run.

Even in the months immediately following the Battle of Buena Vista, Taylor continued to claim he would turn down the presidency if it was offered to him. But this was disingenuous, for at the same time he began directing a political campaign from his encampment in Mexico by incessantly informing his supporters, whom he alleged were bandying his name about without his instigation, about how terrific a candidate he would be. Nearly every letter written by Taylor to his son-in-law, Robert C. Wood, contained inter-Whig politicking: "Between ourselves Genl Scott would stoop to any thing however low and contemptable...to obtain power or place."[6] By mid-1847 Taylor openly claimed he could beat Scott for the Whig nomination and, if it were held later that year, might even win the election. Significantly, by this time Henry Clay had come to prefer Taylor over Scott, although privately he still considered both men ill-suited to be president. Taylor, however, worried he might not be as strong a candidate by 1848. These doubts rested squarely on his fanciful conclusion that a conspiracy was afoot between Polk administration officials and Whigs to "bring Genl S. before the country as the prominent candidate for the presidency."[7]

While some historians argue that the relationship between Taylor and Scott soured over time due to conflicting personalities and mutual misunderstanding, Taylor in fact disliked Scott long before he suggested in August 1846 that Scott was "entirely mistaken if he supposed I am unfriendly to him." By that time, at least in private, Taylor already had called Scott impulsive, flippant, and "crazy." Commenting on Scott's rumored rocky relationship with the Polk administration, Taylor blamed not Scott's politics but rather his delays in coming to Mexico, saying that such hesitancy "disgusted the Secretary of War as well as Mr. Polk." There does not seem to be much consistency in Taylor's accusations against Scott, other than that he disliked him, for at the same time Taylor thought Scott was in cahoots with the administration he ascribed to another theory that the administration was completely sour on Scott.[8]

THE GAINES LETTER

If the Monterrey armistice pushed relations between Polk and Taylor to their edge, the appearance in American newspapers, shortly before the Battle of Buena Vista, of what became known as the "Gaines Letter" pushed them over the edge. In a letter to General Edmund P. Gaines, written in November 1846 following the brouhaha over the armistice, Taylor criticized Polk's overall strategy and went so far as to say that the outcome of the war mattered little because there was no stable authority in Mexico with which the United States could treat. Besides, wrote Taylor, any territory won would be worthless anyway. An indemnity based on the territory already held and enforced by the defensive line established in northern Mexico, argued Taylor, was the only sensible option. Apparently, Taylor had his own opinions after all! Gaines, acting on his own, so said Taylor, had decided to publish the letter, perhaps to get back at Polk for replacing him in consequence of the unauthorized and expensive troop requisitions he had made earlier in the war. Maybe he wanted revenge against Polk *and* Taylor for his earlier reprimand. Whatever the case, as Justin Smith points out, so critical was the letter of Polk and so full was it of suggestions on how to conduct the war and pursue peace that the letter could only be read as "the opening gun of a Presidential campaign."[9]

Polk was naturally distrustful of both his Whig generals to begin with, but the publication of the Gaines letter cemented his anxieties and low opinion of Taylor like nothing else could, not even the Monterrey armistice or his own imaginative suspicions. He immediately asked Secretary Marcy to place an editorial in the administration organ, the *Washington Daily Union*, "exposing General Taylor for writing such a letter" and for making it public. No sooner had the president made these plans than Gaines sent word to Polk that he, in fact, was the recipient of the letter and had decided on his own to publish it. Polk reacted to this news by calling a cabinet meeting to discuss the "highly unmilitary" letter. The letter, Polk fumed, was "calculated seriously to embarrass and injure the pending military operations in Mexico." The cabinet unanimously agreed to censure Taylor and Gaines for the incident, despite Taylor's protestations that the letter had never been meant to be made public. Polk saw no reason not to score some political points out of Taylor's misstep, and so gave orders to time the censure with the publication of Marcy's upcoming editorial. To head off any political damage to his administration and to the Democratic Party ahead of the next year's election, Polk also requested Democrats in Congress to pass a resolution ordering that all official correspondence between Taylor and the War Department be published as soon as possible. This, indeed, is just what happened, although as the war dragged on into late 1847 Americans increasingly started to agree with Taylor's appraisal of the Polk administration's conduct of the war.[10]

Taylor reacted angrily to the fire storm over the Gaines letter and all the criticism flowing out of Washington City. He termed the conspirators against him "Scott, Marcy & Co.," whom he said "have been more anxious to break me down, than they have been to break down Santa Anna." In Marcy's "abusive" reprimand over the publication of the Gaines letter, which appeared at the high point of public adulation of Taylor following Buena Vista, and in the transfer of Taylor's troops to Scott's army, Taylor believed he had been made inactive and left undermanned just to enable Scott to win the requisite military victories needed to secure the Whig nomination. Taylor wanted Scott sent "back to Washington" and Marcy "removed from office" as a result of their role in causing a near tragedy at Buena Vista. "Genl Scott," Taylor remarked, "would stoop to any thing however low and contemptable...to obtain power or place." So, too, would "the party in power," even to the point of endangering the country.[11]

Odd as it may seem, Taylor really believed that Polk and Scott, Marcy & Co. were willing to sacrifice his army to boost Scott's political chances. Taylor found no other way to interpret the orders from Washington and Scott that left him "so completely bound hand and foot...at the mercy of the enemy." Taylor believed had he not disobeyed Scott's "unmilitary and outrageous order" "to fall back to Monterey," which he told his superior officer had not come from "the proper authority" anyway, then the war would have been lost. Most importantly, the victory at Buena Vista worked exactly as he hoped it would: it made him untouchable by Polk, unpunishable by Scott, and wildly popular among Whigs. In spite of the Gaines letter and the subsequent political fallout from it, the president could do nothing other than publicly heap effusive praise on him.[12]

The reality is that politics affected the U.S. Army to a greater extent than that which falls into the simplistic "Polk vs. the Whigs" paradigm. Taylor and Scott were both vain men engaged in a struggle for the nomination of the same party, a struggle Polk and Marcy encouraged with the hope that each might fatally wound the other. Where the two generals differed most was in Taylor's willingness to risk his troops on the battlefield, seeing military glory as the surest means of boosting his own political standing. One thing is for sure; the news of Buena Vista did help to mitigate the Gaines letter's damage to Taylor by overshadowing his public censure. In the long run, Taylor outmaneuvered both Polk and Scott.

A couple of ironies color the long ending to the struggle by Taylor to direct his campaign for the Whig nomination from Mexico while dodging Marcy's actions and Scott's orders, not to mention the Mexicans. First, Taylor suspected Polk's appointee, General Franklin Pierce, was the "Co." in "Scott, Marcy & Co." In 1852, when Scott finally did run for president as a Whig, the Democrat who defeated him was, in fact, Pierce. Polk's hopes that one of his appointees might beat one of his Whig generals reached fruition, but in 1852 rather than 1848. The final irony is that Polk actually all but assured Taylor's nomination once he finished with Scott, for there can be no doubt that despite Taylor's fears and paranoia, Polk feared Scott politically more than he did Taylor.

Whereas Polk only suspected "Ol' Rough and Ready" Taylor of strong Whig inclinations, he knew without a doubt that Scott was a Whig. Polk's dilemma was that he honestly doubted Taylor's wherewithal to command anything greater than a division or to come up with a creative attack plan to take Mexico City. After examining Scott's plans to invade Mexico, Polk—indeed, his entire cabinet—knew "Ol' Fuss and Feathers" was the man for the job. Since General Scott was an avowed Whig, Polk would just have to watch him closely and wait for an opportune time to act. Polk's own summary of his dilemma, written May 21, 1846, says it best:

> I can have no confidence in General Scott's disposition to carry out the views of the administration as commander in chief of the army on the Del Norte, and yet unless Congress shall authorize the appointment of additional general officers I may be compelled to continue to entrust the command to him. If I shall be compelled to do so, it will be with the full conviction of his hostility to my administration, and that he will reluctantly do anything to carry out my plans and views in the campaign.

Indeed, Congress authorized Polk to appoint volunteer generals, and with Taylor being awarded the brevet rank of major general, Scott stayed in Washington for the time being. As late as November 1846 Scott was raving about "how handsomely I had been treated by the President and the Secretary of War."[13] But by that time events south of the border were pointing to the obvious need for taking the fight into central Mexico.

THE LIEUTENANT GENERAL CONTROVERSY

Before deciding to send Scott to Mexico, however, Polk launched his biggest political gambit of the war: the attempted revival of the rank of lieutenant general as a means of placing a Democrat over Scott.

Polk had in mind for this new command Senator Thomas Hart Benton. Benton had worked well with President Andrew Jackson, despite Jackson having once brawled with him. Representing Missouri in the Senate, Benton concentrated particularly on tariff, banking, and land issues. By the 1840s he counted himself among the faction fighting the domination of the Democratic Party by slave interests. Like Whigs, he favored federally funded internal improvements because roads and canals promised to help develop the West. Benton's preference for an agrarian republic of small farmers and Western development had made him a gradual abolitionist. This antislavery position placed him solidly in Martin Van Buren's camp, who had opposed Polk's nomination at the Democratic Party convention in 1844.[14]

Benton's views on expansion also diverged from many other Democrats. He favored systematic settlement through negotiation, not wars of conquest—for this reason, he had sought compromises on Oregon and Texas. In May 1846 Benton confided privately to Polk that he would support appropriations for defending the United States, but never for an "aggressive war." Moreover, Benton criticized Polk's stationing of Taylor's troops between the Rio Grande and the Nueces River.[15] In essence, Benton's was the public Whig position. John C. Calhoun and Benton were longtime political enemies, however, and Calhoun's opposition to the war bill assured Benton's support of it. Both men wanted the presidency, Polk believed, and the Tennessean much preferred the Jacksonian and Westerner Benton in that position than he did the aristocratic South Carolinian.

Polk and Benton began the war on cordial but not friendly terms. For several months Polk met regularly with Benton to discuss legislation and war strategy. Benton probably did not realize it, but this was part of Polk's intensive crash course to verse himself in military theory while on the job. Both men by late summer agreed that invading central Mexico would be necessary to force the peace Polk claimed he desired. In these meetings the president frequently expressed unhappiness with Scott's attitude and Fabian invasion preparations, an opinion with which Benton concurred.

By the fall of 1846 Polk came to see Benton as someone with whom he could work closely, treating the senator almost as one of his cabinet appointees.

On November 10 Polk confessed to Benton that he seriously doubted whether Taylor could be counted on to lead troops on a central Mexican campaign. Taylor, said Polk, might be "a brave officer" but he lacked "capacity enough for such a command." When Polk mentioned that there was little choice but to send Scott after all, Benton quickly expressed "no confidence in him" either. After throwing around several names, Benton presented the idea of a lieutenant generalship—and he offered to fill the post himself. The senator couched this less-than-humble suggestion in political terms the president could understand, noting "that the Whigs were endeavoring to turn this war to party and political advantage":

> You know what my position has been...but let bygones be bygones. I quarreled and fought with General Jackson; I made friends with him and came to his support...Now I will give you any support in this war in my power.

The threat was clear: the war probably would position either Scott or Taylor to defeat whomever the Democratic nominee happened to be in 1848. On the other hand, a Democratic general in chief, especially an anti-Calhoun Westerner (and slaveholder) like Benton who had the support of the Van Buren faction, could attract voters with his own martial glory and unite the Democratic Party at the same time.[16]

Benton and Polk met the next day, again to discuss the war. Concurrently, Polk and his cabinet also were considering a new requisition of troops, what became the Ten Regiment Bill. Polk offered Benton one of the new major general positions, but the senator declined because "the general appointed would be junior officer" to Scott. After several more meetings, Polk on November 17 confided to his diary: "If I had the power to select a General I would select Col. Benton." Conversely, Polk lamented that Scott was the current general in chief but saw no way out of his dilemma. He thus decided "that bygones should be bygones," and authorized Scott to lead the invasion of Mexico. What Polk did not tell the general, however, was that in his mind the leader of the campaign did not necessarily have to hold the highest rank in the army.[17]

Polk used the opportunity posed by the Ten Regiment Bill to request the creation of the office of lieutenant general, reasoning that the temporary increase in the size of the army required it. Members of both parties in Congress, along with the Whig opposition press, disagreed. All confidently surmised that the new generalship would not be offered to Scott, for he already *was* general in chief. Soon, all in Washington learned of the circumstances of Polk's request and realized, to the surprise of not a few, that the president had Benton in mind.[18]

Some opponents of the lieutenant generalship argued the obvious, that Polk's request was a tacit admission that he was really after the complete conquest of Mexico and did not trust a Whig to do the job. Others, including all Whigs and the Calhounites, accused Polk of undercutting Scott and the heroic (and undefeated) Taylor to ensure that a Democrat of his choosing would succeed him in 1848, an accusation not far from the truth. But Whigs did not simply criticize Polk on the grounds that he had sunk to a new low with such despicable politicking. They defended their 1848 presidential hopefuls with a ferocity that showed they knew what was at stake politically, many arguing that putting a civilian in charge of the military was foolhardy. Tennessean Milton Brown pointed out that the office of lieutenant general could be abused so easily that only George Washington, the American Cincinnatus, had been entrusted with it. Polk clearly had overplayed his hand.[19]

This uproar forced a furious and indignant Benton to take to the floor of the Senate to defend both himself and the president. Benton denied the existence of any "ulterior and covert design" by Polk "to appoint his successor" as president. The only true commander in chief, Benton said, was the president anyway, and since Polk obviously could not go to Mexico to lead troops it was his job to appoint someone who could. The president, after all, was a civilian, and *he* was commander in chief. So how could it be foolhardy to appoint a civilian lieutenant general? "The office" of lieutenant general, explained Benton, "was original, and belonged to no person." Indeed, Benton rightly noted that the president could nominate anyone he pleased.[20]

Senator Benton nevertheless went on to play up his own military experience and to deliver what he considered the *coup de grace*: in 1836 President Jackson had "proposed to give me command of the army against Mexico" in case relations during the Texas Revolution seriously deteriorated.[21] Benton did, in fact, possess significant military experience, more than some gave him credit for. He had served during the War of 1812 as colonel of a Tennessee regiment of volunteers, a lieutenant colonel in the regular army, and as aide-de-camp to General Jackson. Still, he was no match for Scott, making Polk's legislative attempt to conquer the army's presumed whiggery all the more remarkable, coming as it did during wartime. Congress took the appropriate, prudent course of action, and even Benton approved Polk's choice of Scott to lead personally the U.S. forces in Mexico. Yet when Benton first learned of the Gaines letter, so "astonished" was he "at the conduct of both Taylor and Scott" that he hurried to the Executive Mansion and met behind closed doors with Polk until nearly midnight, offering now to go to Mexico with any rank, even that of lieutenant colonel, "provided I can have command of the army." This last caveat, of course, kept Benton in the Senate and off the battlefields.[22]

As late as November 1846 Scott had reassured his nervous Whig supporters about "how handsomely" he "had been treated by the President and the

Secretary of War." Scott was in New Orleans when he learned of the lieuten-ant general debate, and he thought little of it, naturally assuming the post would be his. But once it became clear that Polk intended the office for Benton, Scott felt betrayed by Polk's "bungling treachery....A grosser abuse of human confidence is nowhere recorded." Scott believed, apparently correctly, that Polk viewed Scott's whiggery as an excuse to treat him shabbily while trying "to crown Benton with the victory, and thus triumph both in the field and in the polls."[23]

Scott blamed the long delay in approving the much-needed Ten Regiment Bill on the Polk-Benton scheme, which "so disgusted Congress" that it lost trust in the purity of Polk's motives. In other words, Scott thought Polk had threatened the whole war effort, endangered the lives of American soldiers, and irreparably harmed American foreign relations with Mexico for purely political reasons.[24] This may be too harsh of a judgment, for in some sense Polk was following the precedent laid down by Thomas Jefferson, who had tried to make the army personally loyal to him and more politically friendly to the Republican Party. Polk believed he had greater cause than Jefferson, due to the emergency of war. But as an experienced Jacksonian politician, Polk should have realized that while Jefferson had pursued his reforms when the United States was at peace, he had done so buoyed by an overwhelming Republican majority in both houses of Congress. Polk's miscalculation, therefore, was not that he tried to reform the army in his own party's image, but rather that he attempted such a controversial political move during a divisive war without possessing anything close to a mandate.

PARTISANSHIP AND THE OFFICER CORPS

If Polk could not easily thrust aside his Whig generals or appoint some-one who outranked them, he still had much at his disposal as commander in chief, such as the power to appoint general and staff officers. Even so, there was more to Polk's choices in these areas than mere partisanship or calculations about the 1848 presidential election. True, Polk worried about Taylor or Scott riding their battlefield fame all the way to the presidency. But the fact that so many of his commanders or potential commanders belonged not only to an opposition party but also to a party openly critical of his handling of the war deepened Polk's natural inclina-tion to doubt others' motives to a state of near paranoia. He could not overlook the fact that General Taylor, while still in Mexico commanding an American army, had come out publicly against his administration's strategic and tactical goals. Thus, another reason for Polk to appoint Democrats to high positions in the army simply was to ensure the loyalty of the men who would be leading soldiers in a foreign war that lacked full popular support. Polk could make the arguable case that, during a major war where the size of the army had increased by tens of thousands, allegiance to the commander in chief was far more critical than it had been in Jefferson's time.

Another factor in Polk's relationship with his generals and in his choice of officers grew out of certain assumptions that dominated the age of Jackson. The desire to preserve civilian authority over the military and a wariness of standing armies had deep roots in America, each owing its genesis to English tradition, and, more precisely, to events of the colonial and revolutionary periods. The Jacksonian era contributed an element of populism to this mind-set, an initial aversion to professional, high-ranking officers not simply because they posed a potential threat to liberty but because they were elites. For example, Polk looked suspiciously not just at Whigs but at *every* professional officer, especially those turned out by the U.S. Military Academy at West Point, New York. He assumed their concern for their own careers might make them more tepid on the battlefield than citizen soldiers. More likely, thought Polk, their career orientation and elitism might cause them to resist serving beside or under volunteer generals. The only way to ensure success was to place leaders in the army willing to work in tandem with the administration—and for Polk, this obviously meant Democrats. After all, it had been Secretary of War Marcy who some years earlier had first uttered what became the political dictum of Jacksonian majoritarians: "To the victor belong the spoils." The so-called "spoils system" inherent in the politics of the period meant that Polk, as president, was expected to reward supporters and punish opponents when it came to federal appointments.

An additional concern about the regular army unrelated to politics affected Polk's opinion of his generals and other officers. Another Jacksonian habit of the 1840s was the inclination to glorify the common man, this being the other side of the coin to anti-elitism. Polk sincerely doubted whether professional military men were up to the task of offensive operations on Mexican soil. The ones whose abilities he doubted most were those whom he believed had been in the army so long (Scott and Taylor had both received their first commissions in 1808) that they had become indolent or lost the ability to innovate and adjust their long-held but inapplicable assumptions to conditions in Mexico. As Taylor's waste of life at Monterrey and refusal to stay north of Saltillo showed, Polk had good reason to doubt Taylor's abilities. Nevertheless, on the battlefield, certain of Pok's own political appointees—who were not exactly "common" men themselves—fared most poorly of all.

Substantial evidence exists to support the contention that Polk, in choosing his generals, ultimately valued party and nepotism over experience and professionalism. Appointees like the politically ambitious Gideon J. Pillow and Enos Hopping were close friends of Polk and Marcy, respectively. (The appointment of Hopping proved no favor, at least to Hopping, for he died in Mexico in 1847.) But the most telling evidence is that of the 13 volunteer generals confirmed by Congress during the war, there was not one Whig among them. Merely to call these men Democrats ignores the degree to which they were more than just faithful partisans. This group included former and future congressmen and senators, congressmen who resigned to accept their appointment, former state legislators, gubernatorial and congressional candidates, and one future president, Franklin Pierce.

More than unwillingness to trust Whigs to execute his wider war aims guided Polk's volunteer appointments. Polk never lessened his focus on the national political implications of Scott's and Taylor's growing popularity. But knowing how Americans loved to elect war heroes, in spite of all their anti-elitist rhetoric and fears about standing armies, Polk hoped to shape the future of politics at the state level, too. His appointment of generals from traditionally Whig states where politicians disapproved of the war underscores this fact.

Polk's volunteer generals even ran for office while in Mexico. Some lost, like Caleb Cushing in his bid for governor of Massachusetts—no amount of military glory (or lack of, in Cushing's case) could crack that Whig stronghold. Others, like Thomas Hamer of Ohio, won election to the U.S. Congress. Polk appointed Hamer in July 1846 with high hopes that he might take advantage of widespread pro-war sentiment in Ohio and counteract hostility to the war by Governor William Bebb, as well as Joshua Giddings and Thomas Corwin. Unfortunately for Polk and the Ohio Democracy (not to mention for Hamer), their Ohio hopeful died shortly after the Battle of Monterrey.

In Polk's home state of Tennessee political manipulation of the officer selection process provides a telling example of the politicization of officer selection and the intersection during the Mexican War of national and state politics. As occurred elsewhere, companies with Democratic majorities tended to vote for Democratic officers and companies with Whig majorities tended to elect Whigs. The prominent Whig William B. Campbell, who campaigned to lead the First Regiment of Tennessee volunteers as colonel, accused Governor Aaron Brown, a Democrat, of arranging the state's muster of volunteers in such a way that only "the old political companies" of mainly Democrats would be accepted for service. Campbell ended up being elected colonel only because of the overall number of Whigs regiment-wide and perhaps as a bipartisan nod during wartime to the state's Whigs. But all of his officers except one (who, incidentally, ran unopposed) were Democrats.[25]

The man who helped to cement the Democracy in the ranks of the Tennessee volunteers, Governor Brown, did so by ignoring War Department orders and placing 12 companies in the regiment rather than 10. (Probably at no other time during the war was Polk happy to have a state governor flout orders from the War Department.) Brown claimed this was in the interest of speed; not enough companies had arrived yet to fill out the other two regiments and he wanted to help supplement Taylor's meager force as soon as possible. Whigs complained Brown only wanted to ensure that more Democrats than Whigs won laurels in Mexico, but they realized there was little they could do about it since state law and the president were on the governor's side. Once in Mexico, Campbell observed that these machinations did not stop at the Rio Grande: "Politics is somewhat in my way as all my field officers are Democrats and somewhat jealous of any character I may acquire."[26]

Perhaps a Whig leading so many Democrats was some kind of magnanimous gesture meant to maintain the facade that the volunteer army was not politicized or maybe it was just a simple political trade-off in the name of morale, which was usually the case in state militia elections. Whatever the circumstances, President Polk took no chances with the future of the Democratic Party in his home state and appointed his friend Gideon J. Pillow as general and Campbell's direct superior. In so doing Polk was not simply rewarding a crony via the Jacksonian spoils system. He was taking the prevalent understanding of the militia and the partisan nature of its officers and composition during the 1840s and extending it to the national level.

Lest one think Polk unique in appointing generals on partisan grounds, one need only examine the record of William Owsley, the Whig governor of Kentucky. While Tennessee law allowed for the election of colonels, Kentucky law did not. Owsley chose Whigs to serve as colonels in each of the state's three volunteer regiments. As Taylor planned to do at the national level, Governor Owsley hoped to exploit what he considered a Democratic war to boost the Whig Party's popularity in his state. Meanwhile, perhaps with this in mind, Senator John J. Crittenden became one of Polk's most vocal critics during the debates over the Ten Regiment Bill and all other legislation that promised to create officer vacancies.

Just because a volunteer general received his appointment based on politics or cronyism did not mean that he was therefore destined to be a poor leader. To the contrary, some of Polk's generals proved competent, masterly, and even earned the admiration of hard-to-please, prejudicial regulars. General John Quitman, a former Whig who had military experience as a brigadier general in the Mississippi militia, proved so efficient that in September 1847 Scott appointed him military governor of Mexico City, a position that allowed Quitman to utilize his experience as a lawyer and legislator, something no regular U.S. Army general possessed.

Although critics initially criticized him as ill prepared, Brigadier General James Shields won accolades for his anti-elitism and accessibility to enlisted men—two Jacksonian traits hard to find among officers of the regular army, especially those who had been graduated from West Point. Nativists attacked Shields because of his Irish origins, and rumors even circulated that Polk was grooming the general for an ambassadorial post to Rome. But the men Shields led into combat felt differently. Some soldiers even compared him to Andrew Jackson, especially when he continued fighting after being wounded on April 18, 1847, at the Battle of Cerro Gordo.

Cerro Gordo may have marked Shields's rise to hero status, but it marked one low point among many for Polk's most unpopular appointee, Gideon Pillow. At Cerro Gordo General Pillow's brigade arrived three hours late to the battlefield, after marching across unreconnoitered land as Pillow changed the order of battle en route. This resulted not only in the delay but confusion on the battlefield, with Pillow's two regiments marching out in full sight of several Mexican gun emplacements. The result was the loss of any element of surprise and a raking devastation of the Second Tennessee, led by Colonel William Haskell. Meanwhile, a shot grazed Pillow, who then ran from the field without leaving instructions behind to his subordinates. As a testament to Scott's planning and the volunteers' fighting ability, the American army still managed to encircle the Mexicans and force their surrender. Yet Pillow's confounding series of mistakes had needlessly caused hundreds of American deaths.[27]

Perhaps it was Pillow's relationship to Polk that led Scott in his official battle report not to excoriate Pillow for his poor performance at Cerro Gordo. Maybe Pillow by this time had truly charmed or befriended the general. Whatever the reason, Scott's charity toward the man he called "the special friend and partisan of Mr. Polk" did not last long, and it completely dissipated due to a series of public and private letters that caused one of the biggest civil-military controversies of the war.[28]

THE LEONIDAS CONTROVERSY

What precipitated the crisis was the publication in October and November 1847 of a series of pseudonymous letters derogatory toward Winfield Scott in the *American Star*, the most popular American-run newspaper in occupied Mexico City. The first, signed "Leonidas," elevated Pillow to deific proportions as the hero "in command of all the forces" at the Battle of Contreras, and poked fun at Scott for giving "but one order." Leonidas was the hero of Greek legend, mentioned by Herodotus, who fearlessly and nearly single-handedly held the pass of Thermopylae against the invading Persians in 480 BC. Clearly, the "Leonidas" of 1847 intended to lower Scott in the estimation of his fellow citizens while raising Pillow's stock, and all that that meant politically. Other letters signed "Veritas" soon appeared giving General William Worth and Colonel James Duncan the credit for some of Scott's most cunning tactical moves. These letters originally had little immediate effect, because they appeared first in the *New Orleans Delta* and the *Pittsburgh Star*, neither of which Scott read regularly. He did, however, read the *American Star*.

The publication of the "Leonidas" and "Veritas" letters was the final straw in a long line of quarrels between Pillow and Scott, two ambitious, vain men who wanted political power, military glory, and the admiration of their countrymen. The main difference between the two was that unlike

Scott, Pillow deserved none of the three. Scott had first disregarded Pillow's fatal mistakes at Cerro Gordo, but then came Pillow's less fatal but still tragic mistakes at Contreras during the march over the lava beds. In the latter battle, Pillow went so far as to make extravagant claims in his official report about his leadership and heroics. (The similarity of these claims to those made in the "Leonidas Letter" allowed Scott immediately to recognize that Pillow had instigated the writing of it.) Even when writing to his wife, Pillow seemed incapable of telling the truth, instead portraying himself as a wildly popular, Leonidas figure:

> My brilliant...glorious achievement of this war, has covered me with the *praises* of men, of all parties and thrown me, my character and standing as a military man, at the head of the profession of arms....I was in exclusive command of the army....General Scott...told me...that the *fate* of this army depended upon my success.[29]

Scott wrote in his memoirs, that Pillow was "the only person I have ever known who was wholly indifferent in the choice between truth and falsehood."[30] In an earlier incident in Mexico City, a stolen Mexican cannon had been found in Pillow's baggage, trophies of war. Pillow denied responsibility, typically blamed subordinates, then promptly returned the cannon. He also secretly sent a letter to Secretary Marcy begging for protection. Pillow faced a court-martial nevertheless. In its ruling, the court admonished Pillow for returning the cannon only after it had been discovered by others. As soon as Polk got wind of the decision, he negated even this toothless chastisement.

General William J. Worth, though of brevet rank, had proven a confidant and strong ally to Scott up through the siege of Puebla. However, during the Pueblan occupation in the summer of 1847 Worth grew increasingly uneasy about being surrounded by Mexicans with so few troops. Yet some of this unease was of his own making, for Worth had drawn up weak terms of capitulation. Even as morale dropped Worth issued a startlingly weird, unnecessary warning about Mexican attempts to poison the water supply. This resulted in a worst-case occupation scenario: an anxious population guarded by an edgy foreign force already melancholy over its inability to advance toward Mexico City due to a lack of reinforcements. Scott reprimanded Worth for his performance, and this incident helps explain Worth's transformation from trusted confidant to fellow conspirator with Pillow.[31]

Less explainable is Colonel Duncan's rationale for turning this anti-Scott duo into a triumvirate. Other soldiers, including Ulysses S. Grant, noticed Duncan's (and Pillow's) increased hostility toward Scott once Mexico City came under occupation. Up to this time Duncan had been a regular's regular, proud of his reputation as a self-made man. A West Pointer and hero

Gideon J. Pillow during the time of the Civil War (National Archives).

of the Seminole War, Duncan had begun the war as captain of an artillery
unit. His gallant conduct in numerous battles had earned him several brevets
by late 1847, up to the rank of colonel.

   In response to the "Leonidas" and "Veritas" letters, Scott issued General
Order #349, which reiterated an old regulation forbidding officers to
provide military information to civilians. Scott was normally slow to anger,
but in this case his temper got the best of him. In the order he lashed out
at the anonymous authors, accusing them of treason and dishonor. Worth,
who actually had not written any of the letters, responded in kind, admon-
ishing Scott for failing to be "an officer and a gentleman" and slandering

him. Worth thought it best to send a copy of his complaint to Polk. How wrong he was, for when Scott got wind of Worth's letter to Polk, he arrested Worth as well. Meanwhile, Duncan admitted to being "Veritas," and so Scott arrested him, too. Pillow's arrest came only after Scott learned of his secret letter to Marcy, although it already was obvious to all that if Pillow was not "Leonidas," the two men were certainly on speaking terms. Thus, by Christmas 1847 two out of the four American divisions in Mexico lacked commanding officers.

The feud and commotion caused by the Leonidas letter, not as easily buried by Pillow's patron as the cannon incident, led to curious courts-martial of those whom Scott called "three factious officers": General Pillow, General Worth, and Colonel Duncan.[32] It is a testament to Polk's political savvy that he recognized the Pillow affair as the long-awaited opportunity to take Scott down a notch in advance of the 1848 presidential contest. Polk gathered his advisors about him, all of whom agreed that Scott was the one who should be removed. This would have to be done systematically and with much patience.

The first step in Polk's plan was to overturn the charges against General Worth, apparently the most innocent of the three. This was reasonable in the sense that complaining to his superior officer was hardly equal to outright insubordination, and so charges were dropped against Worth. Polk did, however, establish a court of inquiry that included General Caleb Cushing, Brigadier General Nathan Towson, and Colonel W. G. Belknap to look into the accusations of misconduct that Scott and Worth had thrown at one another. Indeed, any dirt against Scott might prove useful later on, and so Secretary Marcy ordered that Worth's charges against his superior be dealt with first. Since Mexico City already lay in American hands, Polk prepared to toss aside his general in chief.

Second, although Polk ordered all three men to be set free, unlike with Worth the charges against Duncan and Pillow were not dropped. Their courts-martial, however, were changed to courts of inquiry. Whatever the result, Polk apparently wanted a spectacular show but no criminal indictments. The "fire from the rear" had finally struck Polk's general in chief. "The President," Scott told Marcy, "has determined to place me before a court, for daring to enforce necessary discipline in this army against certain of his high officers."[33]

Both the president and Scott assumed that each was operating out of politics and personal hatred, Scott in persecuting Pillow and Polk in putting Scott on trial. As historian John S. D. Eisenhower points out, "the authorities in Washington had so couched the terms of the trial that Scott, while still acting as prosecutor, was also a defendant." This was, in fact, the case, even though a string of witnesses spoke in favor of Scott, from Robert E. Lee and David Twiggs to Ethan Allen Hitchcock. Even Nicholas Trist emerged as a staunch defender of Scott, despite the two men's prior squabbles.

Apparently, both could agree on their disdain for Polk, and each blamed Pillow for turning the president against them.[34]

Speaking in Pillow's favor were Quitman and even Marcy himself, the latter joining the fray once the trial moved from Mexico City to Washington in April 1848. The court's findings, issued in July, exonerated Pillow of all charges of insubordination, and even praised him for his gallant exploits at Contreras. As Eisenhower concludes, "Pillow and Polk had both triumphed ...through the sheer manipulation of government power."[35] The administration's success was undeniable (or so they thought), because during the trial the Whig Party dumped all consideration of the beleaguered Scott and instead nominated Zachary Taylor as their candidate in the upcoming presidential election. This was not the ultimate success Polk wanted, of course, since Taylor won the 1848 election.

Gideon J. Pillow provides the best example of the dangers of expanding the Jacksonian spoils system from administrative government jobs like customs officer or postmaster to include military positions where lives are at stake. To be fair, the fact that Pillow was Polk's friend and a well-known Democrat made him a lightning rod for criticism before he even arrived in Mexico. Unfortunately, Pillow in unscrupulous fashion met his critics' low expectations. He proved contentious in his relations with Colonel William B. Campbell, vain to the point of vice, unduly harsh toward his troops, and inefficient in his battle preparations. What made all this worse was that he habitually shifted blame for his failures to others while trying to bask in the light of fame he did not earn—for Pillow, the ends justified the means.

As for Polk's appointment and defense of Pillow, historian Justin Smith puts it this way: "To plant such a person, with urgent recommendations, at open, big-hearted Scott's right hand, to win his confidence, to spy upon, to criticise and undermine him, and inevitably to scheme for his place, was indecent; but Polk did it."[36] Indeed, Pillow did his job all too well, something a dismayed Scott no doubt pondered as he headed for home in the spring of 1848 after being replaced by volunteer general and Democrat, William O. Butler, to become a virtual defendant in Pillow's court-martial. Pillow returned to his law practice after the war, eventually fighting for the Confederate States of America as a brigadier general in the Civil War. During that war, after surrendering Fort Donelson but fleeing to avoid capture, he found himself briefly relieved of duty. He was for the most part placed on administrative duty after that. Pillow died bankrupt after being sued for property he had taken as war booty during the conflict. The other two members of the anti-Scott triumvirate received for their efforts tangible benefits as per the spoils system: Polk appointed Duncan inspector general of the army, and Worth became commander of the Department of Texas and New Mexico. Coincidentally, both men died of disease in 1849.

The extensive spoils extended to questionable witnesses and members of the court-martial, too. Colonel Belknap soon was brevetted a brigadier general and Towson a major general, in Scott's words, "for their acceptable services in shielding Pillow and brow-beating Scott." Colonel Riley, who gave testimony in favor of Pillow, earned the brevet of major general as well, along with the command of California. "Thus a series of the greatest wrongs ever heaped on a successful commander," wrote Scott, "was consummated."[37]

Flooding the army with political appointees and friends could only go so far toward ensuring its loyalty, and it certainly could not transfer public admiration from Scott or Taylor to a man like Pillow. Scott was not alone in his opinion of Pillow as a man "wholly indifferent in the choice between truth and falsehood."[38] Too, undercutting Taylor did nothing to alter the fact that even Polk's advisors early on recognized Scott as the only viable choice to lead the planned amphibious landing at Vera Cruz and march to Mexico City.

CONSEQUENCES OF PARTISANSHIP AND IDEOLOGY

An evaluation of Polk's strategy to keep the army loyal to him and to his war aims while benefiting the Democracy politically and rewarding partisans and friends reveals mixed results. Polk's attempts to weaken the political prospects of Scott and Taylor failed in that Taylor went on to win the presidency while Scott remained general in chief even after the Pillow mess. Maybe this is because, despite Taylor's suspicions, the only real triumvirate of conspirators that existed strove to undermine Scott rather than Taylor. The Gaines letter and Monterrey armistice proved that Taylor could do enough to undercut his own standing all by himself.

The most embarrassing failure for Polk was his transparent scheme to revive the rank of lieutenant general in order to place Senator Benton over Scott. To see the president's supporters rewarded with existing spoils had come to be expected by most Americans in 1846, but to create something as grand as the lieutenant generalship and then to fill it in a preplanned way with a frequent visitor to the Executive Mansion was quite another. Even Democrats refused to support that presidential power grab. Only in his quest to shape temporarily the command structure of the army with Democratic general officers did Polk meet unqualified success.

There is no doubt but that Taylor and Scott made Polk's job easier by sniping at each other in their quest for the Whig nomination. Of the two generals, however, as will be seen in succeeding chapters, Scott acted more professionally in the services he tendered to the intensely partisan Polk and to the U.S. Army. Much later in life, Scott looked back more positively on Taylor, calling him a man of "pure, uncorrupted morals, combined with indomitable courage." Scott never forgave Polk, however, and his opinion of Polk as an "odious" and "cunning" hypocrite only deepened with time.[39]

All of the politicking between Generals Scott and Taylor and between Polk and his generals did not go unnoticed by rank and file soldiers. One accused the "unfortunate jealousy...between Generals Scott and Taylor" of lowering the morale of the volunteers. The Leonidas letter dispute and subsequent inquiry drew the most attention. George Wilkins Kendall, traveling with the army in Mexico as a journalist for the *New Orleans Daily Picayune*, reported that the flap over the Leonidas letter was "the subject of remark and speculation" among the troops. "General Pillow has made himself as it were the laughing-stock of the army" because of his "rasping ambition" to "build a reputation." But while many soldiers found the whole affair "amusing" more than anything, the ignominious manner in which Polk replaced Scott lowered Polk's reputation among the troops.[40]

Did Polk undermine military morale and effectiveness by politicizing to such an extraordinary degree, even for the Jacksonian era, the command structure of the army? Ultimately, no. Events proved Polk right about Taylor's lack of imagination and prudence, for while Taylor's troops won the day at Buena Vista, the general was only there in the first place because he had disobeyed orders. Polk, to his credit, stuck with Scott out of necessity long enough to win the war, before having Pillow take him down. But that was only after first proposing the lieutenant generalship—a risky and stupid political blunder to be sure, made more egregious because it was such an obvious grasp at power by the civilian government over the army.

A more interesting question is whether Polk's military appointments, so obviously political at first glance, were indeed as partisan as they appeared. True, all were Democrats meant to infiltrate an army command structure Polk believed to be "all Whigs and violent partisans."[41] Moreover, the war had ideological and partisan ends in that it was supported by the only major party that favored both territorial expansion and the ongoing spread of slavery. The president's goal of acquiring California and securing the Southwest was not uniformly popular among Whigs and their supporters. Polk assumed that his generals operated on the same democratic, partisan, and populist notions that he did. State governors surely seemed to think so. Governor Owsley's all-Whig appointments to the Kentucky volunteers demonstrates this. In such an atmosphere, would it not be unwise for Polk to appoint Whigs to lead a war so vociferously denounced by the same Whigs who, after all, originally had cast their votes in favor of declaring war? Was not one probable explanation of Taylor's armistice at Monterrey or Scott's interminable delays in leaving Washington City, Polk reasoned, that both generals sought to protect their men while forestalling Polk's expansionist aims? Keeping in mind the social and political context of the 1840s, one can understand why Polk answered these two questions in the affirmative.

The reality is that while Jacksonians like Polk lionized the common man and looked down on professional soldiers, presidential cronies like Pillow made terrible military leaders. Plus, Polk and his friends may have rhetorically claimed to favor a meritocracy but in practice they behaved like an oligarchy of the *ancien regime*. Not a small number of their appointees seemed more like armchair generals than virile Westerners suited to the brave new world of an imperial nation. Benton perhaps would have fared little better than Pillow had he secured the prize of lieutenant general. Yet one would have to ignore innumerable factors to argue in any serious way that the Mexican War was an astonishing success in spite of, not because of, Polk's direction. Polk's decision to keep Scott in the field long enough to achieve victory was one of these factors. Other significant factors, which are discussed in later chapters, were Polk's response to the crisis over the military governance of California, his success at rebuffing the war's critics while at the same time resisting passionate appeals for the conquest of "All Mexico," and his dominant management of war planning. Controlling perfectly the execution of the war, not just on the part of the commanding generals but among the rank and file soldiery, however, was another matter. As the next chapter demonstrates, Polk's authority and efforts, politically inspired or not, could only accomplish so much on the battlefields and in the occupied cities of Mexico.

"A Number of Worthless Men"

The James K. Polk administration wanted a quick war resulting in the annexation of California and the affirmation of the Rio Grande as the southern border of Texas. To prevent a prolonged war or widespread popular uprising, Polk planned to placate the Mexican people by reassuring them that war was being waged only against Mexico's armies and not for the conquest of the entire country. Personal and church property was scrupulously to be protected, supplies were to be purchased, and in most cases rent was to be paid for American-occupied buildings.

Hope and strategy are two things easily undermined by contingent events and unpredictable human agency. As Taylor's success at Buena Vista proved, even generals did not always follow orders. What, then, of common volunteers, many of whom joined the army in the first place hoping to meet *señoritas* and find Mexican gold? This question dogged Polk, who knew he would be forced to trust the judgment and prudence of the American officers charged with keeping discipline and good order in the army while trying to undertake the unprecedented task of ruling whole Mexican cities and provinces.

The president and Secretary of War William Marcy could only do so much from Washington City to ensure that the U.S. Army followed the path best suited to achieving the administration's strategic goals. With soldiers far from the reach of American laws, there existed a great possibility for trouble. Other than outright defeat in combat, looting and atrocities committed by American soldiers posed the gravest risk in country to Polk's hopes for victory and the postwar order. Enraging the Mexican people might lead to exactly what the United States did not want: a lengthy, bloody, and expensive occupation. American officers responded to criminal incidents perpetrated by soldiers under their command in a variety of ways. This chapter explores discontent among the American soldiery with federal or army policy, the connection between this discontent and the criminal activities troops engaged in during the Mexican War, and the response by officers to those crimes. This was one aspect of the war ultimately beyond even President Polk's micromanaging hands.

Potential war booty in Mexico consisted of livestock, church ornaments that soldiers called "golden Jesuses," weaponry, "pretty Mexican gals," and personal possessions of the rich and poor alike.[1] Recruiters, fearing patriotism alone might be insufficient, publicized these tempting facts to lure young men into the army. Loot could be a welcome accompaniment to adventure, steady meals, and a salary of $7.00 per month. Most volunteers, however, joined the army not for war booty, at least not strictly so. They joined out of patriotism, honor, duty, and a masculine desire to impress the ladies. Sadly, the minority who committed crimes and atrocities in Mexico left an indelible impression on the populace there.

DISOBEDIENCE

Mayhem and rowdy behavior occurred in New Orleans and its surrounding encampments even before soldiers embarked for Mexico. Fighting for the same cause did little to quell rivalries between citizens of different states and locales, but just about anything could spark a duel, brawl, or riot. Ethnic differences between companies only aggravated matters, leading in at least one case to a fatal gun battle. Excessive alcohol consumption nearly always played a role in the violence and debauchery. The tent cities that sprouted around New Orleans in mid-1846 quickly gained a reputation as dangerous places to be at night, especially for women. Opponents of territorial aggrandizement and the course pursued by the president in enlarging the regular army and packing its officer corps with Democrats found in the soldiers' behavior additional reasons to oppose "Mr. Polk's War." Democrats faced a real challenge in trying to explain how such miscreants were gathering to spread republican civilization or to defend American honor rather than preparing themselves to embark on an arrogant, destructive war of plunder.

Once in Mexico the deportment of some volunteers degraded further. The first prohibitions broken by transgressing soldiers, not surprisingly, were those against gambling and drinking liquor. Indeed, fighting and general rowdiness inevitably followed the breaking of one or both of these prohibitions. The drunken activities of most soldiers can best be described as mischief and misbehavior. This included shooting out of boredom at the white crosses that dotted the Mexican landscape, intentionally disrupting Mexican religious festivities, and engaging in fisticuffs with fellow soldiers or with Mexican men. In such cases, especially during long periods of occupation or encampment, as long as drinking binges ended with only a few bruises or temporary debilitation and sickness the next morning, officers responded with light punishment.

Particularly in sparsely populated Chihuahua and New Mexico, both of which fell early on in the war to the U.S. Army and therefore faced the longest occupations, American soldiers occasionally robbed private homes. Burgling watches, jewelry, and silverware while pretending to be searching for weapons during house-to-house searches was common, since residents stood at the mercy of the armed soldiers in their midst. Wealthy ranches, located as they were in seclusion away from towns, proved especially tempting targets to Americans, who were under the strictest of orders not to desecrate the most likely source of transportable wealth, churches.

Just across the border at Matamoras, officers stayed busy trying to control their volunteers, who according to one exasperated commander "destroyed the property, insulted the women, and maltreated the men of the country." One soldier, charged with protecting a wealthy Mexican family from bandits outside Matamoras, complained instead about being "called upon almost daily to protect" them "from the unceremonious visits or rude treatments of the volunteers."[2] Moving southward from Matamoras, Americans disobeyed orders by foraging farmland at will and shooting livestock. "Although our orders have been very strict on the subject of private property," wrote a Tennessean stationed near Monterrey, "*yet these men* have not considered themselves subject to the same orders and rules that govern the remainder of the army." By late 1846 depredations at Monterrey became so numerous that to prevent further pillaging Taylor ordered the riding animals of noncommissioned officers, musicians, privates, and laundresses to be sold.[3]

Not all incidents can be blamed on ill-disciplined individuals or criminals in the army willfully acting against clear orders. Some of the troubles are traceable directly to the poor institution of otherwise sound army policy by commanding officers. For example, to conciliate Mexicans army policy required American officers to seek permission before commandeering buildings to use as barracks, stables, or hospitals. In practice, however, American troops, almost always with their officers' blessings, gained entry through threats or outright violence. Volunteer rank and file were not the only Americans bending or breaking army regulations in Mexico.[4]

A second but related policy required that private property owners be compensated in rent when the U.S. Army occupied their homes or buildings. Yet American troops commandeered churches and monasteries without payment, clearly not the most effective way to follow Secretary Marcy's order to pay special heed to Mexican religious sensibilities. Most Americans seemed to appreciate neither the emotional bonds between Mexicans and their churches nor the fact that churches, indeed, were not government property in the first place. (Santa Anna later paid a heavy political price for this same misunderstanding about church property, when Mexicans rebelled against his attempts to confiscate it.) "Nothing tends to incense the people so much," wrote one civilian observer of the army, "as any desecration of their churches."[5]

A third army policy followed irregularly in Mexico was paying Mexican merchants and farmers for foodstuffs and livestock. Besides foraging for both, a few soldiers stole outright, sometimes at gunpoint. For example, at Monterrey in late 1846 several American volunteers rejected the price set by Mexicans for their mules. "They take it without offering them any remuneration and think they treat him better than he deserves," one soldier observed, "for they consider that they give him his life, when they would feel more pleasure in shooting him." The army discharged the perpetrators, a calculated effort designed to ensure ready availability of mules for the invasion force and to keep the populace reasonably friendly. Underpaying was a more common offense. This was accomplished simply by overfilling sacks with produce or grain after having weighed them, and threatening complainants with injury or death. To be fair, however, when it came to foodstuffs and livestock, American soldiers generally paid "in coin." Consequently, Mexicans lined the streets in most towns or all but ran to greet approaching troops in an effort to sell their wares.[6]

Burglaries and street fighting, while obviously not a boon to Mexican-American relations, usually did not end in murder or wholesale violence. But "usually" is not "always," and from time to time fighting got out of control and quickly turned deadly. In late 1847, about thirty miles outside of Santa Fe, New Mexico, in the town of San Pedro, two companies responded to a street fight between a few Americans "and the people of a little town" by raiding the town. About 30 mounted men "ransacked the town, broke open several doors," and robbed the inhabitants of their chickens, blankets, and anything else that was not nailed down. Against strict standing orders about religious property, one soldier hauled off a Catholic statue "as a trophy." Apparently, no one was killed.[7]

ATROCITY

Although at times instigated by burglaries or brawling, atrocities existed on a different scale entirely, and most made the sack of San Pedro seem like mere mischief by comparison. The term "atrocity" refers to violent and deadly crimes committed by soldiers against civilians. Atrocities include rape, mutilation, murder, the sacking of towns or homes, and the burning of crops. Atrocities during the Mexican War almost always invited reprisals against Americans, and so launched a dreadful cycle of death and destruction.

One common thread running through the worst atrocities was intemperance, which demonstrates how disobeying regulations considered to be of small importance could end in morally despicable and, potentially, tactically catastrophic behavior. High-ranking officers constantly struggled to keep liquor out of the hands of their men, but this was no easy task, as Colonel George W. Hughes found out. As military governor of Jalapa, Colonel Hughes resorted to the unpopular measure of forbidding American troops "from resorting to the Hotels of this City" because of the "intoxicating Liquors" found there. Officers serving under Hughes hated this order to such an extent that they openly encouraged enlisted men to disobey it. Even the military police given the task of arresting all "noncommissioned officers and soldiers" caught in hotel bars chose instead to use their authority to compel reluctant barkeeps to serve the men.[8]

The second commonality among atrocities was the motive of revenge on the part of Americans for the massacres committed by Mexicans during the Texas Revolution at Goliad and the Alamo. Revenge of this sort was not limited to Texans or even to Americans who had joined Texas in its cause. Thanks to widely published accounts and memoirs, all Americans were familiar with how they expected Mexicans to treat prisoners. Nevertheless, more often than not Texans committed the worst atrocities of the war.

The third trend most atrocities (or acts of vandalism and looting, for that matter) held in common was a confident feeling among the perpetrators that God and nature were on their side. This took many forms but is best described as Anglo-Saxonism, a belief that Anglo-Saxons (in this context, nearly all white Americans) were a culturally, politically, religiously, and ethnically superior people. Providence had blessed Anglo-Saxons with innate qualities that had produced in them great learning, material advancement, and a love for individual liberty that expressed itself politically in republicanism, economically in market capitalism, and religiously in Protestantism. Bringing "the light of science" to "Priest ridden Mexico" could only benefit the people there, proclaimed one soldier.[9]

This superiority gave Anglo-Saxons not simply the right, but the duty, to dominate inferior races. This domination might take a civilizing form but it could also become an exercise in extermination. Great Britain, Americans believed, had passed the Anglo-Saxonist mantle to the vibrantly democratic United States. Only the blessing of Divine Providence, they reasoned, could explain the United States's frenetic industrial growth, increase in wealth, and phenomenal territorial expansion in the decades leading up to the Mexican War that historians collectively refer to as the Market Revolution. General William J. Worth likened the war as the next logical step in the time-honored, Anglo-Saxon tradition of bringing other lands and peoples under their enlightened rule. As Indianan Henry S. Lane said of Mexico, "The people here are...One Hundred years behind the improvement and spirit of the age."[10]

Anglo-Saxonism formed a key component of the prevailing belief among Americans by the middle 1840s that it was their "Manifest Destiny" to extend their republic's borders to the Pacific, and maybe even as far south as the Andes. Democrat John L. O'Sullivan added the term Manifest Destiny to the American lexicon in 1845 when he accused Whigs, in their opposition to Texas annexation, of "limiting our greatness and checking the fulfillment of our manifest destiny to overspread the continent allotted by Providence for the free development of our yearly multiplying millions."[11] Beginning with Jackson, Democrats had argued that a symbiotic relationship existed between territorial expansion and democracy. Most Americans agreed but hedged at whether such expansion should occur via peaceful annexation, like in the case of Texas, or by the sword, as they feared was happening in the Mexican War. In any case, Americans eventually would spread democracy, Protestantism, and economic vitality all at the same time, for the three were so closely linked together as to be inseparable. One way or the other, they would improve backwards Mexico and make it flourish agriculturally, whether by settlement or by influence.

Soldiers, expansionists, and war boosters applied the term "Anglo-Saxon" to just about all European Americans in the United States, except the Irish. The Irish were excluded because of their Roman Catholic faith, which they shared with the Mexicans. Indeed, to most Anglo-Saxonists devotion to Roman Catholicism was a sure sign of one's inferiority and backwardness. Soldiers marched to war praising in song their "Saxon blood" and "holy right" to conquer Mexico, vowing to tame the priest-ridden "Mongrel Spaniard." If barbaric Mexicans could not be civilized or assimilated into Anglo-Saxon civilization, then they would be exterminated. Expansionists depicted Americans as the new "chosen people," ready to drive the Mexican Canaanites out of North America.[12]

With this exalted view of Americans and lowly opinion of Mexicans in mind, resultant atrocities should come as no surprise. Also unsurprising is that American troops frequently blamed Mexicans for initiating violence. Yet even in cases where Mexican civilians did initiate violence, Americans rarely identified the actual perpetrators before taking action. Nor did Mexicans in their reprisals. One of the most gruesome of such cases occurred on Christmas Day in 1846. A small group of volunteers raped women and girls as they pillaged their way through a ranch near Parras. Mexicans responded by killing an Arkansans volunteer—presumably the first lone American soldier they came across—and dragging him by a rope behind a horse before hanging his mangled, dirty body on a cactus.

The Arkansans proved more than equal to the task of exacting revenge. Around 30 men from their regiment waited until most of their comrades were out scouting the surrounding area. This gave them most of the day and night to act without the watchful eyes of others. They then went on a rampage, indiscriminately massacring over 30 unarmed peasants. The actual killers were already long gone. Not until the next day did other American troops find and tend to the victims. Surrounded by crying women and children, the troops helped wives find and identify their husbands' bodies.

Events like the Parras ranch massacre infuriated most volunteers. One admonished his comrades to "no longer complain of Mexican barbarity... *No act of inhuman cruelty...can excel the work of yesterday, committed by our soldiery.*" The sight of the mangled dead sickened another American soldier, who described the grisly scene: "Most of the butchered had been scalped...a rough crucifix was fastened to a rock, and some irreverent wretch had crowned the image with a bloody scalp." To prevent further reprisals officers stepped in between their companies and the Mexicans for days afterwards, even posting guards over the surviving women and children.[13]

Americans did not just complain about their comrades' atrocities in writing or tend to the wounded and guard the innocent after the fact. Sometimes, to protect civilians they placed themselves in harm's way. When "an unknown criminal" murdered three American soldiers as the U.S. Army traveled along the National Road to Mexico City in mid-1847, "a few comrades of the deceased...took a frantic and senseless revenge, by shooting down in cold blood about thirty unarmed Mexicans." With the death toll already high, it would have been much worse had not Illinois volunteers stepped in and "saved the greater part of these poor people." In a separate incident, several Tennessee volunteers shot one of their own when he fired on guards trying to stop a "drunken row" between Americans and Mexicans at a restaurant in Matamoras.[14]

Volunteers might be willing to save Mexicans from the actions of other volunteers, but out of *esprit de corps* they rarely ratted on their own after the fact. For some reason, the revelry surrounding American holidays tended to provoke soldiers to atrocity. In the name of Independence Day in 1847, a drunken dragoon celebrated by riding down two Mexicans with his horse, killing one and wounding the other. Once sober, he surrendered to his superior officers, only to escape the next day with the help of fellow volunteers.

The Texas Rangers possessed long-standing grievances against Mexicans and consequently showed them little mercy. But Pennsylvanians, Ohioans, and Arkansans proved notable for their atrocities as well. The Polk administration's organ, the *Washington Daily Union*, even took time out from championing the war and praising the president to lament the crimes being committed by "a number of worthless men in the ranks of our army." One war correspondent pointedly thanked God that such men were in Mexico—were they not, they would likely be terrorizing Americans at home instead.[15]

PUNISHMENT

The response by officers to crimes and atrocities committed against Mexicans by American troops varied. Soldiers received mixed signals from their superiors, despite official orders. Commanders other than Worth, like

Generals Caleb Cushing and Commodore Robert F. Stockton, preached Anglo-Saxonism (and Mexican inferiority) to their troops, which only made their men more likely to weaken under the temptation to abuse Mexicans and their property. Moreover, in many cases, atrocities and looting simply went unpunished, accepted instead as one of the unfortunate but unstoppable consequences of warfare.[16]

What did not go unpunished was thievery or ill behavior perpetrated by Americans against Americans. In these cases, rank and file soldiers complained bitterly that their officers punished them far too severely. There is some truth in this, for oftentimes the degree and kind of punishment lowered morale more than had the perpetrator's crime. "The balance of them," wrote one soldier of his commanding officers, "are very tyrannical and brutal toward the men." They "get drunk" and "strike the men with swords and abuse them." Punishments included branding the faces of repeat offenders, forcing soldiers to relinquish up to 80 percent of their salaries, applying the lash, the wearing of a ball and chain, condemning men to survive for days on crackers and water, and inundating offenders with pail after pail of ice cold water. Still other men ended up hospitalized after being forced to stand on a barrel or cower in a covered hole for hours at a time. Complaints to War Department officials about "the brutality of these officers" were rare, for enlisted men quickly learned that "no notice would be taken of it." If officers were willing to overlook atrocities committed against Mexicans as a resultant side effect of war, so, too, were War Department officials and staff officers willing to ignore cases of overwrought officers cruelly punishing their men.[17]

Nativist officers characteristically meted out light punishments to native-born soldiers while whipping and imprisoning Irish- and German-American men, especially those who were Roman Catholic. Recognizing the extent of anti-Catholicism in the U.S. Army and the threat it might pose to peaceful relations with Mexico's influential Catholic clergy, early in the war Polk sent two Catholic priests as chaplains into Mexico with the army. Marcy ordered the two priests to seek amiable relations with the Catholic clergy and people of Mexico, but preserving high morale among Catholic soldiers in the U.S. Army also ranked high on the list of Polk's priorities. Nativist politicians in the Whig and Native American Parties accused Polk of conspiring with Jesuits to bring the United States under papal domination. Some even suggested Polk wanted to annex Mexico in order to swell the ranks of the Democratic Party with more Catholics. Clearly, the anti-Catholic climate of the 1840s made appointing Catholic chaplains politically volatile. The alternative of disorder in the army and the potential of a religious war, however, were enough for the nonsectarian Polk to take the risk. A few soldiers criticized the two priests, but most praised their diligence in ministering to the men in camp and during combat.[18]

Mexican propaganda took advantage of this nativist and anti-Catholic sentiment, encouraging Catholics to desert and join the Mexican cause against the Anglo-Saxonist, Protestant United States. In exchange, Mexico promised land and large bounties. In general, these Mexican appeals fell on deaf ears, but not entirely. The most famous (indeed, infamous) deserters who answered this call, the mostly Irish San Patricio Battalion, fought for Mexico at Churubusco and faced hanging and facial branding afterwards.

DESERTION

Desertion was not limited to Irish-Catholic soldiers weary of oppressive officers or to those enticed by Mexican propaganda. Usually men deserted out of fatigue with army discipline. The militia musters common to the late Jacksonian era rarely entailed serious marching, discipline, or field practice. Rather, a muster was a cause for celebration, drinking, and perhaps the donning of a fancy uniform for a parade. In Mexico, some volunteers viewed just being made to march or stand in a line as an egregious encroachment on personal freedom and one's dignity as a citizen. Apparently, little had changed since George Washington's day in terms of the mind-set of militia and volunteers. Yet soldiers deserted for nonlibertarian reasons, too. The monotony of camp life and restrictions on alcohol consumption compelled some to leave camp in search for liquor and revelry. Those not killed by bandits sometimes regained their sobriety to find themselves impressed into the Mexican military. Others were so afraid of being branded or whipped that they never returned to camp and headed for home instead.

Of the approximately 9,000 men who did desert during the war, most were regulars, not volunteers. Only 6 percent of the volunteers who went to Mexico deserted, as opposed to 13 percent of the regulars.[19] Volunteers, it seems, were more likely to complain and grow restless under even the lightest of army discipline but were also less likely to desert than regulars. Perhaps this is because there was an element of truth in the citizen soldier ethic which volunteers claimed to uphold. Volunteers fought not in the company of strangers like regulars, whom they derided as mercenaries, but beside friends and relatives, under democratically elected officers, and in the name of their hometowns, counties, or states. They might be relatively untrained or ill disciplined compared to regulars, but in Jacksonian America quantitatively unmeasurable factors like liberty and virtue and honor increased the likelihood that volunteers would fulfill their full terms of service.

AMERICAN MILITARY GOVERNMENT IN MEXICO

While American officers—good and bad, well trained and poorly trained—struggled to govern their own men without driving them to desertion, American military rulers in Mexico faced the additional challenge of governing an occupied and potentially dangerous population. This meant cooperating with Mexican officials and influential Catholic clerics while ensuring that their own soldiers behaved themselves and did not stir up the locals. It also entailed following orders that called for a high degree of diplomatic expertise. Keeping the occupied Mexicans passive and maintaining high troop morale despite the fidgety hands of an occupation army ranked highest on the list of priorities.

Military governorships had no precedent in American history, and so General Scott had to establish one that would address these challenges. As historian K. Jack Bauer writes, "The provision for military commissions was...forced on Scott by the lack of any statutory authority to deal with serious crimes once the troops left American soil."[20] The War Department granted Scott no authorization to establish military governments, but it did not disallow it either. And so into the vacuum of authority went Scott, largely in response to the behavior not of Mexicans but of his own troops. Practicality acted as Scott's guiding principle. His General Order #20 established two separate jurisdictions for crimes committed in areas occupied by American forces, effectively insuring that Americans accused of crimes would only be tried by other Americans before military tribunals. Scott was noticeably proud of his guidelines for instituting martial law in Mexico:

> The order worked like a charm...it conciliated Mexicans; intimidated the vicious of the several races, and being executed with impartial rigor, gave the highest moral deportment and discipline ever known in an invading army.[21]

Scott's rosy appraisal of General Order #20 did not always match up with reality, however, when it came to how U.S. military governors instituted it.

General Worth began his stint as Puebla's governor immediately after victory there on May 15, 1847. As governor of Vera Cruz two months earlier, he had done a fine job, establishing order through martial law in the bombed out city and successfully preventing a yellow fever outbreak through his sanitation policies. Unfortunately, Worth failed miserably when trying to repeat this performance at Puebla, largely because he ignored or misunderstood General Order #20.[22]

Before even entering the city, Worth arranged a meeting with Puebla's civic and religious officials. With much-needed reinforcements nowhere in sight, Worth's goal was to smooth the way for what might turn out to be an extended occupation by little more than a skeleton force. In keeping with the U.S. Army policy aimed at avoiding unrest, Worth promised that American soldiers would respect private property and scrupulously honor freedom of religion. All of this seemed reasonable enough, a logical execution of standing orders to conciliate the Mexican population. But Worth, unfortunately for his reputation, went further. He was so intent on ensuring peaceful relations with the Pueblans that he agreed to allow Mexican laws to remain fully intact in the city. In practice this meant that Worth's men would be subject to Mexican law and could be arrested on accusations made by Mexicans. The effect of this rubric also meant that American soldiers could face trial in Mexican courts, a violation of Scott's order. As one of Worth's soldiers wryly observed, the general's propitious terms implied that the U.S. Army had surrendered to Puebla, not the other way around.[23]

Worth did have his defenders, although they were few. Raphael Semmes argued, with some degree of accuracy, that the terms granted by Worth to the Pueblans were no different than policies followed elsewhere by General Scott. Worth granted "protection to religion, life, and property" in order to conciliate "the unarmed citizens of the country." Whether the actual text of the agreement "bore the *form* of a capitulation," thought Semmes, was largely beside the point, because Worth had calmed the bulging, restive city, enlisted support from its most influential citizens by promising them stability, and placated the apprehensive majority by proving to them that the U.S. Army was not "a horde of bloody-thirsty savages" after all. Semmes believed that Worth had approached the governance of Puebla as a professional but practical man, basing it on the ratio of American soldiers to Mexicans and on the prudent realization that "reasoning based upon military technicalities" would have been counterproductive and enraged the populace.[24]

In his zealous professionalism at Puebla Worth ended up angering his own soldiers while simultaneously enraging locals, quite an accomplishment but not exactly the balancing act needed for a calm occupation. Despite relative tranquility in the city, other than occasional cases of Americans burgling churches or brawling with Mexicans (and with each other), Worth became so terrified by the possibility of guerilla attacks that he drove his men to exhaustion by posting them at guard all day long. This became a mounting burden as the undermanned force, largely cut off from the outside during the summer of 1847, waited for reinforcements that did not come for several months.

Worth next convinced himself that Mexicans were plotting to poison American soldiers. In response, he issued a private notice to his officers warning them about nefarious Mexican plans. In spite of the notice's intended privacy, word traveled fast. Soon, enlisted men and the whole city knew. Tension increased dramatically as Americans looked askance at Mexicans and Mexicans eyed Americans with newfound distrust. In the meantime, there occurred scattered instances of Americans looting convents and churches, despite the fact that these places were guarded by other Americans. Unfortunately, Puebla was not the only city to face this treatment during the American occupation.

Scott reprimanded Worth for his many failures at Puebla, including failure to execute General Order #20. Worth responded by complaining about ill treatment from Scott, and he requested a court of inquiry to explain himself and to clear his name. On the court of inquiry, convened in June 1847, sat P.F. Smith, David Twiggs, and John A. Quitman. Without apparently even a second thought, the court condemned Worth's poison warning, especially the botched manner in which he had issued it. The court also reprimanded Worth for the weak terms he had reached with Pueblan officials and for the complaints he had leveled at Scott. Relations between Scott and Worth would never again be the same, as the Gideon J. Pillow controversy later proved.[25]

As the American army marched deeper into central Mexico and approached the capital, concern about U.S. soldiers running amok increased. The *New York Herald*, previously a supporter of the war, predicted that American soldiers would lose altogether their ability to behave themselves once they arrived in Mexico City, "where countless thousands are locked up in the churches and cathedrals—where solid gold and silver vases, candlesticks, and images are scattered in profusion."[26] The worries of the *New York Herald* proved prophetic. Plunder hit its high point shortly before and during the occupation of Mexico City, although not for lack of trying on the part of at least one volunteer general, John A. Quitman.

Quitman, named military governor of the City of Mexico by General Scott, was determined not to repeat Worth's mistakes. After all, he had sat on the tribunal that pronounced a harsh judgment on the latter's failures as governor. Quitman realized the best way to stop American atrocities and curb misbehavior was to act firmly with American malcontents while appeasing the Mexican population to the greatest extent possible. This would ideally give soldiers fewer excuses to abuse civilians or to seek revenge for real and imagined crimes. Thus, Quitman decided to govern the city mostly through extant Mexican officials and institutions. With Scott's approval, he even established a Mexican police force to work alongside American military police. The plan was for the Mexican police to deal with Mexican-only crimes.

Scott's General Order #20 gave Quitman the statutory means to govern Mexico City as he hoped. For a time, this cooperation between Mexican officials and American army officers, plus the support of Mexican bishops which Quitman worked strenuously to gain, worked. Putting his legal expertise and legislative experience to work, Quitman successfully established the two jurisdictions envisioned by Scott: one for Mexicans accused of committing crimes against Mexicans, and one for crimes involving Mexicans and Americans. Significantly, Americans accused even of heinous crimes like rape and murder were to be tried by American commissions. No American was to be left in the hands of Mexican justice, no matter the crime. Quitman's expectation was that if Mexicans saw Americans rigorously punished for their crimes against Mexicans, they might grumble but would not rebel against their occupiers, realizing that at least some justice had been done.[27]

For the most part, this practical combination of overlapping jurisdictions and cooperation with Mexican authorities worked. But General Quitman's hope for a completely peaceful occupation until both nations signed a peace treaty was dashed during his first few weeks on the job as military governor. As the monotony of occupation set in, incident built upon incident until by October the city was abuzz with a palpable friction between American troops and the civilian population. On October 6, 1847, Quitman took the step of promulgating an order, cosigned by a Mexican official, promising to punish all "ill treatment on the part of our soldiers." To reassure an increasingly apprehensive Mexican populace, he printed the order on a broadside in English and Spanish and posted it around the city.[28]

Quitman's posted order failed to deter those Americans who saw the city as their playground. On October 12, intoxicated U.S. soldiers broke down the doors of shops and homes throughout Mexico City, "plundering without restraint." The rioting lasted for two days, at which time Quitman, assisted by Mexican authorities, restored order. The capital remained free of major disturbances but riddled with minor ones and marked by deteriorating Mexican-American relations through the departure of the U.S. Army in June 1848. The events of October 1847 proved that directives from Washington, meticulous occupation planning, and the scrupulous execution of orders by military governors were not enough to ensure an orderly occupation. In the case of Mexico City, there were simply too many variables for which one had to account, such as Mexican insurgents bent on resisting their occupiers, the consequences of inebriety, and Americans seeking to take advantage of a city they believed lay at their mercy.[29]

DISCIPLINE UNDER TAYLOR

The two best known American commanders, Taylor and Scott, each had their own opportunity to demonstrate personally their disciplinary tactics. As in other matters, the two were as different as night and day.

Taylor viscerally disliked and distrusted volunteers but proved lax when disciplining them. His discipline of choice was to discharge a troublesome company or to send it someplace "where it can do less mischief than here." Doing the latter amounted simply to relocating the problem. It also set no example for Taylor's men and left Mexicans wondering why American officers, despite their vaunted proclamations to the contrary, tolerated atrocities. Soldiers did criticize Taylor for profligate use of corporal punishment, but these penalties almost always were given for American-on-American violence or for insubordination and drunkenness, not for atrocities against Mexicans.

Despite his reluctance to mete out harsh punishment to those who committed atrocities, Taylor was not blind to the danger posed by such heinous deeds. "Were it possible to rouse the Mexican people to resistances," said Taylor, "no more effectual plan could be devised than the very one pursued by some of our volunteer regiments now about to be discharged."

Yet knowing this Taylor purposefully neglected to inform the War Department about the extent of atrocities committed under his command until late 1847. At that time, he was still discharging violators and sometimes whole companies. Among the discharged were several companies of Texas cavalry, of which Taylor complained had "committed extensive depredations and outrages upon the peaceful inhabitants." After the grisly scalping episode involving Arkansas volunteers, Taylor likewise ordered the perpetrators back to the Texas border. He soon rescinded the order out of what he claimed was military necessity, presumably meaning that since Scott had left him undermanned, he had no choice but to keep the Arkansas volunteers around.[30]

"The volunteers here," wrote Lieutenant Napoleon Dana from Monterrey in November 1846, "have been behaving shamefully....The officers are...as bad as the men." Dana's list of atrocities committed by Taylor's troops at Matamoras and Monterrey, and ignored by their officers, contained rapes "of the most hellish, devilish kind," including instances of several soldiers holding husbands at gunpoint while others raped their wives. Dana also recounted a series of murders committed by marauding bands of a drunken Kentucky regiment called the Louisville Legion. Mexicans in the region became so scared that they fled their homes to ride out the rest of the war in central Mexico, according to Dana. For some, their treatment at the hands of Americans confirmed widespread rumors that the U.S. Army planned "to send some of them to the United States for slaves."[31]

Taylor's response to this mayhem was to order the Louisville Legion "to the rear," Camargo. He intended to bring shame on the volunteers and remove them from the scene in order to mollify the local population. But the regiment's officers, including its commander, Colonel Rogers, "interceded so hard with the general to save their regiment from disgrace that he has countermanded his order on condition that they shall detach the culprits, officers and all, and offer them for punishment." The punishment was to be left to Rogers.[32]

It is with some irony, then, that one must interpret Captain Ephraim Kirby Smith's statement that the arrival of volunteers "is dreaded like death in every village in Mexico, while the regulars are met by people almost as friends." Smith failed to note that while volunteers may have committed the majority of offenses, it was regulars like Taylor who in most cases were ultimately responsible for order and discipline. These regulars often neglected their duty to punish the grossest offenders in ways designed to deter further atrocities and mollify Mexicans by letting them know that the penalty for atrocities was more than simply being moved from one Mexican town to another.[33]

General Taylor's motivation for underreporting offenses or punishing volunteers only with discharge or relocation stemmed from his embarrassment that Americans commanded by him would "disgrace their colors and their country.'' But what he meant by this was extensive. Taylor knew the propaganda value of such atrocities to the war's opponents in the press and in Congress, and perhaps more importantly, to Polk and the Democratic Party. He also recognized that scandal might harm his campaign to be the Whig nominee in 1848. As a politically ambitious man, Taylor could not afford to be identified with anything other than the Battle of Buena Vista, certainly not with outrages committed by troops he commanded.

Taylor was not the only politician thinking of Buena Vista. So, too, was President Polk, who after that battle was now dealing with a war hero left idle far from the action in central Mexico. What to do with Taylor, Polk wondered? Polk rejected outright the suggestion from his cabinet that he promote Taylor to Scott's second-in-command. That command already belonged to General Robert Patterson, and he was a Democrat. So Polk simply let matters stand. Leaving Taylor in place with too few troops to do anything other than to secure the defensive line across northern Mexico was the best strategy militarily and politically, as far as Polk was concerned.

This weak, defensive posture slowly but decisively wore down Taylor's patience. By the late summer of 1847 the general sounded much like his volunteers, complaining about camp life, the lack of fighting, and the vicissitudes of occupation. He even requested a leave of absence. Unfortunately, the troops under Taylor's command picked up on his negative attitude. A group of North Carolina volunteers, unable to take leaves of absence and lacking the considerable will which restrained Taylor's low spirits, mutinied out of cantankerous boredom. General John E. Wool discharged the ringleaders, and Taylor concurred in the punishment. Yet Polk inexplicably did not, and he overturned the convictions and reinstated the officers. Taylor, it seems, could not impress Polk either with his battlefield victories or with his efforts to maintain discipline in the ranks.[34]

DISCIPLINE UNDER SCOTT

Winfield Scott, although like Taylor a man hungry with political ambition, responded differently and ultimately more effectively to atrocities committed under his command. Scott reacted swiftly and harshly to soldiers' depredations, hoping to set an example for would-be predators. For example, when a mob of volunteers, regulars, and sailors robbed liquor stores, raped women, and burnt homes in a hamlet near Vera Cruz in March 1847, without a second thought Scott promptly arrested the men. He then sent word to Commodore David Conner that he planned to execute "some half dozen, perhaps, of the land scoundrels." Scott urged the commodore to do the same to the sailors involved: "Will it not be just, as well as politic, to make an example of one or two of them?" If the commodore declined or made any pretense of lacking the authority to order executions, threatened Scott, he was prepared to try the sailors under a U.S. Army commission.[35]

Winfield Scott during the Civil War (National Archives).

While Taylor at times, as in the case of the Louisville Legion, seemed to want to rid himself of troublesome volunteers by first disregarding their depredations and then relocating them, Scott was not the type of leader to ignore reality. On hearing news of "disorders and outrages" committed by Americans at Jalapa, Scott did hope the tales were exaggerated "rumours" or "entirely false." But he assured Colonel Henry Wilson that "I will tolerate no disorders of any kind, but cause all to be rigorously punished." Indeed, unlike Taylor, who seemed to measure events primarily by their probable political damage, Scott took such disobedience personally: "No officer and no man under my orders shall be allowed to dishonor me, the Army and the U[nited] States with impunity."[36]

January 1848 was a difficult month for troops in Mexico in terms of discipline. By that time the army had been solely an occupation force for nearly four months, and the dangers arising from boredom paired with anxiety had multiplied. Treaty deliberations dragged on while rumors spread that Polk might recall Scott before the end of the month due to the ongoing Pillow controversy. This combination of factors encouraged disorderly conduct and outright insubordination, especially on the part of volunteers, who had signed up to fight, not to occupy cities and police their inhabitants, or each other, for an indefinite period. In mid-January a court-martial convened in Mexico City for 13 Kentucky volunteers. All came from the 3rd and 4th Kentucky regiments. What distinguished this court-martial from most was that all 13 were officers: Lieutenant Colonel William Preston, Major J. C. Breckinridge, five captains, and six lieutenants. One Georgian captain also found himself under arrest at Mexico City for being "highly insubordinate, disobedient and mischievous." William Walton Morris asked G. M. Henry to place the man on trial immediately in order to restore order to the ranks *and* to pacify the population, because the deteriorating situation in the city showed no sign of abating.[37]

DISCIPLINE UNDER BUTLER

Order and discipline suffered another blow when word reached Mexico that President Polk had recalled General Scott on January 13. This order stunned soldiers who idolized Scott as the exalted figure who had led them to victory. The recall adversely affected morale, especially among soldiers who previously had refrained from criticizing Polk's Mexican conciliation policies or his political appointees. Suddenly, accusations that Polk was using the war for crass political advantage and really was out to get Scott and Taylor simply because they were Whigs did not seem so far fetched. The fact that Scott's replacement, William O. Butler, was a Democrat, did nothing to alter this conclusion. (After the Whig Party's nomination of Taylor for president in 1848, Democrats responded by nominating Butler, a Kentuckian who might help win Henry Clay's home state, to be Lewis Cass's running mate.)

Butler arrived in Mexico in February 1848 to find widespread unhappiness with Polk's recall of Scott. The fact that the recall was issued amid the furor caused by Pillow and the Leonidas letter did not exactly create a hearty welcome for Butler. Men who had waded through blood and disease in Mexico with Scott wanted "Ol' Fuss and Feathers" back. What was needed under these circumstances was an active policy on Butler's part to convince his troops that, regardless of any controversy involving Polk or Pillow, he was now commanding general. As such, he would expect the same level of respect given to Scott. In return, he would command with a firm but fair hand. However, Butler's good intentions had the opposite effect, and he proved inefficient and much less thorough than Scott when it came to maintaining discipline and order.

Encouraged by the politically loaded circumstances surrounding Scott's recall to Washington to defend himself in Pillow's court of inquiry, Butler sought, unwisely, to work his way into his men's good graces through clemency. His General Order #9, for example, addressed the recurring problem of officers gambling and drinking with privates, a practice that lessened the respect and deference the latter paid to the former while weakening the resolve of officers who balked at punishing their drinking buddies. Butler's first chance to enforce this order and to show his firmness came when a military court convicted a group of officers under the #9 rubric. Yet although General Order #9 called such "conduct prejudicial to good order and military discipline," unlike Scott, Butler decided that "the findings of the Court itself administers a sufficient rebuke." Butler merely reminded the men not to gamble and sent them on their way—there would be no precedent-setting and fear-inducing Scott-style punishment.[38]

Two months later, the toll to be paid due to increasingly lax discipline under Butler could be seen in the U.S. Army's field reports. In arrest or confinement at Tampico alone were 144 volunteers. The imprisoned numbered among them more noncommissioned officers than privates. All hailed from the South: Mississippi, Louisiana, and North Carolina.[39]

CRIME AND ATROCITY: CAUSES AND CONSEQUENCES

The circumstances of those imprisoned at Tampico brings to light the disproportionate number of Southerners who committed atrocities and crimes in Mexico. This fact is puzzling and not easily explainable, but one can speculate on its probable causes. The political, social, and economic system of the South rested on a belief among paternalistic whites in the congenital inferiority of black Africans. This system benefited the vast majority of Southerners who were nonslaveholding yeoman farmers as much as it did the small planter class. Perhaps this racialist predisposition helped reinforce in Southerners in Mexico the ugliest side of Anglo-Saxonism, which relegated certain racial and ethnic groups to the category of children at best, exterminable Canaanites or animal-like creatures undeserving of the treatment normally accorded to people by virtue of their humanity at worst. At least in the Southwest and in the not-too-distant past in areas farther east, warfare with Indians was not uncommon. This military experience meant southern militiamen-turned-volunteers were more likely to be better soldiers once battle commenced, but it also provided them with experience fighting a people they deemed congenitally inferior. Like the Indians, Mexicans would fade and disappear before the advance of the civilized Anglo-Saxon.[40]

There also is the matter of the intense concern men paid to their honor that still prevailed in the South of the 1840s in a way that it did not in other parts of the United States. Defending one's honor or that of a comrade, not to mention that of one's home state, conceivably could help explain why the most vile, retributive massacres were perpetrated by southern troops. Taylor showed sensitivity to this drive to avoid disgrace at all costs in his leniency toward Colonel Rogers's Kentucky regiment. For Arkansans, Mississippians, and Louisianans especially, geographical proximity to Texas and familial relations to the Americans living there only increased the likelihood of acts of vengeance. Long-simmering hatred rising from the Goliad and Alamo massacres, and memories of the more recent abuse and execution of American prisoners at Perote in 1841 and at Mier in 1842, also cannot be discounted when explaining atrocities committed (by all Americans, in this case, not just Southerners) specifically in the name of revenge.

Theft, illegal foraging, and brawling certainly were not unique to the U.S. Army and its sojourn in Mexico. Indeed, to innumerable Mexican peasants Americans were just the latest army among many to ravage their homes and farms. Atrocities, however, were something else altogether. Santa Anna and Mexico's Catholic bishops lodged official complaints with Scott about American atrocities and the desecration of churches, accusing him of not honoring the word of his (and Taylor's) proclamations promising to hold private property and Mexico's churches inviolate.[41]

The victims of American atrocities never mounted a serious threat to the U.S. war effort. This is partly due to the fact that only the Mexican Catholic hierarchy possessed the resources, communication network, and managerial skills to mount any kind of organized insurgency. The majority of the clergy supported a negotiated peace, faced on the one hand with the looming threat posed by Santa Anna's confiscatory scheme and, on the other, the potentially devastating consequences were "All Mexico" advocates successfully to shape U.S. policy. The Americans' sporadic desecration of Mexican churches and abuse of prelates was not enough to stir up the populace or change the bishops' minds. In the end, the bishops' own countrymen posed more of a threat to their alleged riches than did the invading Americans. Only the bishops in the state of San Luis de Potosi, a hotbed of support for Santa Anna ever since he had formed his army there in 1835 before invading Texas, attempted to organize an insurgency against the American occupiers. The bishops' attempt ended in failure, for lack of interest.

Guerilla resistance during the Mexican War remained erratic and localized, being led alternately by priests, bandits, and former prisoners of war released by the U.S. Army on agreement to lay down their arms for the conflict's duration. Snipers and thieves did constantly hound the Americans during their occupation. But as long as the occupation seemed to the Americans wishing to return home, the U.S. Army was gone from Mexico within nine months of its arrival at Mexico City. This was no doubt one of the greatest factors in heading off even the possibility of a wider insurgency like that hoped for by San Luis de Potosi's bishops.

Santa Anna's threats to confiscate clerical property and do harm to the Mexicans' much-loved church, when juxtaposed to the pledges by most American officers to protect it, no doubt helped stave off a general uprising as well. In the final analysis, the largest factor preventing any effective, sustained Mexican resistance was not the bishops' passivity or any action on the part of American military governors but the disorganized state of the Mexican government, which changed hands several times during the war. While the Mexican army fought hard in many battles, especially at Monterrey and on the approach to Mexico City, as a general rule it proved less willing to fight the farther north the battle occurred. California and New Mexico fell quickly and stayed solidly in American hands throughout the war, despite brief rebellions in both places. In cities like Matamoras, the Mexican army evacuated without a fight.

President Polk and Secretary Marcy realized early on that during Mexico's occupation they would have to trust to the judgment of American commanders and military governors to encourage discipline among soldiers and maintain relative peace and stability. Looting and atrocities committed by American soldiers risked destroying Polk's strategic goals because these types of crimes risked enraging Mexicans to the point of armed insurrection. Except for his ability to appoint and recall generals, this was one aspect of the war ultimately beyond Polk's reach. The same jingoism and Anglo-Saxonism that drove young men to volunteer to fight the Mexicans inevitably risked the worst consequences of the rhetoric of Manifest Destiny. When combined with a drive to seek revenge for past grievances, the situation became volatile indeed.

American officers responded to criminal incidents and atrocities perpetrated by soldiers, either against each other or against Mexican civilians, with varying degrees of success and failure, and on a spectrum that on one end took such crimes extremely seriously and on the other seemed at best to look the other way and mete out a slap on the wrist for punishment. In the case of nativists punishing foreign-born soldiers, however, discipline sometimes could be excessive and counterproductive. The tough but fair-minded disciplinarian, Scott, met with a great degree of success and generally maintained good relations with local Mexican officials. Scott followed his own orders closely, and expected others to do the same. When they did not, as happened with Worth at Puebla, they suffered a stern rebuke.

But as Quitman's experience proved, even the best laid plans could crumble beneath the weight of occupation.

Although Polk and Marcy could not reach into Mexico other than to remove and replace generals, politics could. Butler discovered as much when he found himself sucked into the political whirlwind with Polk following Scott's removal. Butler's subsequent disciplinary tactics, which backfired, seemed designed above all to maintain morale and enforce order by guarding against charges of political cronyism. Winfield Scott, to his credit, apparently spent little time taking domestic politics into consideration when it came to maintaining discipline or punishing criminals. Nor was he unwilling to risk an interservice clash, as demonstrated by his threat to execute sailors over incidents near Vera Cruz. Taylor, on the other hand, overly concerned himself with the political repercussions of atrocities committed by his soldiers. This inordinate political awareness seems to have dulled his ability to gauge the effectiveness of his policies toward those who committed even the most horrible atrocities. While it is true that soldiers criticized Taylor for using harsh methods, the punishments in question generally were given for insubordination, drunkenness, and crimes against other Americans, not in response to atrocities.

Historian Otis Singletary is correct in arguing that the volunteers who committed the vast majority of offenses were wild, untrained, and poorly officered.[42] Regular officers at the time criticized volunteers for a variety of failures and inadequacies, but mostly for their lack of professional training, poor self-discipline on the march or in camp, and gloomy attitude toward authority. This in part was due to the fact that they had elected their officers based not on military skill but on whiskey, popularity, and promises of plunder. A journalist in Santa Fe blamed nonchalance among officers for the "bedlam" there. Most Missouri volunteers in New Mexico, he wrote, "are, indeed, a reckless ragamuffin band, a disgrace to the name of American soldiers, and will return...a miserable, ragged set, with morals corrupted, and will, ere long, be a great accession to our State Penitentiary."[43] As Alexis de Tocqueville famously explained, democracy does not infallibly ensure the election of good, competent leaders.

Putting too much emphasis on the misbehavior, crimes, and atrocities committed by American soldiers during the Mexican War risks leaving the impression that the majority of U.S. troops participated in such behavior. While volunteers clearly exhibited less discipline and perpetrated more crimes and atrocities than regulars, the vast majority of each maintained a strong sense of honor that, while it might have cracked in places and led to pilfering or brawling, did not inevitably or even commonly end in rape or murder. Just because soldiers were unhappy with army policies designed to maintain good relations with Mexicans does not mean they were therefore more willing to engage in atrocity. To argue such is nonsense. What is accurate to say is that discontent in the U.S. Army in Mexico, whether caused by

Polk's Catholic chaplains, overall Mexican conciliation policy, and his recall of Scott, or by leadership failures among high-ranking soldiers, led many captains and even colonels to look the other way when their men "let off steam." That "steam," although it usually amounted to brawling, drinking, and gambling, sometimes included atrocities. As for volunteers, regulars expected little else from them anyway.

Volunteers chafed under what they considered antidemocratic and excessive disciplinary tactics in the army, but they complained more about the lack of glory in marching, the grinding dullness of long encampments, and manual labor. They also objected to being punished for crimes committed against Mexicans, believing the theater of war and perhaps their Anglo-Saxon superiority endowed them with certain legal protections. This attitude, when combined with atrocities committed by unruly volunteers (and, but to a lesser extent, regulars), posed one of the gravest threats to Polk's quick-war strategy. That strategy aimed at defeating Mexico to secure a peace that entailed a rapid withdrawal from all except newly annexed territories. Importantly, in terms of the dangers posed by prolonged occupation, the only territories Polk insisted on were the least populous ones, California and New Mexico. As the next chapter demonstrates, however, these regions posed their own unique dangers to civil authority and Polk's overall strategic vision for the Mexican War.

5

"I was once viceroy"

Criminals, rowdy soldiers, and weak-kneed officers were not the only threats to come from outside of Washington City to President James K. Polk's quick-war strategy in Mexico. Polk's strategy involved conciliating the Mexican populace to prevent a popular, clerical-led insurgency while convincing Americans that the Mexican War was being fought in self-defense and for honor, not for conquest and territorial aggrandizement. While certain generals out of perceived necessity unlawfully recruited volunteers or issued unauthorized cease-fires, the most significant threat to Polk's war aims and to civilian authority came from officers-turned-military governors in those regions intended for annexation by the United States: New Mexico and California.

This chapter analyzes deliberate and inadvertent attempts by high-ranking American army officers to subvert civilian authority. As mentioned in the previous chapter, occupation governments under martial law had no precedent in American history. California and New Mexico were qualitatively different cases, however, from the urban occupation governments in places like Jalapa, Puebla, and Mexico City. Except for Americans who nursed ambitions for "All Mexico" (a number that, as discussed in the next chapter, peaked and then fell precipitously in early 1848), most Americans confidently assumed that the days of U.S. governance in central Mexico were numbered. Therefore, whether soldiers or civilians governed there mattered little. What made California and New Mexico unique was that the United States, as a republic with a written constitution, operated according to clearly delineated statutes designed to regulate territorial growth and to administer territories. How, then, were occupied New Mexico and California to be governed prior to the ratification of a peace treaty, with respect to the U.S. Constitution and federal law? For those who condemned Polk's influence over the now greatly enlarged army, this was a vital question of executive power and liberty. Others feared an executive too weak to have much influence over distant armies.

In 1803, recognized Constitutional parameters had not prevented President Thomas Jefferson from buying Louisiana, the legality of which even he doubted. About 10 years after the Louisiana Purchase, Americans invaded Canada during the presidency of Jefferson's protégé, James Madison. Although the Canadian invasion occurred in the context of the War of 1812, it nevertheless expressed expansionist aims that had little to do with the maritime issues that sparked the war in the first place. The failure to conquer Canada ultimately meant that by 1846 the United States still possessed no practical model with which to formulate and manage an occupation government. In an era dominated by a classical education, the most illustrative (and most feared) model Americans possessed was that of the Roman Republic. That republic declined into tyranny and empire due to a dreadful combination of territorial conquest, power-hungry generals, and the illiberal political necessities of ruling from afar great populations of foreigners and Roman citizens.

Apprehension of American Pompeys roaming the West, away from Congressional control and lorded over, if at all, only by the president, was neither uncommon nor entirely unrealistic. There existed the unhappy precedent of an incident involving Brigadier General James Wilkinson, Aaron Burr, and several congressmen that occurred while Jefferson was president. Employed by Spain, these men conspired to tear from the Union a vast swath of territory in the Louisiana Purchase, assuming that the lands lay too far west to be claimed seriously by the United States. But trepidation over the viability of a continental union could be traced back to the 1780s, when a sizable number of Americans doubted whether the young republic could survive with its union intact if it expanded west of Appalachia. James Madison and Alexander Hamilton in *The Federalist* assured Americans that a large, diverse union not only would survive; paradoxically and against all historical experience, it also would thrive. In spite of these assurances and heightened nationalism following the War of 1812, anxiety over continued westward expansion increased as the slavery issue entered the politics of the settlement of the Louisiana Purchase beginning with Missouri in 1819. But to govern a territory populated by Americans according to the U.S. Constitution and the Northwest Ordinance was one thing; to annex another nation's land by force and rule or assimilate its people quite another. Americans in and out of Congress debated how these military governments should function, and worried even more about how they *would* function. Many were likewise suspicious of Polk and his relationship to the occupation governments in New Mexico and California. Polk, of course, had profound reservations of his own.

These sentiments about New Mexico and California did not arise in a vacuum, for during the Mexican War Congress set about determining the proper form of government for the Oregon territory. Thus, there existed, in fact, a broader debate over how the United States ought to control the entirety of what was then called "the Far West," and just how Congress might control the controller, i.e., Polk.

The two most notorious cases relating to western governance during the Mexican War involved General Stephen W. Kearny. The first was Kearny's promulgation of a law code, with Polk's approval, for the territory of New Mexico. The second commotion arose when Kearny, Commodore Robert F. Stockton, and Captain John C. Frémont nearly went to blows over whose authority reigned supreme in California. Polk's personal relationship with Frémont and with the brash young captain's influential father-in-law, Senator Thomas Hart Benton of Missouri, added an additional twist to this latter dispute.

THE GAINES REQUISITION

While most incidents of subversion occurred at the hands of commanders forced to improvise in the field, before the U.S. government faced threats to its authority from generals in occupied Mexico, it first had to confront them in a place closer to home: Louisiana. In 1846, the elderly Major General Edmund P. Gaines, in the opinion of Polk and others, was rapidly deteriorating in his mental faculties. Polk seriously doubted whether Gaines, as commander of the army's Western Division, possessed the prudence and temperament to be trusted in any important capacity. Nevertheless, Gaines initially retained his post in New Orleans as commander of the West.

Polk at one time or another seems to have doubted the capacity of *all* his generals (except, perhaps, that of his friend Gideon J. Pillow), but his low opinion of Gaines was not unfounded. In August 1845 Gaines reacted to unconfirmed reports that war had broken out with Mexico by overstepping his authority and convincing Louisiana governor Alexander Mouton to furnish two artillery companies and four regiments of short-term volunteers. Only Secretary of War William Marcy's intervention turned what would have been a very expensive debacle into a moderately costly embarrassment instead. Yet even though Marcy cancelled the volunteer regiments in time, the artillery companies formed so quickly that, in spite of limited funds, the War Department felt compelled to allow them to fulfill their time of enlistment: three months.[1]

Unperturbed, within three weeks Gaines became convinced, based once again on secondhand information, that the United States and Mexico were at war. This time, however, he sought Adjutant General Roger Jones's permission before raising troops. In this instance it was not Gaines's prudence that was in question, but his judgment, for he claimed he could train and field over 125,000 men *and* attack Mexico City within the span of only three months. Sincerely worried about Gaines's reputation, Marcy and Jones chose to bury Gaines's foolish request, allowing the general to discover on his own that the two nations were, in fact, not at war. Whether Gaines understood the substantial difficulties in a northerly, overland invasion of the Valley of Mexico is unclear.[2]

Few were surprised, then, when General Gaines requisitioned over 11,000 volunteers in May of 1846. Gaines was responding to an emergency call for four regiments of three-month volunteer militiamen from Zachary Taylor, whose force had been attacked by Mexicans in disputed territory along the Mexican border. The Louisiana legislature, banking (quite literally) on reimbursement from the U.S. government, agreed to fund and equip the regiments. But Gaines went further, contacting governors of surrounding states for even more troops, chartering and arming civilian ships as troop transports, and ordering regulars stationed at forts in Florida and Louisiana to abandon their posts and rush to Taylor's aid.[3]

Just how many men had Gaines called to arms? Nobody was sure, least of all Gaines. By mid-May about 4,500 Louisianans had signed up for three- and six-month enlistments, an insufficient duration for them to be useful militarily in a war on Mexican territory but just long enough to prove expensive to a federal government that had not yet even appropriated money to pay for them. Secretary Marcy initially approved Gaines's requisitions on the presumption that Gaines was meeting a quota demanded by Taylor. On May 23 Marcy wrote to Taylor, informing him of Gaines's "calls on the governors," but admitting that, "The department is not yet advised of the number sent to join you."[4]

Five days later, when Marcy learned the actual numbers called out by Gaines—over twice what Taylor requested—he promptly changed his mind, firing off a letter to Taylor:

> As it appears that Major General Gaines, in sending forward volunteers to Texas, has exceeded the call made by you for that description of force, it would seem proper that this little excess should be disposed of in such manner as to cause as little expense and embarrassment to the service as possible.

Marcy suggested that Taylor cull from the three-month volunteers men willing to sign up as the 12-month volunteers authorized by Congress on May 13. The governors contacted by Gaines, Marcy promised, "will be requested to aid you in changing them into volunteers for a year." However, to head off the "embarrassment" (though not the cost) of Gaines's requisition, President Polk authorized the acceptance of any full "companies, battalions, or regiments" of three-month men. Taylor doubted the volunteers would stay on for 12 months, thinking that "the larger portion of them have had enough volunteering," but he did as he was told and extended the invitation to them. Meanwhile, within two days the United States promoted Taylor to the brevet rank of major general, putting him, not Gaines, in charge of field operations against Mexico. A few days after that General George M. Brooke (and eventually, Taylor himself) took command of the Western Division, allowing Gaines the time to organize a defense in the investigation that was sure to come.[5]

Already well aware of the president's mistrust for him, Taylor wanted to avoid giving Polk the slightest excuse to punish him. Thus, even before receiving Marcy's letters Taylor had written a preemptive letter to the secretary stating that he had only asked for troops from Louisiana. The new governor, Democrat Isaac Johnson, had obliged, but Gaines alone had extended the call for six-month volunteers to the states, an action "never asked for by me," according to Taylor. Based on a 1795 law and because of the wording of Marcy's letter of May 28, Taylor accepted the three-month men already in his midst. He turned the others away or tried to convince them to reenlist as 12-month troops. One consequence of this was a burgeoning force under Taylor sorely in need of rations and quickly running out of other important supplies, such as tents.[6]

Gaines's broad request for troops resulted in a serious morale problem among the men. Many volunteers interpreted the order to disperse or rejoin for one year as evidence the army and U.S. government doubted their fitness and fighting ability. Worse, maybe their patriotism and honor were in question, too. As citizen soldiers they had responded to their nation's call to arms, but were now told they somehow had been mustered illegally and were unneeded. The governors of their respective states believed the same. Was this war, like that of 1812, to suffer from poor communication and mistrust between the states and the U.S. government?

The situation unnecessarily created by Gaines produced not just an organizational and command problem but also a political predicament for Polk. Once again, Gaines's remarkable lack of prudence unintentionally fostered a contest between state and federal governments over which possessed the power to call forth volunteers and to incorporate state militia into the U.S. Army. In the long run, the latter posed potentially dire consequences to the country's ability to fight a war, something potentially more hazardous than any immediate political damage to Polk or to his party.

An angry Governor Johnson, whose state of Louisiana had given so much in recent years due to its proximity to Texas and to Mexico, labeled Marcy's retroactive exercise of the May 13 congressional act an "*ex post facto* measure of hardship and of flagrant injustice." Johnson informed the secretary that the enlistment of Louisiana troops had been accomplished not under the 1795 law permitting only three-month enlistments but under a Louisiana law allowing six-month terms. Besides, the men had enlisted prior to the existence of the new federal law requiring a yearlong contract. Those volunteers would continue in the service, Johnson asserted, for they were fully legal under Louisiana law and had bravely abandoned their jobs and farms to serve their country. To offer them 12 months or a trip home, said Johnson, was a "harsh and unnecessary" measure sure to cause unrest.[7]

Marcy responded to Johnson with a "carrot and stick" approach—with remuneration the "carrot" and the strong exercise of federal authority over the states in military matters the "stick." He assured the governor (and later his counterparts in Alabama and Missouri) that the patriotism of his state's volunteers was not in question, and promised that all the men, "as a tribute of honor," would be "cheerfully" compensated by the U.S. government. But he also explained that Gaines's call for troops was not just unauthorized—it was illegal. Therefore, contracts existed only with those soldiers "*legally* in service with General Taylor*.*" As for the six-month men, Marcy told Johnson that "by no State law whatever can the militia be called into the service of the United States." In other words, if Johnson continued in his course of action, he would be in "palpable violation" of both federal and state law.[8]

As a further "carrot," Marcy proffered Polk's apology for the mess, even though "it is not in the competence of the Executive to remove the cause of it." What Polk could do, said Marcy, was request from Congress "a liberal appropriation to defray the expenses" to help "mitigate the evils" caused by Gaines. Whether Congress would respond was up to them, and so Marcy laid the whole problem in Congress's lap at a time when the Senate already had begun to investigate Gaines and the War Department to determine who was at fault.[9] Polk was unwilling to go as far with the exertion of federal and presidential power as Andrew Jackson had during the nullification controversy with South Carolina. He instead hoped that money could smooth things over, because he sorely needed Louisiana, Alabama, and Missouri to contribute troops to the war.

Isaac Johnson refused to relent and continued to pressure the Polk administration and Congress on behalf of Louisiana's six-month volunteers. By mid-August 1846 this pressure and Congress's deliberations resulted in a three-part compromise acceptable to all parties. The first part of the solution involved a new, looser interpretation by the Polk administration of the 12-month provision in the law of May 13. As Marcy explained to Taylor, "The President may accept volunteers with an understanding, either expressed or implied, that they shall be discharged at any period short of twelve months." This carefully parsed reading of the law, a very liberal reading to be sure, would allow the six-month volunteers to enter the army legally as 12-month soldiers but still be discharged when their six months expired. This, Marcy and the president hoped, "will avoid all legal embarrassments."[10]

A pair of joint congressional resolutions formed the second part of the compromise between Louisiana and the U.S. government involving the six-month volunteers already mustered or in service. The first refunded the states who had called out their militia and formed volunteer companies in response to Taylor's and Gaines's emergency appeals. The title of the second resolution, dated August 8, was self-explanatory and expressed the predominant opinion congressmen and senators held of the fiasco: "Payment of Troops illegally called out by General Gaines."

With the legal tug-of-war between Johnson and the War Department ended, and with the volunteers insulted but at least paid, the third part of the solution could be undertaken: a court of inquiry to determine whether to punish Gaines. Remarkably, Taylor came to Gaines's defense, at least in private, noting that "if Genl Scott has charged Gen. G[aines] with being crazy, he can with great propriety return the compliment."[11] Held at Fort Monroe, Louisiana, the court reached its decision in mid-August. It concluded that Gaines had disobeyed orders, assumed powers customarily the prerogatives of civil government, and broken several laws. But Polk accurately described the court when he wrote that it had "laboured to give a construction to General Gaines's conduct most favorable to him, and if possible to excuse him." In spite of Gaines's disobedience, which had "greatly embarrassed the government" and cost "many hundreds of thousands of dollars," the court recommended against further action—the venerable Gaines would not appear before a general court-martial.[12]

Indeed, it was not so much in spite of Gaines's violations that the court chose not to punish him, but *because* of the severity of those violations. Polk recognized as much: "General Gaines is now a very old man and although guilty of acts which cannot be justified...if brought before a general court-martial, he would without doubt be punished....He is now, however, removed from that command and cannot repeat the mischief." Polk, it turns out, was wrong on this last point. When Taylor resigned from the army in 1849 in order to become president, he appointed Gaines to replace him at the head of the Western Division.[13]

Gaines was not without a direct, more immediate revenge. As discussed in Chapter 2, in mid-1847 he acquiesced in the publication of the so-called Gaines letter, General Taylor's letter to him criticizing Polk. The letter's publication infuriated the president as well as Taylor, for both thought Gaines once again had demonstrated astonishingly poor judgment. The resulting uproar led to the publication of Taylor's entire correspondence with the War Department in an effort to vindicate Polk and Taylor against the accusations of the other's supporters. As Otis Singletary points out, "Such was the feeling of [Polk and Taylor] by this time that neither could bear to hear the name of the other mentioned."[14]

THE ARMISTICES OF TAYLOR AND SCOTT

If President Polk and War Department officials experienced difficulty ensuring that generals still inside U.S. borders did not work at cross purposes with federal law and civil officials, they encountered greater problems the farther into Mexico the American army ventured. Unsanctioned cease-fires instituted by Generals Taylor and Scott are sufficient to demonstrate the limits of civilian authority over generals in the field who need to make quick tactical decisions based on larger strategies.

Military historians and theorists have criticized General Taylor's attack plan at Monterrey for leading to the needless loss of American life. This critique is accurate, and it helps to explain why after four days of bloody fighting in and around the city, Taylor felt compelled to agree to General Pedro Ampudia's request for an armistice. Taylor's army moved into the city, the surrendering Mexican army departed, and Taylor and General William Worth garnered honors in Congress and among the American public. The victory, however, earned Taylor few applause from Polk and Marcy, because the armistice violated orders. The Battle of Monterrey confirmed for Polk his worst suspicions about Taylor.

Beyond Polk's political interpretation of the Taylor-Ampudia agreement, the structure and timing of the armistice elucidates, at least in part, his low opinion of it. The armistice called for an eight-week period, during which Taylor agreed not to advance against Mexican forces. The Mexicans departed the town safely, still armed with their personal weapons and even a field battery. Allowing the enemy two months to regroup and rearm was not Polk's idea of the way to force a peace and win the war quickly: "I regret that I cannot approve his course. He had the enemy in his power and should have taken them prisoners, deprived them of their arms...and preserved the advantage."[15]

Polk's cabinet agreed that Taylor's armistice was "a great error," but now that the general was a hero they faced a delicate political situation. After lengthy discussion they unanimously agreed to order Taylor to rescind his armistice immediately, but formulated the rescission in such a way as "neither to approve or condemn" the general's behavior. In other words, out of political considerations the Polk administration overlooked Taylor's insubordination but promised to continue the war "to conquer a peace."[16]

Taylor had not reached his decision to grant an armistice lightly, and even Polk acknowledged privately that there could be sufficient reasons for allowing the enemy to depart armed and intact. The president was not in Mexico and was at least two weeks away in terms of round trip communication. Taylor hoped that eight weeks might be enough time for the American and Mexican governments to reach a peace settlement, and was not securing a peace by making a show of U.S. force in northern Mexico the stated aim of the president in the first place? Moreover, his troops were tired and the unconditional surrender he first requested would undoubtedly have led to deadly urban warfare against a well-entrenched foe. In the opinion of Taylor, who realized that issuing the armistice disobeyed his instructions from Washington, the smart move militarily *and* geopolitically was nevertheless to grant an armistice.

The lost opportunity to destroy the Mexican Army at Monterrey played a key role in Polk's decision to invade central Mexico via Vera Cruz rather than from the north. Taylor would secure and hold a defensive barrier in northern Mexico, thus isolating Mexico City from the north, but no more than that. While Taylor chafed at this, he accepted it, at least until February 1847. Early that month Taylor again disobeyed his explicit orders when he moved south of Saltillo and led his outnumbered army to victory at the Battle of Buena Vista.

Taylor's disobedience of War Department orders at Monterrey and in moving beyond Saltillo could have undermined the American war effort, if not destroyed it entirely. Of the two, the latter posed the gravest risk. Had Mexicans wiped out Taylor's outnumbered force at Buena Vista, it is doubtful Scott would have landed at Vera Cruz on March 9. Conceivably, the Mexican army could then have retaken northern Mexico, invaded American territory, or at least made raids into Texas and Louisiana to force a peace. American forces already in control of California and New Mexico may have had to abandon their posts.

As was commonly the case throughout the war, General Winfield Scott learned from Taylor's mistakes. Prior to advancing on Mexico City from Tacubaya, Scott granted an armistice that lasted from August 24 to September 6. He hoped, as had Taylor at Monterrey, that diplomats might reach a peace without the need for more bloodshed. When Nicholas Trist's negotiations with the current Mexican government failed, however, Scott advanced with fury, engaging the Mexicans in three major battles between September 8 and September 14. When the obviously defeated Santa Anna offered terms at Mexico City similar to those offered by Ampudia at Monterrey, Scott refused. Whig presidential contender or not, Scott recognized his army's superior position and clearly understood that Santa Anna must step down from the presidency in disgrace for the war to end. That occurred on September 16. Negotiations between the two nations followed, leading to the signing of the Treaty of Guadalupe Hidalgo on February 2, 1848.

The U.S. Army left Mexico City on June 12, 1848, just three days after Taylor had beaten Scott for the presidential nomination at the Whig Party convention in Philadelphia. But U.S. troops had occupied California and New Mexico since the summer of 1846. If generals making snap decisions based on troop morale or military necessity could sometimes undermine the proper power relationship between the civil government in Washington and the army, then military governorships in Mexican territories posed an even greater risk. How exactly did a republic occupy and govern conquered lands? Moreover, a temporary occupation was one thing, but Congress and the American public well knew that Polk wanted to annex California and possibly New Mexico. How, then, to hold or govern these two Mexican territories, conquered so early in the conflict, until the war's conclusion?

By which nation's laws would Mexicans be governed prior to any treaty? Perhaps most important of all, who or what actually governed New Mexico and California: Congress, the president, or American army officers? Would American military rulers be as troublesome to Polk as state governors like Isaac Johnson and William Owsley? The potential for confusion, abuse of power, unconstitutional behavior, and outright tyranny was immense.

KEARNY'S NEW MEXICO GOVERNMENT

Born in 1794 in New Jersey, after receiving a classical education at King's College (later Columbia University), Stephen Watts Kearny joined the U.S. Army as a 1st Lieutenant in 1812. Kearny's education in the Greek and Roman classics, combined with what he perceived as the militiamen's lack of discipline and the servility of volunteer officers to the men who elected them, influenced his Whig politics and shaped his firm belief that the army was no place for democracy. Good morale and fighting form, in Kearny's opinion, depended above all on consistent discipline, especially when on the march. But it also depended on a solid knowledge of human nature and how to treat raw recruits. As Kearny's biographer states about the young lieutenant's experience in the War of 1812, "Nearly everything that happened in that campaign was an excellent example of how not to fight a war."[17]

In 1836 Kearny received promotion to colonel and became commander of the 1st Dragoons, based at remote Fort Leavenworth, Missouri. His primary task was to protect the lucrative Santa Fe Trail. By 1846 Kearny had traveled extensively in the West, amassing administrative, combat, and diplomatic experience. For good or ill, Kearny personally knew all the soldiers who played so prominent a role in the conflict with Mexico, from Gaines and Frémont, to Scott and Taylor. Colonel Kearny proved such an astute diplomat and methodical administrator that Presidents Tyler and Polk, recognizing the need for improvisation in the vast, distant lands of the West, trustingly delegated important decisions to him. The consequences of that delegation helped create the first of two major controversies involving Kearny during the Mexican War.

In June 1846, Colonel Kearny received two bits of news. First came orders to conquer New Mexico and Alta California. While on the march, he learned that he had been promoted to the brevet rank of brigadier general. While Polk could only hope that Kearny's Whiggery ran far less deep than Taylor's and Scott's, he knew for sure that Kearny harbored few if any dreams of ever holding political office. This explains why the president and his cabinet unanimously agreed that Kearny's resourcefulness made him far and away the best person for the mission, since no precedent existed for conquest, the rule of subject populations, and the establishment of civil government in a territory not yet annexed or organized by the United States.

Polk and Marcy entrusted Kearny with "a large discretionary power" to supplement his force of 1,650 soldiers with volunteers recruited from Missouri, Americans living in California, and Mormon migrants. By mid-August Kearny firmly controlled Santa Fe. Leaving enough men to guard New Mexico, he personally led a contingent to California and dispatched another to Chihuahua.[18]

Marcy's instructions to Kearny enjoined him to "establish a temporary civil Government" in California and New Mexico, "abolishing all arbitrary restrictions." To accomplish this, Kearny would rely on his own judgment to identify and then bind by oath of allegiance Mexicans friendly to the United States.

> It is foreseen that what relates to the civil government will be a difficult and unpleasant part of your duty, and much must necessarily be left to your own discretion.

As long as Kearny established duty-free trade in Santa Fe and conciliated New Mexico's inhabitants, Polk left all else to his discretion. Still, Marcy promised to send "a proclamation in the Spanish language" to guide Kearny in this process.[19]

No such proclamation was ever sent. Marcy did send Kearny copies of Taylor's proclamations, but warned against using them without considerable alteration. Left with this exiguous guidance, Kearny issued proclamations on July 31 and September 22 that together declared the United States had invaded New Mexico with the purpose of welcoming it into the Union. "A free government" would be instituted soon, Kearny announced, and friendly New Mexicans who swore allegiance to the United States would henceforth be considered full U.S. citizens.[20]

Kearny followed up these initial proclamations with the extensive "Organic Law for the Territory of New Mexico" and the "Laws for the Government of the Territory of New Mexico," both of which he promulgated on September 22, 1846. These law codes, compiled by Kearny himself, along with lawyers Willard P. Hall and Alexander W. Doniphan, were meant to be long lasting and comprehensive. Kearny's "Organic Law" established a civilian executive, judiciary, and legislature, and even provided a bill of rights. Claiming that he was "duly authorized" by Polk via Marcy to do so, Kearny made civil appointments, including that of governor, to the new government of "New Mexico, a territory of the United States."

The latitude given to Kearny by the Polk administration was based not just on confidence in his temperament and practicality but also on a coherent but somewhat twisted interpretation of the U.S. Constitution. Under the Constitution, Congress retained the sole right to organize and govern territories. However, New Mexico fell into a questionable gray area, because it had not yet been annexed. So, who was in charge? Polk would have committed political suicide to claim any right to govern the occupied territory by virtue of his status as commander in chief. Marcy put forth the most persuasive argument, citing historical European precedents to demonstrate that Kearny's civil government and law code were lawful under the right of conquest. Therefore, supportive legislation, the U.S. Constitution, and executive authority were useful but in the end unnecessary to legitimate Kearny's government and law code.[21]

Democrats praised Kearny's New Mexican government as good for trade and beneficial for the "down-trodden race" of Mexicans who never before had enjoyed "the blessings of civil and religious liberty."[22] New Mexico was not just conquered territory to be held temporarily out of military exigency, Democrats reasoned. Presumably it would be annexed at the war's conclusion. Kearny's first proclamation to the Mexicans had promised as much. So why quibble and delay before organizing it? A general unilaterally transforming conquered people into American citizens did not seem to bother Democrats.

Whigs, however, expressed alarm at a general declaring conquered lands to be U.S. territory. They charged that Kearny's law code exceeded the reasonable leeway granted him by his superiors, and then some. Indeed, they doubted that his superiors possessed the authority to grant any degree of civil power to Kearny in the first place. Whigs also refuted the Democratic claim that Kearny possessed authority to relieve Mexicans of their national allegiance, declare them citizens, and command from them oaths of allegiance to the United States. More important politically, Kearny's mass naturalization of that "down-trodden race" made New Mexicans not just citizens but, presumably, voters. By imperial decree and no doubt at Polk's urging, Whigs argued, General Kearny had swelled Democratic ranks by extending suffrage to another foreign-born Catholic group who, like the Irish, would not shed their unrepublican habits easily. Nor could a people so bereft of all experience with liberty be expected to resist the demagogic tactics of the Jacksonian Democrats.

CALIFORNIA AND THE FRÉMONT CONTROVERSY

On September 25 Kearny, having "performed his duty well" in Polk's opinion, departed Santa Fe and headed to California.[23] On his arrival in Los Angeles he became embroiled in the most notable civil-military (and interservice) clash of the war: the quarrel involving himself, Commodore Robert F. Stockton, and Captain John C. Frémont over who governed California and commanded the American forces there. This dispute escalated until it included President Polk, Senator Thomas Hart Benton, the famous mountain man Kit Carson, and even Frémont's wife, Jessie.

About 800 Americans lived in California in 1846, and most were there illegally. California's Mexican citizens, known as *Californios*, governed themselves with near autonomy, thanks to their remoteness from Mexico City and moderately successful rebellions in 1836 and 1844. This virtual autonomy meant that the Americans were mostly left to their own devices, especially since their settlements were located in areas most subject to Indian attack, like the Sacramento River Valley. But rumors persisted of an impending British takeover supported by the governor, Pio Pico, and the inevitable attempt by General José Castro to tighten his grip on power. These fears made the Americans, and not a few *Californios*, nervous.

In 1845 the 33-year-old Frémont officially had been on one of his 10 exploratory missions in the West, with orders to map the headwaters of the Arkansas River. But merely mapping one western river among many did not earn one the glory Frémont so desired, and so he had disobeyed these orders and headed off to explore California (and to blaze a trail to it) instead, arriving there in December 1845. After nearly coming to blows with Mexican forces who considered him and his company more an invasion force than a band of innocuous topographers, Frémont departed with his men for Oregon in early March 1846. There, on May 9, he received a letter from his father-in-law, Benton, encouraging him to hasten to California to head off a British invasion. Here was the opportunity for fame for which he had so long waited. Frémont immediately left Oregon and hurried south.

Frémont arrived back in California in early June. His confident bearing and gutsy behavior gave the impression that he had come on military business, perhaps even with secret orders. Commodore John D. Sloat, the 68-year-old commander of the U.S. Navy's Pacific Squadron, certainly seemed to think so. For whatever reason, though, Sloat initially did not ask Frémont to see his (nonexistent) orders.

By June 1846 anxiety among American settlers in California had evolved into a readiness for rebellion. Only a spark was needed, as was a leader. Captain Frémont filled both of these needs, assisted as he was by reliable reports that the United States and Mexico were officially at war. In several skirmishes 224 "Bear Flag" rebels under Frémont's command secured the entrance to San Francisco Bay, routed leading (and formerly friendly) *Californios*, and captured the town of Sonoma. On July 4 they declared California to be not a U.S. territory like Kearny's New Mexico, but rather an independent republic.

At the time war broke out between Mexico and the United States, Commodore Sloat possessed standing orders to occupy and blockade, in the event of a declaration of war, "San Francisco and other Mexican ports."[24] Sloat's temperament was just the opposite of Gaines's—it was not in his character to take liberty with orders or to go one inch beyond explicit instructions. Nor was he like Kearny, who felt confident enacting steps only implicit in broad orders. Moreover, Sloat's replacement, Commodore Stockton, was scheduled to arrive any day. Sloat more than anything feared making his last action as commander of the Pacific Squadron a repeat of Commodore Thomas ap Catesby Jones's abortive, embarrassing takeover of Monterey in 1842, when Jones mistakenly thought war existed between the United States and Mexico. If Kearny was the man one wanted in the West, where resourcefulness was a necessity, Sloat was the man one wanted behind a desk in the office down the hall.

In June 1846 Commodore Sloat complained in a letter to Secretary of the Navy George Bancroft that he had received no communications for so long that he would "avoid any act of aggression," despite word from several quarters of war, unless he heard unequivocal word from Bancroft that war had been declared. "I have...come to the conclusion," Sloat announced, "that your instructions...will not justify my taking possession of any part of California." In essence, Sloat demanded new orders and refused to operate on the old ones.

New orders were, in fact, on the way—orders that emphasized the conquest and annexation of California rather than the temporary occupation of its ports—along with copies of Polk's war message and the Congressional declaration of war. "Much must be left to your discretion," Bancroft told Sloat, due to the "great distances" between Washington and California. When Bancroft finally received Sloat's request on August 13, he responded by saying that while the Department of the Navy would not charge Sloat with disobedience because of "the purity of your intentions...your anxiety not to do wrong has led you into a most unfortunate and unwarranted inactivity."[25]

Sloat's pusillanimous inactivity had ended by the time Bancroft wrote those words, and unbeknownst to the secretary Sloat already had left California. What had changed Sloat's mind, although Bancroft had no way of knowing it on August 13, was Frémont's arrival and subsequent military actions. Sloat took great solace in the conviction that Frémont possessed special orders from President Polk, and Frémont did nothing to relieve the commodore of this erroneous assumption. Therefore, even without new orders telling him so, Sloat now assumed the United States and Mexico must truly be at war. After a final bout of hand-wringing, on July 7, 1846, Sloat gave the order to occupy Monterey and San Francisco. He also issued a proclamation to California's inhabitants and dispatched marines to reinforce Frémont.

Sloat's proclamation mirrored Kearny's to New Mexico. It announced "henceforward California will be a portion of the United States" and promised trade could commence "free of any duty" throughout the region. Those not wishing to become American citizens and unwilling to live peacefully under the new regime would have to "dispose of their property and... remove out of the country." *Alcaldes* and others could retain their political or judicial offices "until the government of the territory can be more definitely arranged."[26]

Unlike the conquest of New Mexico, the Bear Flag rebellion in California had a precedent, of sorts: the Texas Revolution. The major difference between the Texas Revolution and the Bear Flag Revolt in California, however, was that the United States under Sloat officially supported the rebels in the latter. Moreover, the Republic of Texas subsisted as an internationally recognized, independent nation for nearly 10 years before its annexation by the United States. The Bear Flag Republic, on the other hand, lasted less than 10 days, for American marines quickly replaced the Bear Flag with the Stars and Stripes. Polk, after all, wanted to annex California, not set it up as an independent, competing republic with the West Coast's best harbors and most fertile valleys.

After issuing his proclamation, Sloat decided his next order of business should be to meet with Frémont. Likewise, Frémont wanted to see Sloat, and so he headed to Monterey on July 10 while the Bear Flag still waved over Sonoma. "Each," according to historian K. Jack Bauer, "looked forward to the meeting as the source of justification for his actions."[27] The nervous Sloat craved reassurance for his takeover of Monterey and for his ensuing proclamation. Frémont coveted the requisite glory for having secured the California interior, and he wanted the official command that he believed he deserved.

Meanwhile, on July 15 Robert F. Stockton sailed into Monterey Bay, and Sloat told him he would relinquish command by the end of the month. Frémont arrived four days later to meet with Sloat, who was still making preparations to depart and had not yet handed over his command. He told the commodore that he had been unaware that war had been declared when he led the revolt, and furthermore informed him that "I had acted solely on my own responsibility, and without any expressed authority from the Government to justify hostilities." According to Frémont, Sloat exploded, telling him that he had occupied Monterey only "upon the faith of our operations in the north." Frémont, surprised, thought it strange that a naval commander needed to rely on him "to justify his actions" when there already was proof of war and Secretary Bancroft's orders were so clear in the first place. Visibly shaken, Sloat promptly ended the meeting and prepared to leave California—and therefore, he hoped, any potential trouble— as soon as possible.[28]

By July 29 Sloat was gone from California. By November he was back in Washington. Stockton, now in command, proceeded to finish the conquest of California. He immediately promoted Frémont to the field rank of major, placed him in charge of land operations, and incorporated the Bear Flag rebels into the U.S. Army. After dispatching this new "California Battalion" to San Diego, Stockton led a separate force to Los Angeles, where he claimed the city for the United States on August 13 without firing a shot.

On August 17 Stockton issued a proclamation, meant to supersede Sloat's, to "the people of California." Unlike Sloat, Stockton forcefully asserted

American rights to California with a definite sense of finality, pronouncing California "entirely free from Mexican dominion." Stockton also declared martial law and a nightly curfew, both of which were to last until a territorial government could be established according to constitutional and legal guidelines. He then set about organizing a governmental structure much like the one established by Kearny in New Mexico. The key difference between the two was that in California the governor and commander in chief of the army were to be one and the same person, until removed by the president. Stockton would appoint no civilian to rule the territory over which he later joked he "was once viceroy." The man he had in mind for this unprecedented, august post was Frémont.[29]

The invasion and subjugation of California proved to be more difficult than blockading less than a half dozen ports, expelling a few *Californios* from the interior, and ensconcing Frémont in the military governor's chair. Between September 1846 and January 1847 the American conquerors faced a large-scale revolt at Los Angeles, previously considered pacified by Stockton. Into this fighting marched Kearny's force from New Mexico, winning what at best must be described as a Pyrrhic victory at the Battle of San Pascual on December 6. After another skirmish Kearny's army limped into San Diego on December 12. For the time being, whether the commodore or the general controlled California seemed inconsequential next to the need for military collaboration between the two. Their cooperation resulted in the fall of Los Angeles to American forces, for the second and final time, on January 10, 1847.

Two days later Frémont's California Battalion finally reached the Los Angeles vicinity. By this time Frémont knew Los Angeles was in American hands, for he possessed instructions from both Stockton and Kearny to avoid hostilities and meet up with Kearny's army as soon as possible. Fully expecting to become governor of California as soon as the rebellion ended, Frémont decided to make his future job as trouble free as possible. So, instead of joining Kearny he treated with the enemy, resulting in the munificent Treaty of Cahuenga. Unlike Kearny's New Mexico code, the Treaty of Cahuenga offered U.S. citizenship to Mexicans but required from them no oath of allegiance until the ratification of a peace treaty by both nation's governments. Frémont signed the agreement on behalf of the United States without prior authorization by either Kearny or Stockton, although the latter retroactively approved the treaty merely out of relief that the uprising was over.[30]

The fighting between *Californios* and Americans may have ended on January 12, 1847, but the struggle for the control of California between Frémont and Stockton on the one hand, and Kearny on the other, was just beginning. For over four months Stockton had been promising to depart California and appoint Frémont governor in his stead, and the young adventurer knew it. Technically, Frémont had received the gubernatorial appointment on September 2, 1846, but the rebellion had intervened and so Stockton, unable to leave as planned, had continued in the position. But Frémont's appointment as governor (along with a promotion to lieutenant colonel) explains much about his increasingly independent behavior in the intervening months, such as his unilateral negotiation of the Treaty of Cahuenga. Kearny's arrival further complicated this transfer of authority and threatened the aggressive young soldier's rise to power. The fault in the dispute over California's governance, however, belongs to all the involved parties, not least of all, Kearny.

Stockton and Frémont together had conquered, organized a government for, and then reconquered California. When Kearny arrived Stockton ruled California, and Frémont, already military commandant, was preparing to take on the additional title of governor. Rather than speak with either man, as one might have reasonably expected him to do, Kearny instead fired off terse letters to them on January 16. These letters informed them that only

John C. Frémont during the Civil War (National Archives).

he, Kearny, possessed civil and military authority in California. As a career military man of few words, Kearny believed personal ego should never get in the way of clear orders, and so had no qualms about offending the sensibilities of California's conquerors. Thus, the general, who days before had seen his troops pulled out of the fire by Stockton, ordered the commodore and the colonel to desist immediately from all civil and military activities.

Stockton and Frémont refused to acquiesce to Kearny's forthright challenge to their authority. Stockton informed the general that he would not relinquish authority, based on a strict interpretation of Kearny's original instructions from the War Department. These instructions, when read literally, said that Kearny must conquer California in order to be the one to establish a civil government. Since conquest and government formation had occurred prior to the general's arrival, Stockton argued that that part of Kearny's orders was null and void. Hardly trying to hide his position in isolation like some renegade warrior, Stockton sent a letter to President Polk informing him of the dispute and requesting that he relieve Kearny of command.

For his part, Frémont decided to meet alone with Kearny to discuss matters. This was not their first meeting. In 1843 the two men had engaged in a minor row that Dwight L. Clarke, Kearny's biographer, contends probably soured Kearny's opinion of Frémont for good. Kearny, trying to do a favor for Senator Benton's son-in-law, had loaned Frémont a howitzer as the then-captain prepared to leave St. Louis on one of his western exploratory expeditions. The War Department, realizing Frémont might encounter Indians allied with Great Britain and not wanting to risk providing the British an excuse for war, countermanded Kearny's loan. Frémont's wife, Jessie, intercepted and burned the War Department's orders. This allowed Frémont to depart and later say in all honesty that he had seen no such order. Kearny received a reprimand for the incident and, if he did not bear a grudge (which Clarke suggests but is unlikely in light of Kearny's temperament and behavior elsewhere), at the least he now knew firsthand Frémont's penchant for disobedience.[31]

Whether Frémont, in his meeting with Kearny in January 1847, refused to follow Kearny's orders only when the general declined his request to be appointed governor, is subject to debate. Kearny later claimed this to have been the case, but Frémont consistently denied it. In the end, Frémont informed the general that since he had received his commission from Stockton, until Kearny and the commodore could "adjust between yourselves the question of rank...I shall have to report and receive orders, from the commodore."[32]

The flaw in Frémont's argument is that it ultimately rested on the branch of the service to which his superior belonged. While Stockton as commodore had named Frémont a major, Frémont had since accepted promotion to lieutenant colonel in the U.S. Army. Kearny, and rightly so, therefore saw no interservice rivalry in the matter, only ego and ambition, and considered Frémont unquestionably under his direct command. As a subordinate, Frémont deserved no explanation, as far as Kearny was concerned.[33]

The reaction by Stockton and Frémont to Kearny's letters placed the general in a delicate situation. Stockton commanded the loyalty of the vast majority of American troops in California, and the California Battalion was loyal to Frémont. All this might change on the arrival of the Mormon Battalion and other volunteers being sent from New York, but in the meantime Kearny had no muscle to back up his orders. Moreover, the day after the letter fiasco Stockton went ahead and officially appointed Frémont governor. Kearny's political friends in Washington were too far away to be of any help, and besides, his most influential patron was none other than Frémont's father-in-law, Benton. Kearny's only noteworthy supporter in California during the early days of the controversy was W. Branford Shubrick, who arrived on January 19 to replace Stockton, who then promptly left the scene.

The bleakness of Kearny's status should not be overemphasized. As Frémont's biographer, Tom Chaffin, points out, Frémont's political allies grew thinner by the day. Frémont's familial connections led career naval and army officers to doubt his military fitness, the new naval commander in the region now backed Kearny, Stockton was gone, and orders dated November 6 from the new secretary of the navy, John Y. Mason, were already on the way. Mason's orders left no doubt who was in charge: control of the U.S. Army in California as well as complete civil authority in the territory belonged entirely to Kearny.[34]

In spite of these facts and against Kearny's warnings to the contrary, Frémont threw himself into the role of governor and began assembling California's new government. Of course, in doing so he did not relinquish his army commission. Other than amassing a rather large debt in a few short months, Frémont actually proved adept at the position, even successfully undertaking measures to soothe influential *Californios*. To Kearny's consternation, Frémont issued military orders in the region, calling up three-month volunteers in a move Kearny considered mutinous.

Kearny wisely remained silent for the time being and did not press the issue. His silence and correspondence reveal a sagacious man who understood the very real danger of civil war in California. This was just the kind of reasoned, prudent behavior Polk and Marcy had expected when they sent Kearny west in the first place. Kearny informed the War Department of Frémont's and Stockton's refusal to recognize him, and then patiently waited for several months. In February 1847, when Mason's orders finally arrived, Kearny acted immediately and decisively. The newly arriving Mormons and New Yorkers sided with Kearny, as per their orders. This left Frémont and his tenuous claims on power out in the cold.

Kearny now chose to ignore Frémont entirely, and proceeded apace as if there was no feud at all. He relayed the new orders and Polk's wishes to military personnel. On March 1 Kearny proclaimed himself governor of California. From Frémont he requested troops—indeed, he declared the California Battalion disbanded and announced its incorporation into the newly created Southern Military District, under Lieutenant Colonel Philip St. George Cooke. Frémont, insensible that his time as California's ruler was up, initially refused to cooperate. Only after holding a personal meeting with Kearny did Frémont agree to disband his only remaining group of allies in the territory, the California Battalion.

Kearny's methodically won success was a victory for civil authority over military power, although his critics argued just the opposite and accused him of being a tyrant. Whigs saw only a conqueror issuing laws and bringing territories into the Union by fiat at gunpoint. If he was dangling from Polk's marionette strings, Whigs thought, that was bad enough; scarier still, they predicted, if he was not. But the reality is that the general had patiently faced down an upstart, politically well-connected officer for the rightful control of California, avoiding civil war and its unforeseeable but surely devastating consequences in the process. By June both Kearny and Frémont were on their way to Washington, and a civilian government established by Kearny ruled California.

THE TRIAL OF FRÉMONT

Only during the journey eastward did Kearny risk informing Frémont that he was under arrest and would face a court-martial upon their arrival. To Kearny, Frémont was little more than a pretender whose desire for glory had led him to risk civil war by exploiting California's isolation and using his personal army of Bear Flaggers in a bid for raw power. This pretense at power had far reaching and unintended consequences. While Kearny and Frémont were en route to Washington, the U.S. Navy resorted to arresting the recently elected *alcalde* of Sonoma, John H. Nash. The authorities appointed by Kearny had first asked him to resign. Nash refused, on the grounds that he had been elected legally while Frémont was governor—an argument not unlike Frémont's that named as the source of his authority Stockton's legitimacy at the time of his appointment.

President Polk met with many concerned visitors in the months leading up to Frémont's trial, and the California controversy consumed several cabinet meetings. Kearny and Frémont each visited with Polk, separately of course. Neither man mentioned the upcoming trial. They simply made courtesy calls. Polk found Kearny to be "a good officer and an intelligent gentleman."[35] Senator Benton and his daughter, Jessie Frémont, visited the president's mansion again and again, trying each time to convince Polk that John C. Frémont's accomplishments in California outweighed any alleged misdeeds. Benton threatened to bring charges against Kearny while Jessie simply wanted to ensure her husband could stay in the service.

Polk, however aware he was of the political value of appeasing Benton, privately approved of Kearny's treatment of Frémont and Stockton. He suspected that Benton, not having received the abortive lieutenant generalship, was now preparing to distance himself from the Polk administration and was using the Frémont trial as the pretense with which to do it.

Despite his private feelings, Polk refrained from expressing his opinion either to the senator or to Jessie Frémont. Both Polk and Benton agreed they would operate in their official capacities "without reference to any former friendship between us." Polk actually wished to avoid a court-martial, since at this time he was already dealing with having to rescue his friend, Gideon Pillow, from a similar fate. He hoped the "unfortunate collision between the officers of the army and navy in that distant region" could just be buried and forgotten. Polk, consummate politician that he was, realized of course that this was a false hope.[36]

At the court-martial, which opened on November 2, 1847, the arguments of Kearny and Frémont went head to head. Frémont stood charged with illegally raising troops and a prolonged mutiny lasting from January 17, 1847, to May 9, 1847; disobedience of orders; and "conduct prejudicial to good order and discipline." For the prosecution, Kearny simply submitted his orders, Frémont's responses to them, and recounted the details of their January 17 meeting. He also accused Frémont outright of trawling for the governorship, and turning mutinous and risking civil war like some Roman conqueror when denied the job.

Frémont responded to these charges with a mix of the Jacksonian and Shakespearean: "I consider these difficulties in California," said Frémont, "to be a comedy...of three errors." These "three errors" consisted of "the faulty orders sent out from [Washington]," "the unjustifiable pretensions of General Kearny," and "the conduct of the government in sustaining these pretensions." Frémont considered the last "error" to be "the greatest of the three," for Polk had allowed Kearny to co-opt the heroic and democratic brilliance of Stockton and Frémont's Bear Flaggers.[37]

As for the actual charges proffered against him, Frémont argued that there had been no mutiny or disobedience because his authority had originated with Commodore Stockton. The only pertinent question, therefore, was whether Stockton possessed the authority to appoint him territorial governor and commander of the California Battalion. Frémont thought he did, and added that "General Kearny was, at the time of giving the order, suspended from the command of the forces at that place by order of Governor Stockton."[38] If Stockton had the authority, Frémont reasoned, then his own actions were legitimate. Otherwise, Stockton himself ought to be on trial. If anything, Frémont continued, he should be *rewarded* for preventing civil war not just between Stockton and Kearny, but between himself and Kearny "by consenting to be deposed."[39]

Frémont's blustery tactics proved so tortuously ineffective, and comedic in their own right, that the court's verdict on January 31, 1848, was unanimous—guilty on all counts. However, Frémont's argument was not without some effect: each judge issued separate recommendations relative to Frémont's proposed sentence of dismissal from the army. While two of Kearny's friends on the panel (including George M. Brooke) found that the general's "honor and character are unimpeached," even Brooke signed a statement with three others recommending lenience due to the confusion caused by the dispute between Stockton and Kearny. Three others recommended clemency.[40]

For several days Polk and his cabinet debated what action to take in the Frémont verdicts. As usual, they had to take into account not just morale and military issues like discipline and the chain of command, but also politics. Frémont had publicly accused the Polk administration of conspiring with Kearny to rob him of his accomplishments. But Polk knew from recent experience how to and how not to undermine a military commander. He also knew, of course, that in this case he had done no such thing. The charge that Polk would undercut anyone who had won for him California was simply ludicrous, and all acquainted with the president, especially Benton, knew it. Remarkably, Polk let none of Frémont's melodrama color his opinion of the matter. Frémont had clearly disobeyed orders, yes, but Polk could not decide whether he was "guilty of the legal definition of mutiny." For its part, the cabinet could reach no consensus. Finally, on February 16 Polk took action. He approved the sentence but granted clemency and remitted Frémont's dismissal from the army, due to "the previous meritorious and valuable services of Frémont."[41] Really, only one "previous" service of Frémont's mattered. Winning California for Polk, it seems, had its advantages.

POLK AND THE THREATS TO CIVIL AUTHORITY

Before 1846, instituting martial law on foreign soil as a result of conquest had no precedent in American history. The greatest potential threat to Polk's war aims and to civilian authority more generally came from military governors in regions the president planned to annex. From start to finish, however, the Mexican War provided a variety of opportunities for American army officers to subvert civilian authority, although not all such opportunities (or attempts) were created equal. Edmund P. Gaines's foolish acts and impetuous call-ups of volunteers and militia resulted more from imprudence and inability to improvise in emergency situations than from a conscious desire to be an American Napoleon or Caesar. Likewise, in spite of his public criticism of Polk's war strategy in the Gaines letter, Taylor's disobedience at Monterrey did not arise from some ardent desire to subvert civilian authority. Rather, Taylor sincerely believed that his armistice with Ampudia was the right move militarily, in terms of saving American lives, and geopolitically, if Polk really did want peace as soon as possible.

In this latter sense, one could interpret Taylor's armistice with Ampudia as a shrewd challenge to Polk personally, although not necessarily one with ill intent toward the executive branch or federal government. Conceivably, Taylor may have concluded that the unauthorized armistice actually could work to preserve civilian government by precluding what Whigs saw as Polk's reckless use of the army for conquest. Since Polk wanted California he knew he would continually have to ratchet up the pressure on Mexico until it agreed to cede its most northerly state. The only peace Polk wanted was one that included California. If the Monterrey armistice led to a negotiated settlement of the Texas border issue, whether Taylor knew it or not he would have thwarted Polk's key war objective.

Yet consequences care not for one's intent, and Gaines's behavior and Taylor's armistice each had damaging consequences. For Gaines, these were mostly political. His expensive actions inadvertently dragged Governor Isaac Johnson of Louisiana, a Democrat, into a legal battle with the U.S. government and a tug-of-war with Polk, two things neither man wanted. Taylor's armistice permanently soured relations with Polk. It so incensed the president because, as Polk foresaw but apparently Taylor did not, Mexico was not about to capitulate so easily after escaping Monterrey with weaponry and such a large part of its army intact. This, indeed, proved to be the case, and so commenced the planning for Scott's amphibious landing at Vera Cruz.

Taylor's near disaster at Buena Vista, however, was not the unintended consequence of a well-meant but misguided act. It occurred precisely because he despised Polk and Winfield Scott for ordering him back to Monterrey, and he was bound and determined to leave. He told the War Department that he felt compelled to move the long 18 miles south of Saltillo to Buena Vista because "of the pernicious moral effect upon volunteer troops of falling back from points which we have gained" and due to unspecified but "powerful military reasons."[42] But the core of the matter is that Taylor believed he had been made to linger in order to prevent him from securing a place in the pantheon of American battlefield heroes. That charge may have been true, but true also was the tactical necessity of not having the American army charged with cutting off central Mexico from California and New Mexico, and tasked with guarding the northern flank of Scott's invasion force, wiped out in a foolish drive for a Roman-style quest for glory—a Jacksonian and democratic *cursus honorum*—on the battlefield.

If ever the potential for tyranny and military rule within the United States existed, it came during Kearny's occupation of New Mexico. Without Congressional approval, as called for by the U.S. Constitution and the Northwest Ordinance, General Kearny declared New Mexico to be U.S. territory and personally organized its government and laws. Kearny conquered a territory, claimed it as U.S. property, and then—as a general—briefly ruled it. Mexicans were hanged as traitors under Kearny's code. The temporary nature of the government and laws established by Kearny, with the qualified support of lawyers and politicians, cannot negate these facts nor the act of a general declaring conquered foreign lands U.S. territory. Nor can hindsight approve of Polk's (successful) gamble that Kearny would behave like George Washington and not Julius Caesar or Marc Anthony. Subsequent events and acts of Congress placed New Mexico peacefully on the road to statehood, but things easily could have turned out much differently.

The conquest of New Mexico threatened to subvert the American tradition of splitting civil and military authority but the dispute over the governance of California, due to the personalities involved, lingered far longer in the minds of Americans. The case of John C. Frémont presents a career of a perpetually insubordinate officer with aspirations for glory and the personal, political connections to repair the negative consequences caused by those aspirations. From the U.S. government's point of view, Frémont's abandonment of his exploratory mission to lead a revolt in California was entirely forgivable, for annexing that state was the American commercial elite's and Polk's primary goal of the war.

Frémont's deceptive and anguished excuses in the dispute with Kearny and Stockton was another matter, however, for it threatened the chain of command and revealed the pitfalls of having military commanders establish civil governments and rule by right of conquest alone. That Polk's and the American people's opinion of Frémont's actions differed from Kearny's is proven by Frémont's subsequent political popularity. Frémont simply gave in to the Jacksonian impulses of the day. Like Taylor, Frémont got what he wanted out of the Mexican War—the nomination for president by a major political party. (Frémont was the Republican nominee in 1856.)

No military governor, soldier, or general set out with the intention to undermine civilian government and to rule permanently as an autocrat unimpeded by the distant Washington bureaucracy, not even Frémont. But patriotic zeal, lack of precedent, political ambition, an absence of practical knowledge of just how to govern an occupied territory, and especially isolation from Washington produced several dangerous incidents. As it turned out, the conquest of New Mexico and California did not prove fatal to civilian control of the military. Nor did it lead to extended governance by generals over lands of the Mexican cession. Public opinion supported territorial expansion. Moreover, the officers involved so well served the president that he was willing to use his pardon power to absolve them.

The Polk administration and Democratic Party defended the military governments of New Mexico and California, arguing that those territories had been conquered in a declared war under the law of nations. Kearny's measured administration in New Mexico and prudence in the California feud, not to mention the subsequent court-martial of Frémont, did not make the general's life any easier but they did validate Polk's confidence in him. (Indeed, Polk appointed Kearny governor of Mexico City on May 23, 1848, exactly two weeks after Frémont's trial ended.[43]) Accusations continued that Polk had appointed Kearny "Executive Viceroy" to rule with nearly unlimited powers. Whigs put the question this way:

> Is not the new civilian still a Brigadier General in the Regulars of the United States? And can there by any thing more contrary to all the spirit of our institutions, or to every thing republican, than this uniting in the same person the civil and the military functions?[44]

Whigs were left with asserting that no such right to military government existed under the Constitution, and that New Mexico and California simply could not be declared U.S. territory and their inhabitants made citizens by the president or a conquering general. Only a ratified treaty and Congress could do that.

The disposition of New Mexico and California were soon solved, first by the Treaty of Guadalupe Hidalgo in 1848 and finally by Congress in the Compromise of 1850. The civil-military divide in the United States had been preserved, although not without near civil war by politically hungry and glory-seeking officers in far-flung conquered territories. California and the New Mexico territory belonged to the Union; and while Taylor's subsequent political career ended due to his untimely death in 1850, Frémont's continued into the 1860s.

6

Serving "the Great Body of the People"

From the moment news reached the United States of the skirmish on April 25, 1846, between American and Mexican troops, the U.S. war against Mexico faced several challenges. Among the greatest of these were mismanagement at the War Department and in the army, impassioned opposition from Christian voluntary societies and social reformers, eager appeals for the Protestant evangelization of Catholic Mexico, demands for complete conquest of the continent, intensely partisan debates in Congress, and squabbling between President James K. Polk and his generals (not to mention, among Polk's generals). One could add to this the potential, successfully averted in New Mexico and in California, for the subversion of civilian control over the military. Yet in spite of these obstacles, on September 14, 1847, the U.S. Army embarked on what was to be a nine-month occupation of Mexico City after waging a seemingly unstoppable campaign. On September 16 Santa Anna resigned the Mexican presidency, allowing serious treaty deliberations to begin.

This chapter explores the role of President Polk in this remarkable achievement of American arms, an outcome at variance with what knowledgeable European observers initially predicted. Considering the above-mentioned obstacles to American victory, as well as the Mexican army's numerical superiority, Europeans naturally assumed odds favored the Mexicans. Successfully navigating through a maze of antiwar opposition, political hostility, confrontational War Department personnel, and appeals for "All Mexico," Polk not once altered his original, limited territorial goals. As a result of the Mexican War, the United States annexed no more—and no less—than New Mexico and California.

Historians account for the unexpected American victory in the Mexican War in a variety of ways. In interpreting the outcome of this conflict, the scholar's task is not simply to recount the battles leading up to the American victory and the Treaty of Guadalupe Hidalgo. He or she also must account for just how amazingly triumphant the American military campaign was, from the conquest of New Mexico and California to the invasion of central Mexico. An important addendum to this story, as detailed in previous chapters, was the overall success of Polk's conciliatory policies toward Mexican civilians and clerics, in spite of atrocities committed there by Americans, and the preservation of civilian control over the military in New Mexico and California.

Historians' interpretations of the Mexican War's outcome are wide ranging but fall into three broad categories. First, some explain the American victory neither in terms of social and political circumstances in the United States nor in terms of American military technology and capability. Rather, they focus on Mexico's defeat, concentrating primarily on the detrimental effects and military consequences of national disunity and the behavior of belligerent demagogues. Mexico thus lost the war, the United States did not win it. Had Mexicans and their Catholic bishops and politicians united to support their numerically superior, European-style army, Mexico easily could have repelled the American invasion, and maybe even brought the war to U.S. soil.

Other historians, most of whom predate the 1940s, do just the opposite. They explain the victory by maintaining an almost exclusive, American perspective. Wearing blinders they look at the American war effort in great detail but neglect important causal factors on the Mexican side. Volunteers' *esprit de corps* and a talented group of West Pointers, along with General Winfield Scott's able leadership and General Zachary Taylor's good fortune, won the war. Presupposing American military superiority, these scholars assume the United States could only be defeated by its own mistakes, and that Mexico never had any realistic chance of success. This ultimately means that studying the potential pitfalls to American success becomes an effort merely in using hindsight to explain an inevitable victory.

Finally, a few scholars point out that to interpret properly the United States's unstoppable march to Mexico City and to the shores of California, one must take into account Mexican and American politics, organization, and public and elite opinion. Neglecting one in favor of the other, they argue, invariably leads to a skewed, one-sided understanding of a two-sided war. These historians are correct, if one's goal is to paint a comprehensive picture of the war. Yet examining civil-military relations in the United States during the war goes a long way toward explaining how the U.S. Army overcame obstacles and how James K. Polk maintained his focus on the war's limited objectives while steering clear of the "All Mexico" advocates. Indeed, Polk's policies and governing style—colored though they were by his own rabid partisanship, Jacksonian attitudes, and an instinctive mistrust of others that united a penchant to micromanage with insecurity and even paranoia—played a vital role in undermining Mexican unity and in encouraging Mexico's Catholic bishops not to cooperate with Santa Anna. At the same time, ironically perhaps, Polk's policies precipitated divisions and arguments among American civilians and soldiers.

POLK'S LEADERSHIP STYLE

Polk's difficulty in choosing commanders and formulating strategy at the beginning of the war was mostly a political quandary of his own making. All of the army's top commanders were Whigs, and Polk, though practical, did not wish to hand the opposition party the popularity that might come with a Whig general's victory. When the Whig William Henry Harrison had been elected in 1840, he had done so on a platform that shamelessly proclaimed his heroism at the Battle of Tippecanoe. After Harrison's untimely death and John Tyler's accession to the presidency, influential Whigs discovered to their horror that they had little in common with Tyler. In the middle to late 1840s Democrats, including Polk, convinced themselves that despite the apparently equal influence and political strength each party possessed, the Whigs required the boost of military glory to stir the souls of voters when it came to winning the presidency in a contest that had been profoundly reshaped by populist, democratic politics.

Jacksonian America's religious-like faith in the *demos*—what Andrew Jackson referred to as "the great body of the people"—along with its republican mistrust of a large standing army commanded by an elite, professional officer corps, meant that any war must be fought by a large volunteer force. These volunteers, drawn from existing militia or newly formed companies, would always be needed in national emergency. In fact, this was something of which to be proud, for virtuous volunteers would fight out of patriotism or in defense of their homes, not simply for pay and three meals per day. For American democrats to remain ideologically coherent, "the great body of the people" themselves simply *had* to be the army.

This democratic sentiment played into Polk's personality and buttressed his broad conception of his powers as commander in chief. Since the United States lacked a regular army of any significant size, Polk like other Americans knew volunteers would form the bulk of any army sent to Mexico. True, disputes arose between certain state governors, regardless of political party (Kentucky's William Owsley was a Whig and Louisiana's Isaac Johnson a Democrat), and the U.S. government over who possessed the greater authority in constituting these volunteer forces (especially their officers). But all accepted, however grudgingly, that the gap between the number of regulars and West Point–educated officers on the one hand, and the numbers needed to wage a major war on the other, all but predetermined

that an active and unabashedly partisan president—especially one as uncon-
cerned about accusations of cronyism as Polk apparently seemed to be—
could wield considerable power in the event of a declared war.

West Point, in the opinion of Jacksonian Democrats, constituted an unrepublican remnant of a bygone era. What is more, it had become a bastion
of the Federalists' northeastern political descendants who formed the core
of the Whig Party. Considering that the academy was founded to counter
Federalism by Thomas Jefferson during his first term as president, this was
ironic indeed. But the political situation had changed dramatically since
Jefferson's time, and so during the Jacksonian era "the Whig Party seemed
to be friendly to the army, while the Democrats openly doubted its worth."[1]
In fact, congressional Democrats in 1846 were seeking to close the U.S.
Military Academy for good. In part, this was an extension of the Jacksonian
belief that the virtue and patriotism inherent in the yeoman farmer majority
of the *demos* far surpassed anything either regulars or their officers
could attain. Just as President Jefferson had tried to break the back of the
Federalist Party by attacking its last stronghold, the judiciary, Polk hoped
to accomplish the same, viewing West Point as he did through this ideological, Jacksonian prism of party, class, and section. Thus, he hoped to circum-
vent the army's professional officer corps and weaken the U.S. Military
Academy's influence, and therefore New England Whiggery, if at all possible.
And what better way to weaken the influence of the antidemocratic,
northeastern elites than to turn to the South and West for troops, who then
would be commanded by Democratically appointed officers?[2]

Based on these class, sectional, and party concerns, Polk endeavored to
use his war powers to bring advantage to the South, West, and to his party.
Yet like any politician who also adheres to the principles he or she asserts,
Polk strongly believed that what benefited the Democracy inevitably served
American national interests as a whole. Of course, Polk recognized the con-
verse to be true: victory under a Whig general, although good for the country
in the sense that defeat at the hands of Mexico would be a disaster for
all Americans, was neither good for the Democratic Party nor ultimately
for the mass of people who had moved westward in search of a prosperous
independence or who hoped to do so and therefore supported territorial
expansion. Thus, had there been an able or well-known candidate other
than just the willing but unpopular Westerner, Thomas Hart Benton, Polk
early on would have replaced his Whig commanders with Democrats.

Polk's partisanship, friendships, suspicious nature, and Jacksonian view
of the world led him to make some terrible decisions during the war.
Most notable among these was the appointment of the militarily inept
but scheming Gideon J. Pillow. In the disputes that followed, Polk sided
with Pillow and used his old friend to thwart General Scott's political
ambitions. Yet overall Polk was pragmatic when dealing with the conver-
gence of his political concerns and wartime necessity. He refused to support

John C. Frémont in the dispute with General Stephen W. Kearny over the governance of California, despite Frémont's status as son-in-law to the Democrat, Benton. Kearny, a Whig but a professional general in every sense of the term, had performed an important service in conquering New Mexico and California—a far more important objective to Polk than pleasing Senator Benton.

Polk also understood the finite limits of the U.S. Army, and realized what was possible with its current staff of officers, including the army with which he had to work. Thus he made use of Zachary Taylor as much as the situation demanded, often hoping for the best but from the beginning convinced that Taylor lacked the temperament, prudence, and intelligence to command more than a single regiment. He also suspected, rightly as it turned out, that Taylor harbored presidential ambitions. The general's private complaints about Polk and the war, and his public criticisms of the administration in the Gaines letter, obviously did little to endear him to Polk. Despite the victory at Buena Vista, Polk never thought much of Taylor as a leader of men.

Winfield Scott, on the other hand, Polk recognized to be a capable general. Not that this pleased Polk or provided him comfort. Polk, Jacksonian democrat that he was, craved admiration and was always attuned to the political ramifications of events. But in spite of Scott's well-known presidential ambitions, Polk had little choice but to order him to lead the advance into the interior of Mexico, and both men knew it. As soon as Mexico City was firmly in American hands, Polk, Pillow, and company maneuvered Scott into controversy. Scott's reward from the Democratic administration in Washington for conquering Mexico and forcing a peace on its hapless government was a recall notice.

Does this mean Polk as a wartime president was able, despite the Second Party System's vicious partisanship that was reaching its zenith (or, depending on one's point of view, its nadir) during the 1840s, to be aware of but overlook political consequences when it came to the Mexican War? Yes and no. Fearful of political plots at all times and from all quarters, Polk's devotion to party was not so rigid as to lead him to sacrifice an American victory against Mexico in the name of hurting Scott's, Taylor's, or any other Whig's political chances. After all, Polk was commander in chief, and so he assumed that that Constitutional title counted for something when calculating the political benefits of a successful war. Polk's political goal, then, was to maintain a balance between handing the Whigs a presidential candidate with popular, military credentials while winning what he viewed as a popular, Democratic war—popular especially in the Democratic strongholds of the country, the South and the West. Fortunately for him, sustained Whig opposition to the war in Congress and in the pages of the *National Intelligencer* made this job easier than it might have been had Whigs tried to absorb Democratic constituencies by supporting the war in a more open, coherent fashion. But the Whig Party divided over the choice of whether to support soldiers and Whig generals but oppose the war and Polk's handling of it or to oppose it entirely on principle. One thing Whigs could agree on, however, was that they despised Polk, whose policies, in the words of Michael F. Holt, single-handedly "revived the Whigs' cardinal principle of opposition to executive tyranny."[3]

As might be expected, Polk, as president, formulated the political strategy used by the Democratic Party in Congress to oppose Whig accusations of patronage and abuse of executive power while securing funding and other support for the war effort. He also, as always, worked through the national organ of the Democratic Party, the *Washington Daily Union*, to influence public opinion. At times during the war the paper's editor, Thomas Ritchie, ignored his putative bosses and published politically damaging statements in the pages of the *Union*. For example, in April 1847, against clear administration policy, he suggested the United States ought to seize the wealth of Mexico's Catholic Church. He recanted following an upbraiding by Polk and a fire storm in the Whig and Catholic press.[4] Other than this incident, however, Polk overall maintained a tight grip on editorials that appeared in the *Daily Union*.

Polk brought this systematic attention to political details to the nuts and bolts of war planning and execution. The vigorous Tennessean, inclined already to micromanage his subordinates, was not one to delegate his powers as commander in chief. Like Abraham Lincoln after him, despite possessing little military experience Polk instinctively grasped what would be politically and militarily necessary to achieve victory. What he did not understand intuitively he studied hard to learn. "Whatever his deficiencies," writes military historian Russell Weigley, "control of the war was probably better in his hands than in those of anybody else available."[5]

Even competent, trusted subordinates like Secretary of War William Marcy demurred to Polk, who devised the multi-theatre invasion strategy and took an active role in coordinating its execution. Cabinet meetings in the early weeks of the war consisted mostly of the president presenting his "plan of conducting the war," the cabinet briefly discussing and then approving Polk's plan, and lastly Polk contacting Democratic congressmen and senators to provide them with their marching orders.[6]

The breadth and detail of Polk's instructions is staggering. They included, for example, delineating the exact numbers of troops needed for the Santa Fe and Chihuahua campaigns, declaring what sort of soldier (that is, cavalry or dragoon) was best suited for conquering California, and castigating staff officers and military professionals for not seeing early on that pack mules would be more useful for transportation in Mexico than horse-drawn wagons that required fine roads. In an effort to disabuse Mexicans of the notion that the largely Protestant United States might be making war on Mexico's religion, Polk also met with American Catholic bishops and convinced them to send two priests with the army as unofficial chaplains. Although a politically unpopular act in the highly anti-Catholic 1840s that led to a flowering of wild nativist conspiracy theories about Polk being in cahoots with Rome, Jesuits, and Austria, the president overlooked no factor in his quest for victory. He knew that, in the end, nothing is as popular as victory.[7]

Politics did, however, lead Polk to hold his tongue and quash his own opinion on at least one occasion. In May 1846 Polk disagreed with General Scott over the estimated number of soldiers needed for the initial advance into northern Mexico, which Polk hoped would convince Mexico to sue for peace without the need for an all-out invasion. In this matter Polk's partisanship got the best of him. Although he earnestly believed that Scott's request was far too large, Polk avoided even expressing his opinion to his cabinet, "not being willing to take the responsibility for any failure of the campaign by refusing to grant to General Scott all he asked."[8]

In the case of the Catholic chaplains, Polk concluded that sending them to Mexico was worth risking any political damage that might come from anti-Catholic attacks on the administration. German- and Irish-Catholics as a bloc already supported the Democratic Party, and most nativists voted Whig or belonged to the small, upstart Native American Party, whose role in two deadly, anti-Catholic riots in Philadelphia in 1844 had tarnished its name for good. The number of political friends to be earned by preventing a dangerous, popular uprising in Mexico over religion and thus winning the war far outweighed any new political enemies or temporary furor created by an appointment of Catholic chaplains. Likewise, Polk's political sensitivity, not to mention common sense, told him that *losing* the war merely to stand his ground in a tactical disagreement over troop numbers with Scott was not, to say the least, good for the country or for the Democratic Party.

Polk's close supervision of war planning, along with his sensible implementation of strategy, pressed the limits of executive power and sets him apart from all prior presidents, except perhaps George Washington. Washington, as a former general, had few reservations about interfering with his Indian-fighting generals, Arthur St. Clair and Anthony Wayne, whom he often told where to make camp, what supplies they might need, how to track or approach the enemy, and what time of year was best suited to engage them in battle. But without a doubt Polk played a far greater managerial role in the Mexican War than did President James Madison during the War of 1812. Thus, while Whigs and even a few Democrats in Congress eyed Polk suspiciously as a patronage king and worked to thwart his political appointments to the army, they could do little but grumble about the president's treatment of Marcy and his dealings with the War Department.

POLK AND THE WAR DEPARTMENT

Secretary of War Marcy was not so much easily dominated by Polk as he was consumed with protecting the "Hunker" faction of New York's Democratic Party against its rival, Martin Van Buren's "Barnburners." Despite his presumed influence as secretary of war, Marcy shied away from challenging or removing influential, turf-conscious career officials at the War Department. As for the appointment or removal of Indian agents, however, he wielded the weapon of patronage to the fullest. When war came, he sought to do the same in filling officer positions in the newly created regiments. As a result, while Polk increasingly assumed the strategic role commonly filled by secretaries of war, Marcy inadvertently dragged the president into the mire of New York Democratic squabbling, much to Polk's irritation.[9]

The minimal structure of the War Department in 1846 suited Polk's temperament and controlling personality. The president issued directives to the secretary of war, who then issued orders via the general in chief or through one of the army's 10 staff departments. During wartime the most influential, important departments were that of the inspector general, the quartermaster, and the adjutant-general. Of the three, the last, headed by Whig and War of 1812 veteran, Colonel Roger Jones, possessed the most influence. Virtually all army correspondence and orders passed through the adjutant-general's hands at some point. But all the men who headed these staff departments, remaining as they did in their positions through successive administrations, consistently challenged their boss's authority, practiced delay tactics in implementing orders they disliked, and worked to subvert Polk's exploitation of temporary officer appointments for patronage.[10]

Adjutant-General Jones stands out as the shrewdest and most effective bureaucrat who continually frustrated Marcy and opposed Polk's energetic management style. When Polk derided his commanders as "Whigs and violent partisans," he unquestionably included Jones in that group. During the war Polk accused Colonel Jones of "highly censurable" conduct after he discovered Jones had conspired with General Scott to stop the creation of additional major generals and brigadier generals. Marcy consistently failed to detect such machinations and seemingly lacked the fortitude to replace War Department personnel, and so early on Polk realized that his secretary of war would be of little help against the likes of Jones. Scott and Jones together, Polk believed, "seem disposed to throw every obstacle in the way of my prosecuting the Mexican War successfully." This was no doubt an exaggeration, but Polk more than once forcefully reminded Jones that he expected his orders to be obeyed. Agreeing, Jones always did obey—after long delays that left the president exasperated.[11]

Except for the actions of U.S. field commanders, the Washington bureaucracy's disruption of the commander in chief's desires on myriad issues probably posed the greatest challenge to Polk's ascendancy over war planning and execution. This, in combination with his propensity to take control, explains Polk's energetic exercise of authority over the War Department. Polk even had to watch out for Marcy, who clandestinely attempted in the 1847 budget to appropriate War Department monies for internal improvements in the name of military necessity. Marcy clearly was responding to Polk's recent veto of a river and harbors bill that would have benefited New York. In effect, Marcy was trying to maneuver around Polk's veto in order to make the U.S. government fund internal improvements, a central policy of the Whig "American System" but anathema to Jacksonian Democrats. In response to this incident and what he considered wastefulness in general, Polk broke precedent and assumed direct responsibility for overseeing the War Department's annual budget estimates. Prior to Polk, and again after him, treasury officials undertook the budgetary review of the War Department. Also in 1847, at Polk's behest, Marcy issued new, streamlined army regulations. Significantly, the revised *General Regulations* all but ignored the role of the staff departments that had become so troublesome for Polk.[12]

POLK AND THE NAVAL DEPARTMENT

The Department of the Navy remained headed by George Bancroft until September 1846, just long enough to see California come under the Stars and Stripes, but not long enough for Bancroft to experience firsthand the interservice squabbling that resulted. That unfortunate feature of the job fell to Attorney General John Y. Mason, who took over as secretary of the navy upon Bancroft's resignation. Bancroft's departure was not due to conflicts with Polk, political differences with his administration, or unhappiness with the war. Indeed, Polk publicly heaped effusive praise on Bancroft. Rather, the resignation was part of Polk's reward for Bancroft's successful leadership and strengthening of the U.S. Navy, for Polk appointed Bancroft American minister to Great Britain, a post he had long desired.[13]

The visceral mistrust, and even distaste, that Polk had for most elites—whether generals or bureaucrats—he seems not to have had for Bancroft. If insecurity was the cause of much of Polk's anti-elitism and efforts at domination, it seems to have had the opposite effect in this case. The two men's relationship was an uneven mixture of the political and the personal, highlighted by Polk's obvious but restrained admiration for the New Englander. The two men occasionally took their horses on tours around Washington City, conferring as they rode about historical and political matters. Polk and his wife, Sarah Childress, rarely dined out in people's homes during their time in Washington City, but the Bancrofts were among the select few who warranted such a visit.[14] The secretary also routinely acted as social intermediary between Polk and influential, New England elites like John Quincy Adams and Marcus Morton.[15]

As for the two men's working relationship during the war, Polk did not oversee Bancroft's governance of the navy in the same way he overshadowed Marcy at the War Department. Nor did he feel the need, for he trusted in, and apparently was intimidated by, Bancroft's intellect and command of his underlings. Unlike Marcy, in cabinet meetings Bancroft periodically disagreed with the president, and Polk greatly respected his opinion. When the cabinet found itself evenly divided over issues, such as the wording of Polk's messages to Congress, the president usually sided with Bancroft's camp. Beyond Polk's singular respect for Bancroft, the politically savvy Tennessean well knew that unlike Secretary of the Treasury Robert J. Walker and Secretary of State James Buchanan, Bancroft had no presidential ambitions. One must never underestimate the role of politics in every decision Polk made and every relationship he formed.[16]

Whatever Polk's motivations for his dominant role in devising strategy, his leadership style at the War and Navy Departments, and his use of the war as an opportune moment to take the career men in the army's staff departments down a notch, the ultimate result was American victory in the Mexican War. Polk maintained his focus on the war's goals and on strategy, and an important part of this maintenance was his micromanagement of subordinates like Marcy. Whether this focus was due to an overcompensation for feelings of intellectual inadequacy compared to men like Bancroft or whether Polk was just an inveterate micromanager is not as important as the fact that, in the end, Polk's management of the war played a vital role in the U.S. victory.

POLK AND CONGRESS

However, Polk's triumphs within the Executive Branch and as commander in chief of the army did not always translate into political victory in his dealings with Congress. He could browbeat his own subordinates or exert his perceived presidential powers to their fullest extent within his own branch of government, but these tactics would not work with senators and congressmen. Polk's politicization of officer appointments, his drive to weaken the political prospects of Whig generals, and his embarrassing and misguided scheme to revive the rank of lieutenant general all met with failure. Only in his quest to shape temporarily the command structure of the army with Democratic general officers did Polk meet unqualified success, although one can hardly count Gideon Pillow's battlefield exploits at Cerro Gordo or his behavior toward Scott in Mexico an "unqualified success."

Whigs in Congress opposed what they saw as a war to expand slavery and to enhance the Democratic Party, and this opposition found form in resistance to nearly all of Polk's requests, especially his moves to enlarge the regular army and the force of volunteers, and to staff their respective officer corps. Unfortunately, as discussed previously these political fights in the halls of Congress sometimes caused organizational difficulties and increased the likelihood of disaster on the battlefields of Mexico.

To be fair, the Jacksonian sentiment that enlivened Polk and his supporters was equally dangerous, for it encouraged the short-term enlistment mentality that at Puebla left the American army dangerously undermanned. This same sentiment also reinforced a blind faith in volunteer citizen soldiers and their elected officers that all but belied reality. Popular democratic sentiment combined a mix of anxiety and optimism over the future with demands for more territory on which to settle yeoman farmers and slave-owning planters. Jacksonian Democrats believed that only through westward expansion could democracy be preserved and economic opportunities be created. In 1846, this ideology, called "Jacksonism" by Winfield Scott, nearly caused armed conflict with two nations but ended up producing war with only one: Mexico.

Beyond the ability to stifle Polk's officer appointees by denouncing them as little more than the spoils system and the Democratic patronage machine in action (both accusations, of course, were accurate), the only genuine power held by Congress was the power of the purse. Majority rule or not, sometimes the *demos* could act contrary to its own interests when swayed by demagoguery or misguided by the passion of the moment, or so the Whigs convinced themselves. The president might solely represent the majority and be commander in chief, but it was Congress which funded the army and navy Polk commanded. These debates over funding posed a grave risk to the American war effort. Democrats tried to capitalize on Whig resistance with patriotic and historical arguments. The Whigs certainly realized that enervating the U.S. Army in time of war was politically and ethically out of the question, and they were not about to repeat the mistake of the Hartford Convention Federalists. Yet they also recognized that they could serve their party and regional constituents (and therefore, they believed, the republic) by undercutting Democratic territorial ambitions. Whigs believed the most effective way to keep a tight hold on Polk's treaty-making powers was to make political hay over funding requests and to refuse to hand the president full control over large amounts of war monies. The closer the U.S. Army came to Mexico City, the harder Whigs fought to restrict federal funds.

THE THREE MILLION DOLLAR BILL

On February 2, 1847, Democratic senator Ambrose Sevier of Arkansas introduced a bill for the appropriation of up to $3 million, designed to enable the president to expedite an end to the war. The debate and vote over the Three Million Dollar Bill, which began in February 1847, illustrates the concerns of both Democrats and Whigs, and the manner in which Whigs could best oppose "Mr. Polk's War." It also reveals that the Second Party

System and, more precisely, the Whig Party, already were fraying due to sectionalism. In debating this bill both sides employed patriotic, republican/democratic, and historical arguments, proving that Jacksonian political rhetoric could be made to serve both parties, a lesson first learned when the Whig William Henry Harrison used populist and rugged Jacksonian rhetoric to trounce the real "common man" of the presidential election of 1840, Martin Van Buren. The Democrats were soon to experience a devastating repeat of "Tippecanoe and Tyler, too" campaigning.

In accordance with the provisions of Sevier's bill, the president would be given complete control to direct the spending of the money, informing Congress of expenditures only after the fact. Sevier cited the precedents of the Louisiana Purchase in 1803 and a proposal to buy Florida soon afterwards, noting that in both cases President Jefferson had received from Congress the authority and money needed to secure a treaty. Thus, with only one month left before Congress adjourned to flee the sweltering heat of summer at Washington City, Sevier anticipated a vibrant but quick discussion and speedy vote. Instead, Whig senators' delay tactics dragged out the debate until 1:20 in the morning on March 1.

Despite its namesake, the Three Million Dollar Bill faced a debate not so much about money but about slavery, territorial expansion, states' rights, and the proper balance of power between the legislative and executive branches of government. Even those who ended up voting in favor of the bill still took advantage of the debate to contest and undermine Polk's dynamic use of presidential authority. Polk, after all, would not always be the president, and in fact he seemed oddly intent on carrying out his pledge to serve only one term. Democrats wisely feared a Whig who might be as energetic and controlling as was the Tennessean. Knowing that their speeches would be read by citizens of their home states, senators crafted rhetorical arguments acceptable to their constituency and, perhaps as importantly, to their state legislators.

Much of the debate centered around amendments offered by presidential hopeful, Democrat Lewis Cass of Michigan, and the Pennsylvania Whig, William Upham. These two amendments revealed the respective parties' fears about and hopes for the postwar order. Cass's amendment provided for obtaining an indemnity from Mexico, but the actual result of it would have been to use the $3 million to bribe the Mexican army and secure an indemnity in the form of territory. Whigs rightly suspected a territorial indemnity was the real goal of the bill in its original form anyway, but Democrats heartily denied this.

Upham's amendment was the senatorial equivalent of the House's Wilmot Proviso, an attempt by the Pennsylvania Democrat David Wilmot to prevent the war from benefiting the slave states of the South at the expense of the free labor states of the North. The proviso had gone down to defeat, but not before stirring the cauldron of the slavery issue to a boiling point and widening the sectional chasm between northern and southern members of both parties. The fight over the Wilmot Proviso also had threatened Polk's request, in August 1846, for $2 million to prosecute the war, because Wilmot had attached his amendment to the appropriations bill. A sectional vote had, in the end, killed the proviso, which survived the House but failed to come to a vote in the Senate. What also lay dead in the Capitol after the Wilmot Proviso debate was the illusion of unity each party tried to maintain.

Upham's amendment, like its more famous predecessor, forbade the introduction of slavery into any lands ceded by Mexico to the United States as a result of the war. Yet the timing of Upham's amendment precluded serious consideration of it, for despite inflaming sectional tensions "Mr. Polk's War" had significantly hardened partisanship since 1846, and all wanted to end the conflict as soon as possible. The Three Million Dollar Bill in its final form included neither amendment, yet debate over each offered the two parties the oratorical opportunity to put their positions before the "great body of the people" in the historically informed, republican rhetoric of the day.

Whigs denounced the war as unjust and blamed Polk for starting it in the first place by sending U.S. troops into the disputed territory between the Nueces and Rio Grande. Southern and western Democrats responded, arguing in favor of the bill, that the war against Mexico was as just as any past conflict, including the Revolutionary War and the War of 1812. Mexico, not the United States, was the imperial aggressor, possessing as much right to retake Texas as England had to reconquer its former colony of Massachusetts. In response to the "Mr. Polk's War" rhetoric, Senator Benton defended the president:

> I do not consider the march to the Rio Grande to have been the cause of the war any more than I consider the British march upon Concord and Lexington to have been the cause of the American Revolution.

Senator Sam Houston smugly tried to educate his fellow senators on Texas history, favorably comparing the Texas Revolution to the Revolutionary War.[17]

Whigs fired back at this Democratic tutorial in American and Texan history. James Pearce of Maryland dragged out a series of maps, the oldest one dating to 1685. Among them, much to Houston's chagrin, was Stephen F. Austin's own map, drawn up during the Texas Revolution in 1836, which clearly labeled the western boundary of Texas as the Nueces River. There could be no doubt, said Pearce, that the war against Mexico was "a presidential war" of territorial ambition. This war was not a fulfillment of the American Revolution, said New Jersey senator Jacob Miller, but instead was an embarrassing consequence of an American republic in decline. The United States was conquering a weak, neighboring republic, and behaving more like Alexander the Great or the Goths and Huns, rather than Washington and the valiant Continental Army. History, it seems, could cut both ways.[18]

To southern Democrats, this war certainly was not a clash of two republics, for Mexico could hardly be called a functioning country where the people ruled in democratic fashion. Military strongmen in power due to coup or revolution ruled over a people who suffered under a form of peonage not far removed from slavery. Senator Houston denounced as "sacrilege" even referring to Mexico as a republic, portraying Polk as a Mosaic figure, straining to hold his tired arms aloft as he waited for Congress's support in his fight against the Amalekites.[19]

Continuing the Whig history lesson, Senator Upham tediously reviewed past American territorial acquisitions in light of the American Founders and the slave question. Arguing in *a priori* fashion, Upham asserted the Founders never would have included the three-fifths clause in the Constitution if they supported the future expansion of slavery. Therefore, said Upham, the creation of slave states violated the will of the Founding Fathers. Even Jefferson, "the great apostle of democracy," had denounced slavery in his early drafts of the Declaration of Independence, condemned the South's peculiar institution in his private writings, and sought to exclude slavery from the western territories while president. This opinion continued into the early years of the republic, culminating in the latitudinal clause of the Missouri Compromise, which Upham argued conclusively showed that Congress possessed the authority to restrict slavery.[20]

In general, arguments in favor of the bill and of Cass's amendment appealed to the American Revolution, the U.S. Constitution, the Louisiana Purchase, the War of 1812, and any historical precedent that could be rhetorically massaged to approve of the expansion of slavery and Polk's strong exercise of executive power. Some senators pointed out that the Constitution condoned slavery, and argued that the statesmen of the late eighteenth century trusted one another enough not to be concerned about whether free or slave states were in the majority. Others noted that money had been allocated for direct presidential expenditure in the past, as in the case of Jefferson and Louisiana. They equated the Revolutionary War with the Texas Revolution, and compared the Federalists of Hartford Convention fame to the Whigs of 1847. Above all, the Union had admitted several slave states since 1787.

Whig senators who opposed the bill cited much the same historical precedents, for outside of analogies drawn from classical history and Greco-Roman mythology, these were the only extant traditions and precedents to which citizens of the still young United States could directly appeal. Whigs, however, made far better use of the Revolutionary era, in order to lambaste Polk (and Andrew Jackson, for that matter) for trying to shatter the traditional Constitutional relationship between president and Congress. Sure, Congress had given Jefferson money with which to purchase Louisiana, but it had painstakingly spelled out to him exactly how to spend those funds. The Federalist comparison likewise was inapplicable, since the War of 1812 was a purely defensive war and the conflict with Mexico was one of conquest.

Support for or opposition to the bill was not only partisan in nature, but sectional as well, and sensitivity to regional interests intensified the core issues for both parties. This built on the Wilmot Proviso debate. It also foreshadowed the dissolution of the Whig Party in the mid-1850s and the subsequent splintering of the Democracy in 1860 that enabled Abraham Lincoln to win the presidency without even appearing on the ballot in much of the South. Southern Whigs who opposed the bill could hardly condemn the war on grounds that it was a plot of a secretive slaveocracy. They instead tried to out-Jacksonian the Democrats with populist, libertarian rhetoric. The war, they said, was best seen as a contest between states' rights and congressional authority on the one hand, and the potential for tyranny on the other, for President Polk had provoked the conflict, forced a congressional declaration of war after the fact, and since then had sought additional, unchecked wartime powers. The only two Whigs who voted for the bill, David Atchison and Henry Johnson, were strong expansionists who represented the western/southwestern slaveholding states of Missouri and Louisiana, respectively.[21]

The only Democrat who sided with the Whigs in their vote against the bill, Simon Cameron, represented the increasingly antislavery and nominally abolitionist state of Pennsylvania. (Cameron later joined the Republican Party in the 1850s.) Connecticut Democrat John Niles accused the South of being recklessly aggressive toward the liberal and patient North. Democrat John Dix of New York portrayed Texas's admission to the Union as a unique case. Texas already was a slave state at the time of its annexation, and there had been slaves in Florida and in parts of Louisiana at the time of their annexation. Dix, however, who soon joined Martin Van Buren's new Free Soil Party, strongly attacked slavery's expansion, and he defended Congress's right to restrict the expansion of slavery, as per the Northwest Ordinance and Missouri Compromise. John C. Calhoun spoke against the bill in terms of the threat it posed to congressional authority and to states' rights. Yet in a vote that was 29 in favor and 24 against, all three dissenters cast their vote with their party in favor of the bill.[22]

Barely mentioned in the nearly month-long debate was the $3 million. Obstructing Polk's grab for power might be a poor replacement for defeating it, but this was the best the Whig Party could muster in Congress in February 1847. They used the opportunity to its fullest while delicately balancing their harsh opposition to Polk and the expansion of slavery with grudging, lukewarm support for a war many Americans accepted as the unavoidable consequence of Divine Providence. Americans were destined, after all, to transform the wilderness of North America into an Anglo-Saxon Protestant republic that left little or no room for a neighboring country weighed down by despots and shackled mentally by Roman Catholicism. (Whether there was to be "little" room or "no" room was, in fact, the central question in the coming "All Mexico" debate.) Van Burenites on their way to becoming the Free Soil Party used the bill to elucidate their position, as did perhaps the Polk administration's most vocal Democratic critic by March 1847, Calhoun. At the very least, the debate over the Three Million Dollar Bill, because it did not directly affect the welfare of U.S. soldiers in Mexico, offered great leeway for senators of both parties to set before the public their positions on the most far-reaching issues surrounding the war: the limits of state and congressional checks on wartime (and peacetime, for that matter) presidential power, the extension of slavery, and the wisdom of a large territorial indemnity. As one senator put it, "The great defect of our government is the publicity to which all our movements, intentions, negotiations...are exposed. They uniformly read us through the debates in Congress."[23]

ANTIWAR DISSENT

If Polk had trouble getting Congress to cooperate and follow his leadership, in the arena of public opinion he faced dissenters of all kinds. Most were rhetorically and financially well-armed, published newspapers or journals of some kind and could not be identified easily as either Whig or Democratic. Politicians may have liked to believe that the "publicity" of congressional debates affected larger public opinion, and this was to some extent accurate. However, that "publicity" often was only a pale reflection of expansionist zeal or antiwar opinion, because of the unwillingness of men facing reelection or party superiors' orders fully to express arguments against "Mr. Polk's War" or against the president's more modest territorial goals.

Elected officials opposed to the war had to manage carefully their rhetoric, but critics unaffiliated with a particular party did not. These dissenters liked to point out the obvious contradiction between Whig antiwar rhetoric and the rush to be the first Whig to congratulate U.S. generals and soldiers— especially Whig generals and volunteers from one's own state—on the occasion of each new American victory. This eye for contradiction and hypocrisy was especially sharp among Christian pacifists, along with their close kin with whom they often affiliated, abolitionists. The two-party system was failing them, and there was little politically they could do by 1847 but support the seven-year-old but dying Liberty Party or, by 1848, the Free Soil Party, which with the help of Van Buren rose out of the ashes of its predecessor. Yet for abolitionists neither of these parties commanded unequivocal support, because both sought merely to limit slavery's extension, not to eradicate it altogether.

Pacifists, on principle, would presumably oppose all wars, but for several reasons the conflict between the United States and Mexico especially rankled them. The Mexican War, in their view and contrary to the president's claims, was a poorly camouflaged offensive war of conquest designed to spread the evil of slavery onto Mexican lands while infecting Christian, republican Americans with an imperial mentality and nationalistic jingoism. Unlike politicians, pacifist writers and ministers had no reason to moderate their denunciations. New England's Congregational and Unitarian ministers accused Americans of gross arrogance and criticized volunteer soldiers as deluded or dishonest. Even those who predicted or hoped for an Anglo-Saxon, Protestant republic encompassing all North America, like Theodore Parker, denounced war as a means of achieving it. The American Peace Society, as pacifist as it was evangelical, argued that the millions of dollars spent on the war could be better spent funding scores of Protestant missionaries in Mexico.[24]

Historian John Schroeder argues that pacifist opinion of the war never evolved or wavered between 1846 and 1848 as did that of politicians because pacifists never saw the war as anything other than an evil crime perpetrated against a peaceable neighbor. A more limited territorial conquest might lessen the war's diabolical consequences both for Mexico and for Americans' morality, or the expansion of slavery might deepen the evil for both populations, but in any case evil the war would remain.[25] Abolitionists clearly could not support a war that extended the institution of slavery, not to mention one provoked by a slaveholding president. But as the Civil War later demonstrated, abolitionists were not uniformly pacifist, so whether they admitted it or not the size and location of the territory to be acquired played a considerable role in their antiwar arguments. Abolitionist newspapers like *National Era* worked extensively to influence in a practical way the character, size, and extent of the territories the United States was sure to gain from the war.

While impassioned, moralistic attacks on the war were popular in pockets of New England and New York, nationwide they did little to alter American support for the war. True, Americans were growing tired of the war by mid-1847, but most blamed Mexico's stubbornness, not Polk's leadership or an amateur, insufficiently supplied, and ill-equipped army, for continuing the war. People began to grumble about punishing Mexico with a territorial indemnity or perhaps even taking the whole country if necessary. This only played into Polk's hands, who had not lost sight of his plan to annex, one way or the other, California. Timing is always important in politics, and news of the victories at Buena Vista and Vera Cruz arrived almost immediately after the Three Million Dollar Bill debate ended in March 1847. For the next several months, U.S. troops under General Scott's command won battle after battle as they marched through central Mexico, from Vera Cruz to Mexico City. By August, Americans stood ready to strike the capital itself but paused for a few weeks during a failed armistice.

By September 1847 the principal challenge to Polk's war leadership, as well as the greatest threat to the American army's efforts to stabilize and hold areas of occupied Mexico, was not Whig politicking or biting attacks by pacifists and abolitionists. Neither was it weariness with what had evolved from a predicted defensive war of short duration into one and a half years of fighting. Rather, the most significant challenge to Polk's comparably limited designs for the war came after the U.S. Army occupied Mexico City on September 14, after which all major combat ceased.

THE "ALL MEXICO" DEBATE

Whigs and antiwar protestors were not the only Americans who equated territorial aggrandizement with the expansion of slavery. So, too, did proponents of the largest land acquisition of all, those who wanted to annex the entire nation of Mexico, or as their slogan put it, "All Mexico." Most All Mexico supporters belonged to Polk's own party, and their moment seemed to have arrived now that U.S. generals stood in Mexico's National Palace and American soldiers quartered themselves in finely built convents and monasteries. This group counted among them soldiers, congressmen, cabinet members, and a sizeable number of Americans interested in some combination of the following: westward expansion, the growth of slavery, a jingoism fueled by the emotional and psychological satisfaction engendered by victorious conquest, and a desire to punish the vanquished for their unwillingness to surrender earlier. Polk fought to rein in the nascent All Mexico movement because it stood in stark opposition to his goal of securing the earliest possible, permanent peace and the annexation of the territorial prize he valued most, California. By necessity, Polk believed, this also meant annexing New Mexico, as General Stephen W. Kearny's actions confirmed when on presidential orders he established U.S. rule there.

Although soldiers debated the wisdom of taking All Mexico once they occupied Mexico City, most had been considering the annexation question since they had first laid eyes on the fertile Rio Grand Valley. As one Tennessee volunteer noted, "it is contrary to the genius of the Yankee to suppose that when once his greedy eyes have fallen upon so extensive a tract of fair and fertile country, he will be long finding the means to possess himself of its soil." In general, this sentiment governed soldiers regardless of their sectional origins or views on slavery. This does not mean every soldier who admired Mexican lands wanted to annex the country in its entirety, but it is fair to say that the more of Mexico American soldiers saw, the more they became convinced that they as Anglo-Saxons could more worthily utilize its mines and agricultural lands than could the Mexicans themselves.[26]

Also in Mexico by this time was Nicholas Trist, the diplomat charged with negotiating a permanent peace with Mexico. That is, Trist was the American minister plenipotentiary until November 1847, when for several reasons Polk recalled him. For one, Trist showed a readiness to disobey explicit orders involving the setting of borders and the amount of money which the United States would pay Mexico for annexed territory. But this was not the primary cause of Polk's mistrust and intense dislike of Trist, for although Trist, when he first swaggered into Mexico, had initially run afoul of the vain General Scott, in December 1847 both men reconciled and became political allies. That same month General Pillow informed Polk just how far this reconciliation went, when he accused both men of conspiring against the president, the intent being, Pillow surmised, to craft a treaty that pleased Whigs like Scott but not the president. General Scott soon arrested General Pillow (along with General Worth and Colonel Duncan) and Polk, in turn, recalled Scott and replaced him with the Democrat, General Butler.[27]

In December 1847, amid these travails, Congress began to debate what to do now that the two nations seemed no closer to establishing a permanent peace even though the American army controlled Mexico's northern departments, occupied its major cities, and in effect already governed, however dubiously under domestic and international law, New Mexico and California. Reflecting opinions voiced in leading newspapers, Democrats pushed for the annexation of All Mexico by arguing that such a measure was the only sure means to bring the war to a close. Others proclaimed that since Providence had awarded Mexico to the United States, Manifest Destiny demanded no conceivable result but All Mexico—anything less would dishonor U.S. troops and God at the same time. Proponents of this view tried to soften it by claiming that incorporating Mexico into the United States would benefit Mexicans through the establishment of true republican government all the way to the Isthmus of Tehuantepec. The popularity of this sentiment left All Mexico's opponents, most of whom were Whigs, lamely arguing that Mexicans were too inferior—congenitally and culturally—to enjoy the blessings of liberty after the manner of Americans. Not a few Whigs feared that Mexicans would find religious affinity with German- and Irish-Catholics, thereby forming a whole new constituency for the Democratic Party. But it was left to the leader of the anti-Polk Democrats, Senator Calhoun, to state succinctly the position of those opposed to All Mexico: "Ours is the government of the white man." To believe that Americans could spread "civil and religious liberty" among Mexicans as the first step in doing so "over all the globe [was] a sad delusion."[28]

As among congressional Democrats, there existed in Polk's cabinet no consensus on the annexation issue. In discussions between September 1847 and February 1848 the cabinet divided between Secretary of the Treasury Walker and Attorney General Nathan Clifford on the one hand, and Secretary of State James Buchanan and Secretary of the Navy John Y. Mason on the other. All supported securing right of travel through the Isthmus of Tehuantepec, annexing New Mexico and Baja and Alta California, and in some manner using the Rio Grande as the basis for the boundary between Mexico and the United States. But Walker and Clifford, both ardent expansionists who by May 1848 were busily trying to convince Polk to invade and then annex Yucatan and Cuba, pushed in late 1847 for the annexation of the Department of Tamaulipas, which included the port of Tampico. Buchanan and his clique opposed Walker and Clifford on all of these efforts. Polk actually regarded the annexation of Tamaulipas as a good idea, but only "if it should be found practicable." Whether practicality was to be determined by politics, military capability, funding, or something else entirely, Polk did not say.[29]

By January 1848 opinions within the cabinet, and the president's own position, had shifted somewhat. Buchanan now supported annexing Tamaulipas on the grounds that since the previous September the United States "had spent much money and shed much blood." Interestingly but not unexpectedly, Polk now mirrored Calhoun, opposing the annexation of Tamaulipas because he considered "obtaining a country containing so large a number of the Mexican population" impracticable. Unlike his suspicious Whig critics, the president did not see in the Mexican population a whole new Democratic constituency. At the most, Polk said, the United States ought only to "secure the port of Tampico."[30]

TREATY OF GUADALUPE HIDALGO

What ultimately and rather abruptly caused the demise of the meteoric All Mexico movement, however, were not any exertions on the part of Polk or Calhoun, but the arrival in Washington City on the nineteenth of February of a treaty, negotiated by Trist. Against orders the recalled diplomat had remained in Mexico to take advantage of what he saw as an unrepeatable opportunity to end the war. There was but one matter on which Trist and Polk could agree: neither wanted to annex the entirety of Mexico. Both increasingly feared that the lack of a peace treaty increased the chances either of an interminable occupation or the complete conquest of Mexican territory, the two outcomes being virtually indistinguishable. Either would likely result in a sustained and bloody insurgency, which the United States thus far had been able to avoid.

Dated February 2, the Treaty of Guadalupe Hidalgo promised a permanent peace while insuring adequate territorial gains for the United States without the unwanted addition of a large Mexican population. It called for $15 million to be paid to Mexico in exchange for California and New Mexico. The fee was designed to prove to the war's critics and to the world that the Mexican War was waged by the United States for indemnity, honor, and self-defense, not conquest, for conquerors do not pay the conquered for their right to rule. This fiction did little to persuade Polk's multifarious opponents to change their opinions and relent from their criticism but seems to have convinced the president himself. When Polk received in his hands a treaty that included the cession by Mexico to the United States of New Mexico and California (but not Tamaulipas), along with an affirmation of the Rio Grande as the border between Texas and Mexico, he grudgingly but with some relief decided to accept the treaty negotiated by his disobedient diplomat. Polk could thus claim in March 1848 that he had not waged a war of conquest or a war to extend slavery, for the Mexican Cession was to be paid for and neither New Mexico nor California would enter the Union with constitutions allowing slavery.

The U.S. Senate approved the Treaty of Guadalupe Hidalgo, with some revisions, on March 10. Both nations exchanged final ratifications three months later, at which time the last of the occupying U.S. troops, now led by General Butler, departed northward for the United States rather than southward toward Yucatan.

So much diversity existed among the expansionists of the 1840s that one should not be surprised by the complexity of the debate over Mexican annexation. Frederick Merk famously identified a belief in a religious-like, republican mission as the underlying motivation for American expansion. As other historians have shown, however, while some Americans may have misguidedly sought to elevate Mexicans with the blessings of liberty, most desired only to ensure freedoms for themselves or to encourage the United States's development as a white, Anglo-Saxon, and Protestant republic. The idea of mission downplays or ignores the diplomatic, commercial, ethnocentric, racialist, market capitalist, anti-Catholic, and other aggressive drives that united in thought, word, and deed under the capacious banner of "Manifest Destiny."[31] Thomas R. Hietala adds to this list the argument that the Mexican War (and expansion more generally) was the product of "fundamental" Jacksonian doctrines found prevalently but not exclusively in the Democratic Party which had their origin in older Jeffersonian principles.[32]

Polk may have been a Jacksonian, but he was no strict agrarian in the Jeffersonian sense. He envisioned for the United States not a landed, agrarian empire of virtuous and vigilant yeoman farmers, but instead a bicoastal commercial empire leavened with a large agricultural base of both slave and free states. In Polk's view, such a nation could not be controlled by northeastern, federalist Whigs any more than it could be manipulated by southern planters and men like John C. Calhoun. Instead, in true Jacksonian fashion, a continental United States engaged in commerce and agriculture would be built, expanded, and governed by the common people of the West, South, and North who, as it happened, were also the faithful of the Democratic Party. If they were not Democrats, Polk thought, then they ought to be, for as John L. O'Sullivan had argued when he coined the term "Manifest Destiny" in 1845, Whigs had opposed U.S. continental dominance every step of the way.

This conception of Polk's expansionist views fits Norman Graebner's emphasis on the precise goals of American expansionists, such as harbors on the West Coast (and nearly one at Tampico). Even maritime, commercial New Englanders initially viewed this type of expansion enthusiastically, but during the war they experienced second thoughts, in no small part because of proslavery sentiment in the Democratic Party, calls by influential men for additional territory further south, and the brief but pervasive and popular All Mexico movement. Nevertheless, as Graebner shows, "For Whigs who had flayed Polk's Mexican policy, San Francisco Bay possibly made somewhat more palatable the huge swallow of territory acquired by the war." Thus, when all was said and done, for economic reasons most Whigs and their supporters acquiesced to the limited territorial objectives that Polk had held all along. Ironically, in the debate over Mexican annexation, the president's own party had been the one to challenge Polk in his desire for a limited cession.[33]

In terms of public opinion and political activism, the biggest danger to Polk's war aims and to the safety and morale of American soldiers was not the dissent voiced by pacifists, abolitionists, or Christians who believed the war to be unjust. Neither was the ultimate peril to the administration's strategy or to the soldiers that posed by Whigs in their partisan but often principled opposition to the conflict. While Whigs did succeed in killing the lieutenant generalship, that was more a political setback for Polk in terms of patronage and Democratization of the officer corps than a real defeat that weakened the army. Even the Whigs' delay tactics in Congress, as displayed in the Three Million Dollar Bill debate, which could well have endangered American troops by postponing peace negotiations, can best be understood as a protest against territorial aggrandizement and executive tyranny.

The calls by evangelical Protestant preachers, officers, or army chaplains, who viewed the conquest of Mexico as a God-given opportunity to Protestantize a subjugated Catholic country and bring it out of the darkness of Romanism, probably posed a greater threat than any of these. Indeed, this anti-Catholic sentiment cut both ways, running as it did through Whig and theological arguments against the war and against the incorporation into the Union of a large number of Mexicans. Still, the greatest danger to Polk's limited territorial war was the drive by expansionists to annex All Mexico, always a nascent movement but one that exploded in the period between the fall of Mexico City and signing of the Treaty of Guadalupe Hidalgo.

The ultimate success of the American war effort is traceable to three factors: the fighting ability and fitness of American soldiers; the actions, political craftiness, and controlling personality of Polk; and events within Mexico and among the Mexicans themselves. In spite of the difficulties posed by relatively untrained men, short-term enlistments, struggles between volunteers and regulars, unruly behavior, and atrocities, the American army in Mexico met with remarkable success in battle. This was not entirely due to the leadership of Scott or of West Pointers but to fighting ability and the willingness of the men to rush into combat chanting slogans like, "Our Country, Right or Wrong."

As early as October 1845, President Polk already had been considering preemptive military action, under the guise of the Monroe Doctrine, to ensure that California (and Cuba, for that matter) did not fall into the hands of Britain or any other "powerful foreign power."[34] During the war Polk faced a chorus of critics in Congress, the press, and among antislavery or pacifist dissenters, obstructionist career professionals at the War Department, and ardent expansionists both inside and outside his cabinet. Yet he was able to steer a course through this ocean of criticism and build and sustain an army capable of achieving his territorial goals. Meanwhile, he dominated members of his cabinet like William Marcy in an effort to make the War Department work efficiently, even as he used the opportunity to beat down career bureaucrats in the army's staff departments.

THE FIRST MODERN PRESIDENT?

Does Polk deserve the title, then, of "first modern president" for his forceful expansion of executive powers during the war with Mexico? Or was he simply following in the footsteps of his mentor, Andrew Jackson, and flexing as much democratic muscle as possible as the one federal representative elected by all the people? In other words, is Polk's domination of military strategy and of the War Department best seen as an exhibition of the Jacksonian leader of the people in action, attempting to take down elites who thwarted the will of people at every turn or as the response of a paranoid and insecure man naturally inclined toward a domineering managerial style?

To account for Polk's behavior as a war president and for his style of micromanagement, one must understand both his personality and his political sensibilities. Ideologically incapable of trusting elites, he nevertheless could rationally assess a given situation and, for example, cooperate with Whig generals or bureaucrats when necessary. He also could admire and trust men like Bancroft. Like Jackson, as the servant of the country's majority and as commander in chief Polk believed that he ought to control as much or as little of war strategy as he might wish—whatever was necessary to achieve his objectives. But Polk's Jacksonian democratic views meshed with his natural paranoia and insecurity to create a personality that, at least during the Mexican War, enabled him to control just the right things or people needed to steer a course toward victory: obstreperous bureaucrats and generals or obstructionist politicians on the one hand, and overzealous expansionists within his own party and cabinet on the other. Polk seems to have given little consideration to the nonpartisan, moralistic, antiwar protestors, probably because they existed outside the Whig-Democrat dichotomy which shaped his view of the world. After all, the dissenters clearly were in the minority, always a key determinant in the mind of any Jacksonian.

This Jacksonian sentiment that enlivened Polk and his supporters could be equally as dangerous as Whig obstructionism for more reasons than the consequences, seen at Puebla, of its accompanying short-term enlistment mentality. Popular democratic sentiment, a complicated mix of anxiety and self-reliance and demagoguery, found its greatest expression in the All Mexico movement that very nearly undid the limited political (that is, territorial) objectives of the war, itself the result of Jacksonian impulses. To uncork the bottle that contained expansionism was one thing; to use it in a limited way and then lock it up again quite another.

Polk's tight managerial style did not threaten or hinder the overall ability of the U.S. Army to be successful on Mexican battlefields. Polk's uneven but ultimately successful balancing of his partisan leanings with the need to command the U.S. war effort proved critical to American efficiency and victory in the war against Mexico. Second to this was his ability to wade through the mass of antiwar propaganda on the one hand, and overzealous, expansionist *pro-war* propaganda on the other, in order to achieve his territorial aims. President Polk's territorial goals remained largely unchanged throughout the war, even as the thirst for territory waxed or waned among members of the public, Congress, or his own cabinet. Apparently even "Young Hickory" was willing at times to temper the passions of the *demos*. Thus, the United States annexed no more—and no less—than New Mexico and California. These goals, and the manner in which Polk pursued them, were based not just on the president's temperament, insecurity, and penchant to micromanage. They were rooted in a Jacksonian awareness of the partisan, class, and sectional implications of not only the outcome of the war, but also just how and by whom the army was to be organized and led, and how war strategy itself was to be formulated and executed.

7

The Mexican War in the American Civil-Military Tradition

In his memoirs, published 20 years after the end of the Civil War, Ulysses S. Grant judged the Mexican War "as one of the most unjust ever waged by a stronger against a weaker nation," more so because Americans had attacked Mexico solely from a "desire to acquire additional territory." But this was not the worst of it, as far as Grant was concerned, for the unjust war had produced terrible consequences for Americans, too. "The Southern rebellion," he wrote, "was largely the outgrowth of the Mexican War." Grant's opinion as a young soldier, however, had been quite different, for he well knew that despite his West Point education, there is nothing like actual combat to train a soldier. And so in 1846, while in Matamoras, the young lieutenant confided to his wife: "I would volunteer to come to Mexico as a private if I could come no other way." As president during the crucial, waning years of Reconstruction between 1869 and 1877, perhaps Grant sometimes wished he and no other American soldier had ever gone to Mexico in the first place.[1]

After the Civil War, Grant was not the only American who remembered above all the invaluable experience the Mexican War provided to those who later fought the civil war it spawned or identified its origin as the inevitable result of land-hungry Americans "following the bad example of European monarchies" by engaging in conquest.[2] Historians have typically assessed the war against Mexico in much the same way, which explains, for example, why the vast majority of edited and published Mexican War journals and letter collections are those of soldiers whose names most Americans recognize only because of their Civil War exploits. Yet the Mexican War was more than a training ground for future generals or a bold imperialist move in the name of "Manifest Destiny." The Mexican War tested U.S. military readiness and demonstrated the need for a more organized, professional army, even as it put a strain on civilian control of the military and, indeed, reintroduced the quarrel over just whom the civilian controllers ought to be—the president, Congress, or the states. It furthered the debate about the role of the military in American society. The war also helped Americans answer the question of whether citizens—as individuals or as members of political parties—could oppose a war or condemn a wartime president without suffering adverse legal consequences or lasting political damage, as had been the case, respectively, during the Quasi-War with France in 1798 and in the War of 1812. Likewise, the Mexican War presented the first opportunity for the United States to wage war since states had extended suffrage to nearly all white males during the period historians call the Jacksonian era. Finally, it threatened to put to rest the myth of the superiority of the citizen soldier, thereby strengthening the important leadership role that became the province of the U.S. Military Academy at West Point, New York.

Viewing particular incidents or trends in later wars in light of the Mexican War and Polk's tenure as commander in chief is instructive. The effect of the Mexican War on the relationship between the U.S. and state governments on the one hand, and the U.S. Army and Navy on the other, reached farther than just the Civil War. The Mexican War inaugurated a century-long process that culminated in the modern commander in chief, who initiates military hostilities without congressional declarations of war and who in wartime seeks expansive powers in the name of Constitutional prerogative and practicality. In a collateral process that occurred over a much shorter time, the Mexican War marked an important milestone in reminding Americans of the need for professional, well-educated military leaders. At the same time, it added another facet to the citizen soldier tradition. Finally, in hindsight the Mexican War provides the first important vignette in the often contentious interplay between the country's top generals and its presidents. The evolution of these four processes is the subject of this chapter.

Democrats, having failed to shut down the U.S. Military Academy entirely, hoped that what their political opponents called "Mr. Polk's War" would prove decisively that the regular army, dominated as it was by Whig officers, should remain but a bit player in the American drama, and so they hoped Polk's attempts to Democratize the army would reduce West Point's influence once and for all. In this, they were disappointed. True, Polk did leave the regular officer corps more Democratic than he had found it. But the Mexican War only boosted respect for West Point, proving that both it and a standing army were needed, even if neither quite fit republican principles and Jacksonian rhetoric. The esteem which West Point graduates earned on Mexican battlefields prodded even the most Jacksonian of Democrats by 1848 to admit to the value of the institution they had long vilified as elitist.

In the 1840s, the attitude of U.S. Army regulars toward the militia and volunteers differed significantly from the opinion of most Americans. When the United States went to war against Mexico, Americans operated on widespread myths and misconceptions of their nation's performance in the War of 1812. There was much, therefore, for Americans to learn from their collective and individual experiences in the Mexican War beyond the fact that once again, as was the case with the War of 1812 under President James Madison, a major war failed to bring about the weakening of civil liberties. As dominant and bent on controlling the government as Polk was, he wisely followed Madison's, and not Adams's, course. The U.S. government, soldiers, and Americans more generally, applied what they interpreted as the lessons of the Mexican War in their initial approach to the Civil War. Sometimes this benefited military preparedness, organization, and efficiency, and sometimes it caused more harm than good. Certain of the major issues that plagued civil-military relations during the Mexican War were not necessarily unique to it, such as the jockeying for power and prestige among generals, regulars' derision of civilian appointees, turf battles among the branches of government, and power struggles between the commander in chief and his generals or War Department staff. In these matters, nearly all of America's wars show a remarkable continuity. Accordingly, during the Civil War relations between each government fighting it and their respective militaries built on precedent, tradition, and memory, although as historians like James M. McPherson and T. Harry Williams demonstrate, experience during the long, bloody conflict ended up playing the more fundamental role.

THE CIVIL WAR

Presidents Polk and Madison may have avoided using their wars to undermine civil liberties in the name of emergency, but emergency was exactly how Abraham Lincoln perceived the perilous situation of the United States during the Civil War, itself a not entirely unexpected outgrowth of the genie unleashed by the American defeat of Mexico over a decade earlier. During the intervening years, the United States had done relatively little in terms of improving military preparedness and organization. Williams points out that the United States "had in 1861 almost no army, few good weapons, no officers trained in the highest art of war, and an inadequate and archaic system of command." The Mexican War had proven that armies could be formed quickly via appeals for volunteers, but the Civil War was to demonstrate that "it took time and battles to train generals." Most importantly, "it took...bitter experience to develop a modern command system."[3]

In keeping with the American tradition Polk had ignored during the Mexican War, Lincoln responded to the Confederate attack on Fort Sumter with a requisition of 75,000 militiamen from the various states. In Polk's case, state governments had wanted to avoid incurring debts as they had in the War of 1812. Because of Constitutional uncertainty over which governmental entities were responsible for funding the militia once it was called into federal service, most governors in 1846 actually preferred new volunteer companies as more practical and cost efficient. Their fighting ability was not necessarily the major consideration. Polk early on had realized that the three-month federal service limit on militiamen and their well-known lack of offensive capabilities made the militia exactly the wrong type of system to use in a foreign war, but most Americans expected any civil war to be a short affair. Clearly, Lincoln was not so much expressing confidence in the myth of militia superiority as he was attempting to face the unique problems posed by a civil war. Thus, the militia, whose stated purpose in the first place was to put down insurrections or repel invasions, seemed the logical choice in April of 1861. The element of necessity in Lincoln's militia call-up was that since the Mexican War, the size of the regular army had grown relatively little, and it certainly was too small to be able immediately to fight a war. Three months, some hoped, ought to be enough time to make Southerners reconsider their dream of independence. In contrast to the treatment Whig governors like William Owsley gave Polk, the only flack Lincoln received from northern governors of either party was appeals to increase their states' troop allotments, for just as in the heady early days of the Mexican War the craving by young American men for what they expected would be the glorious adventure of combat was tremendous.[4]

State governors in the upper South, however, accused Lincoln of violating the Constitution and acting tyrannically, and so they refused to comply. Instead, they prodded their states to vote for secession, and joined the Confederacy. In Kentucky, where Governor Beriah Magoffin refused to send his state's militia and instead welcomed Confederate recruiters, the state legislature declined in May 1861 to support either the Union or the Confederate cause. It instead declared an uneasy neutrality. Lincoln meanwhile continued to cultivate Unionist sentiment in Kentucky. In the end, by force and persuasion he stopped Kentucky's secession. By November Magoffin resigned and a convention tried to trump the legislature by voting for secession. Kentucky thus became a battleground anyway.[5]

Missouri, too, was a state where, in the words of McPherson, "the Unionism of the state convention elected to consider secession" thwarted the avowed wishes of its governor, Democrat Claiborne Fox Jackson. Like Magoffin, Jackson refused to meet Lincoln's militia requisition, calling the war against the Confederacy "an unholy crusade." Ignoring his state's decision to remain in the Union, Jackson called a rump congress that declared secession. But three out of every four of Missouri's white men opted to fight for the Union. As with Kentucky, the supposed Confederate state government found acceptance in the Confederate Congress but never held any real sway in the state itself. Consequently, Missouri became one of the worst middle grounds of the war, torn apart by guerilla warfare and banditry.[6]

In 1861 Mexican War veterans were plentiful in the U.S. Army, and filling its highest posts were two heroes of that war, Winfield Scott and John E. Wool. Both were men whom Polk had tried to undermine or drum out of the service as "Whigs and violent partisans." Scott was still general in chief of the army but so addled that he could not even mount a horse. Wool, a veteran of Buena Vista who had also successfully fought off Polk's politically motivated invalidation of his punishment of mutinous volunteers, was the only other general in 1861 who had led anything larger than a brigade into combat. He was older than Scott.[7]

As a former Whig, now a Republican, Lincoln of course had no qualms about his two top generals' history of Whiggery or the fact that Scott had campaigned for the presidency in 1839 and 1852. He did, however, want vigorous generals who could lead men into battle and win a war, and Scott and Wool did their best but soon confirmed they were past their prime. Yet having shrunk the number of generals and officers after the Mexican War, as promised by the Ten Regiment Bill, there was in the army not much in the way of personnel for Lincoln to work with. Thus began his famous search for a general who would pursue and destroy the Confederate army with the dynamism needed to force the South's surrender. Only in 1864 did the U.S. Army finally possess what Williams describes as the logistical efficiency and qualified generals demanded by Lincoln.

In the meantime, Lincoln sacked or demoted numerous generals until he selected Mexican War veteran and graduate of the U.S. Military Academy, Ulysses S. Grant. Grant had resigned his commission in 1854 because of his chronic drunkenness, but after joining the Union army in 1861 he quickly rose through the ranks due to modest competition and political favoritism. But it was his willingness to expend much blood in order to win battles that brought him to Lincoln's attention, who heavily weighed present accomplishments and not past failures or future political prospects when choosing field commanders. In the spring of 1864, Lincoln named Grant Lieutenant General and Chief of the U.S. Army, facing none of the problems associated with Polk's ill-fated and transparently political attempt to revive that rank. As Polk had surmised, however, the rank came with political benefits. Four years later Grant, as a Republican, won his first of two terms as president. Grant's inadequacy in the executive was not cut short as had been that of the last ill-prepared, war hero-turned-president, Zachary Taylor, and his administration ranks among the most corrupt in history.[8]

Abraham Lincoln proved less partisan than Polk in the way he promoted or demoted his generals, even though he, too, was forced to juggle individual political ambition with ethnic, sectional, and state rivalries. Unlike Polk, Lincoln worried less about generals' presidential aspirations than he did about ensuring that Democratic opposition to his administration's conduct of the war did not succeed in establishing a peace that entailed disunion.

This was a much more difficult job than Polk had faced, and the Union's fate hinged on its success. Lincoln's own Whig Party had opted for the pursuit of political advantage when it successfully balanced its opposition to "Mr. Polk's War" with adulation of the army's Whig commanders and the cultivation of voters in predominantly pro-war states. Whigs had even netted the presidency the same year that a Democratic president won a war. But in Lincoln's mind, his political opponents sought not to gain political advantage but rather to emasculate the U.S. government and end democracy itself, destroying the whole American experiment.

Democrats still mocked the president as "Spotty Lincoln" for his impetuous and colorful demand in 1846 that President Polk take him to Texas to show him the exact spot where Mexicans had "shed the blood of our fellow citizens on our own soil." Most Democratic congressmen in 1861 still viewed Republicans as Whigs gripped by the same antislavery sentiment that in part had instigated their opposition to the Mexican War. Politically savvy, Polk had welcomed Whig opposition to his war policies and tried to gain public favor from it while undermining his Whig generals. But Lincoln faced an enemy whose capital was less than 100 miles away in Richmond, Virginia, and a national emergency that threatened the Union. Even if he wanted to do so, Lincoln could not afford to engage so crassly in politics as Polk had done. Plus, he knew with a good deal of confidence that while Democratic politicians opposed his administration and the war, the majority of the people in the North who had elected them were wildly in favor of giving the South a good drubbing.

Besides Scott, the other former presidential candidate also of Mexican War fame who turned up in Lincoln's coterie of generals was John C. Frémont, who had run for president on the first Republican ticket in 1856. Lacking enough leaders, the U.S. Army had to hunt far and wide for available, qualified candidates, and Frémont was all too pleased once again to offer his services to the U.S. Army. It was not long before Frémont went at loggerheads with the civilian government. Nearly two years before Lincoln decided that emancipating slaves in the rebellious states had become indispensable to victory, Frémont issued orders to free slaves in Missouri when he declared martial law there in 1861. Once again assuming he could safely formulate his own policy in what amounted to a frontier region far from (so he thought) the president's control, Frémont seemed to have learned nothing from his shakedown at the end of the Mexican War following his mutinous acts in California. In this case, too, Jessie Frémont rushed to his aid, meeting with the president to convince him of the righteousness of her husband's actions. Without a second thought, however, Lincoln removed Frémont from command. While Frémont's impulsive glory hunting may have helped President Polk secure California, his disobedience on the slavery issue in 1861 threatened to end any possibility of the seceded states voluntarily rejoining the Union, and it risked the loss of those slave states that by choice or force had remained in the Union. A president simply could not allow his generals to make policies of such great consequence on the grounds that a degree of flexibility was needed in the field. Beyond that, Lincoln knew Frémont's actions provided political fuel for his Democratic opponents.[9]

Despite all of Lincoln's efforts, it was still a general whom he removed for military, not political, reasons that became his greatest political opponent, George B. McClellan. As Williams argues, Lincoln removed McClellan because the general "was not a fighting man," and what was needed, in Lincoln's opinion, was a leader who realized that only "tough fighting" and not delays and "strategy" could win the war.[10] In effect, McClellan was creating his own policy, too, by refusing to follow the administration's directives to attack and pursue the enemy. McClellan's snail-like speed in prosecuting the war in 1861 was qualitatively different then Scott's dawdling at the beginning of the Mexican War or Taylor's unauthorized armistice at Monterrey, but the major distinction to be made here is that Polk's displeasure with Taylor and Scott is indecipherable without understanding the partisanship that existed from the very beginning of his relationship with each man. Party differences between Lincoln and McClellan came to light only later, for as the 1864 Democratic presidential candidate, McClellan nearly defeated Lincoln on a peace platform that promised a settlement Republicans and Southerners alike recognized as pro-Confederate. A timely victory at Atlanta under William T. Sherman and soldiers' votes helped propel Lincoln into a second term, but barely.[11]

The Mexican War had by most accounts proven the value of the U.S. Military Academy, and civilians who received generalships due to politics or favoritism in both the Union and Confederate armies contended with opposition from West Point–educated officers who dominated their respective armies. As in the past, graduates of West Point or experienced, battle-hardened regulars derided these citizen soldiers as ignorant political hacks. This sentiment glossed over the unpleasant truth that even Grant and Sherman owed their initial commands to political favoritism. Moreover, although bungling on the part of a few political appointees led to their troops' untimely deaths, some of the U.S. Army's vaunted professional soldiers performed no better.

The relationship between Polk, Lincoln, and their respective generals presents stark contrasts. Polk, political animal that he was, never really inspired confidence in his leadership among his regular generals, who were always looking over their shoulder for what Scott had so colorfully termed the "fire upon my rear," waiting for the axe to fall. President Lincoln, however, tended to inspire loyalty among his generals, but not because he avoided being a micromanager like Polk. He was, in many respects. But he did allow his generals to do the fighting and even appointed men like the ambitious Mexican War veteran, Joseph Hooker, who had all but threatened to lead a revolt early in the war. Personal disdain existed also between

Hooker and his superior, Henry W. Halleck, that was every bit equal to the ill feelings between Scott and Taylor. Yet Lincoln, for a while anyway, thought Hooker could fight, and that was enough. All that can be said of Polk by way of comparison is that once his lieutenant general proposal bombed, he continued to employ his Whig generals until he considered them no longer necessary to achieving his strategic and political objectives. Then he conspired with men like Gideon J. Pillow to weaken or remove them.[12]

Polk may have taught Lincoln how not to act in certain cases, but Mexican War experiences and the lessons Americans during the Civil War drew from them did not always translate into positive developments for the Union. For example, based not on prejudice but on personal experience with disobedient volunteers during the Mexican War, Scott made the fateful decision to keep regular regiments separate from volunteer regiments. This unintentionally created a vacuum of talented and experienced officers who could have better prepared the volunteers for the long, bloody fight ahead. But this proved to be the least of his problems. Union generals behaved no more amicably toward each other than had their counterparts during the Mexican War. All knew from the last war the important role battlefield exploits could play in promotions and political power. McClellan, according to Timothy D. Johnson, "learned more through personal experience in Mexico than he did from the classroom at West Point," and once gushed that he owed everything he knew to Scott's tutelage there. Indeed he did, but unfortunately that education included Scott's propensity for condescension and irritation whenever others questioned his proposals. After his promotion to head the Army of the Potomac, McClellan seemed intent on thwarting Scott's every move. Scott had faced supercilious obstinacy before from both political appointees (Gideon Pillow) and hardened regulars (Zachary Taylor), but such games were for younger men, and Scott knew it. So, too, did McClellan.[13]

The U.S. Congress during the Civil War also tried to take some practical lessons from the Mexican War and translate them into effective policy. In fact, Congress, on the surface at least, appeared to behave almost in direct contradistinction to its conduct during the war with Mexico when it came to forming and manipulating the army's command structure. It phased out the election of officers by 1863, and established a system to appraise the qualifications of nominees. Congress also created a board to evaluate their conduct and performance once they had become officers. Congressmen rigorously scrutinized every battle's outcome, something that had been unnecessary during the Mexican War's long string of victories. Yet this is about as far as the apparent improvement in congressional oversight and recognition of the limits of democracy in forming a military command structure went, for just as in the years 1846–1848 partisanship and rivalries continuously intervened. As a result, the remedy of federalization applied to the ills of the old elective, state-run system that prevailed during the Mexican War proved worse than the disease. Congress unfairly scapegoated a number of officers following defeats. In these after-the-fact evaluations by the armchair generals at the capital, Democrats and Republicans tended almost always to blame each other. Meanwhile, cabals within the army itself schemed to promote their own candidates. One of these plots, engineered by Halleck, resulted in convincing Lincoln to replace the talented Hooker with George Gordon Meade.[14]

In such a charged atmosphere, Lincoln needed to be careful politically. As the leader of a new, untested party, he occupied the presidency mainly due to divisions in the opposing party. Consequently, Lincoln wanted to ensure that Republicans got credit for victories, including those won by Democratic generals. In this sense, he was every bit the politician as Polk. But it is accurate to say that while Lincoln was as partisan as his contemporaries, he was noticeably much less so than Polk when it came to his conduct of the war overall. Lincoln had learned from the clash of parties during the Mexican War, and still smarted personally from his brief but memorable quarrel with Polk. Now president himself, Lincoln appointed generals with state or federal politics in mind, but overall the system of nomination under Lincoln functioned more like the ideal merit-based system he thought might generate the kind of leaders needed to outmaneuver brilliant tacticians like Robert E. Lee and Thomas J. "Stonewall" Jackson.[15]

The Confederate Army faced more of a problem due to the practice of electing officers than the Union, and the jealous Jeffersonian affection for individual and state liberty, along with the Jacksonian urge to democratize all positions, persisted throughout the war. These principles, after all, were what most Southerners claimed they were defending in the first place. Even though the Confederacy lacked an organized, professional army in 1861, the men who filled the Confederate volunteer officer corps were generally better prepared than their northern counterparts. The laudable exploits of successful Mexican War volunteer generals like John A. Quitman had owed a lot to the abilities and talents they brought from civilian life. But the reason for the initial high quality of many Confederate officers was that, in keeping with the more militant tradition in the South, many of them had attended The Citadel in Charleston, South Carolina, or the Virginia Military Institute in Lexington, Virginia. During the height of the Jacksonian era, in 1841 and 1839, respectively, these institutions had been founded as military colleges or upgraded to that status. Indeed, the South was home to seven out of the eight military academies in the country, even though in the 1840s southern Democrats had participated in the failed drive to shut down the alleged Whig stronghold of West Point.[16]

Jefferson Davis, president of the Confederacy, was himself a graduate of West Point, and had served with distinction in the Mexican War under General Taylor. (He had even been married briefly to the general's daughter, Sarah Knox Taylor, but she died the same year they wedded, in 1835.) Partisanship in the most precise meaning of the term played little role in

Davis's relationship with his generals, because while factions multiplied after secession, only one organized political party existed in the Confederacy, and that was the Democratic Party. Nevertheless, civil-military relations did not proceed smoothly, and Davis generally produced the opposite effect on his generals than did Lincoln. In that sense, he was much like Polk. However, unlike both Lincoln and Polk, Davis proved exceptionally tolerant of his officers' failures.

This tolerance was insufficient in the long run, though, for another side of Davis's personality overshadowed it. Lincoln at times self-deprecatingly spoke of his minimal service in the Black Hawk War, and Polk, lacking even that, consistently made the pretense of at least consulting cabinet members and senators who possessed military experience. But Davis seemed fond of using his Mexican War hero status and West Point education as a blunt weapon when it came to planning strategy, dealing with the Confederate States of America's (C.S.A.) War Department, and relating to army officers. Even before the fall of Vicksburg in July 1863, for example, Davis's behavior produced a rift between himself and the army's commanders in the western part of the Confederacy. There, Davis tried to manipulate the officer corps and angered many career soldiers by not carrying their U.S. Army ranks over into the new army of the Confederacy. In other words, from the soldiers' perspective Davis was promoting out of line, and this bred mistrust and then disillusionment. Davis trusted fellow West Pointer Robert E. Lee, however, and rarely second-guessed him. The result was that Confederate civil-military relations in the east were amicable. This was due, however, more to General Lee's tactfulness and ability to sooth Davis than to anything else.

It is quite probable that civil-military relations in the Confederacy were uniformly horrible not in spite of the vast southern reservoir of militarily educated men and Mexican War veterans, but because of it. President Jefferson Davis generally weighed essential military needs first, but the rifts between his government and its generals appear to have been created more by Davis's tactless, West Point bravado than the states' rights principles avowed by the C.S.A.'s governors. Davis apparently learned the wrong lessons from the Mexican War when it came to the value of the U.S. Military Academy. Clearly, this broad claim about the relationship between civil-military relations in the C.S.A. during the Civil War and in the U.S. government during the Mexican War must be qualified by factors too lengthy to explore here. For example, one must take into account the inability of the C.S.A. to collect taxes and to communicate with the West. What is fair to say is that while Davis may have been a micromanager like Polk, he did a poor job of it. Polk's paranoid-like need to control all angles in any given situation actually served him well during the Mexican War. For Davis, just the opposite was true, and this lessened his value as a leader of a nation at war.

There can be no greater insult imaginable to the American citizen soldier tradition and wartime voluntarism than the draft, and yet both the Union and the Confederacy eventually resorted to conscription. Lincoln and Davis, in enacting drafts, appealed to military necessity. In the Mexican War Democrats had barely been able to add a company of dragoons to the regular army or to offer boons to enlistees without accusations that they doubted the valor of volunteers or that Polk was conspiring to steal the people's liberty by building a permanent regular establishment. But again, participants in the Civil War may have honed their skills or gained knowledge about warfare and command strategies during the Mexican War, but the two wars were qualitatively different in one important way—the first being fought on foreign soil and the second being a lengthy civil war in which one of the belligerents, the Union, demanded unconditional surrender. These mitigating factors make some of the alleged lessons to be learned from the Mexican War inapplicable to the Civil War. Partisanship, congressional and presidential power grabs, feuding generals, and the chasm between regulars and volunteers were all present in the Civil War, but they played out in different ways with dissimilar consequences. For example, the temporary draft did not mark the death of the volunteer spirit that comprised such an important facet of the citizen soldier ethic, but it did firmly plant the seed of the notion that quickly trainable volunteers might not be enough to fight a modern war. In addition, Americans would have to adjust ideologically to the fact that without the U.S. Military Academy or similar institutions, there might not be enough men of needed intellectual quality to rise to the rank of general due to the extensive training, education, and experience that in the Civil War, unfortunately, had to be learned on the battlefield.

The upshot of any comparison between James K. Polk and Abraham Lincoln as commanders in chief is that unlike Polk, President Lincoln tended to consider military necessity first and more successfully compartmentalize his virulent partisan leanings. This was partially due to personality differences between the two men, but overall Lincoln's leadership grew out of the simple fact that unlike in the Mexican War the Union and federal government were threatened. Consequently, there was nothing for Lincoln to learn from Polk's role as a *political* leader during the Mexican War other than what not to do. What Lincoln had to learn from Polk as *commander in chief*, however, was that a president must closely supervise his generals but still allow them to fight, and at all times must be aware of and able to manage cabals and political machinations within Congress and the army. On this last point, Polk had Lincoln beat, hands down. These facts form an important part of the overall context in which one must view the Mexican and Civil Wars in order better to understand the impact of the former on the latter.

In the minds of most Americans after 1865, the Mexican War quickly became known as the conflict that helped cause the Civil War and prepare the generals who fought it. Americans immediately attuned themselves to the irony and discomfiting romance of soldiers who, having once marched and fought as compatriots in a foreign land, later faced one another from the opposite ends of American battlefields. In the late nineteenth century, lessons about warfare and organization and management learned in the Civil War greatly overshadowed any that lingered from its predecessor. As for the citizen soldier tradition that so dominated Jacksonian America, it survived the Civil War in spite of the high death toll and the draft. In the years between 1865 and the outbreak of the Spanish-American War in 1898, however, it should be noted that neither militia nor volunteers but U.S. Army regulars systematically ended armed Indian opposition to the increased migration of Americans into the West, where the issue of free vs. slave states had been solved once and for all.

THE SPANISH-AMERICAN WAR

By 1898 the fears of tyrannical presidential power voiced during the Mexican and Civil Wars had dissipated. Wealthy industrialists or bankers like John D. Rockefeller and J.P. Morgan overshadowed presidents as a new power bloc. With their allies in the press and in legislative halls, men like Rockefeller and Morgan served business interests in the name of serving the nation. This was a far different state of affairs than what had existed in the antebellum period, although the agrarian myth still lingered in rural America even as a new generation of imperialists looked longingly to the Caribbean and to the Pacific, just as the expansionists of Polk's day had hoped they would. By 1898 the pendulum of presidential power had thus swung fully, and the more accurate label for the Spanish-American War, according to its opponents, ought more appropriately to have been "Mr. Hearst's War" than "Mr. McKinley's War." It was William Randolph Hearst's newspaper empire, not the administration of President William McKinley, that highlighted events in Cuba between Spanish forces and rebels and encouraged American entry into the conflict.

After the sinking of the *U.S.S. Maine* under questionable circumstances in Havana Harbor, in a popular move seen as altruistic by many Americans, Congress declared war against Spain. In the fighting that followed, the United States defeated Spain and captured its colonies of Cuba, Puerto Rico, Guam, and the Philippines. America was now an imperial power beyond the bounds of its own continent, a rising force in the world with colonies stretching from North America to Asia. The consequences of the addition of California and the Oregon Territory to the Union under Polk had helped bring the dreams of the commercial expansionists of the 1840s to fruition: the United States finally was poised to insert itself into the lucrative Asian trade and one day to dominate the Pacific Rim. Americans understood that this warranted a larger navy to protect U.S. territories and to guard trade with Asia, but they were still not ready to accept a massive standing army of infantry.

THE PHILIPPINE INSURGENCY

President McKinley promised independence for the newly conquered territories of Cuba and the Philippines, but that independence was a long time coming, especially for the Philippines. Consequently, by 1900 the United States found itself bogged down in the Philippines fighting the type of bloody insurgency Polk had successfully avoided in Mexico by annexing only the least populated (but most highly valued) regions. The Spanish-American War also continued the long American tradition begun by the Revolutionary War and furthered by the Mexican and Civil Wars by contributing to the creation of a war hero who soon became president, Theodore Roosevelt. Along with compatriots like Alfred T. Mahan and Senator Henry Cabot Lodge, Roosevelt had been one of the driving forces behind an unabashed American imperialism that saw empire and naval power as the hallmarks of a great and modern nation. As assistant secretary of the navy, Roosevelt had been instrumental in the takeover of the Philippines, giving standing orders to take Manila in the event of war during his brief moment as acting secretary. At the start of the war, Roosevelt had even resigned his naval department post to fight as a volunteer in Cuba, and he won much fame there for leading the "Rough Riders" into the Battle of the San Juan Heights. For a time, this reinvigorated the myth of the virtuous and vigorous volunteer, even as the United States embarked on an unprecedented naval buildup, a navy having been considered since Thomas Jefferson's time as indispensable to the defense of liberty.

On McKinley's assassination in 1901, Roosevelt, now vice president, took to his new role as commander in chief with all the vigor for which he was known. Roosevelt was determined to swing the pendulum of power back to the president, and then some. In domestic affairs, he pursued progressive policies like trust-busting, with Rockefeller's Standard Oil a primary target. In foreign affairs, he served notice to the rest of the world that the United States had come of age as a great power. One of his first international challenges involved cleaning up the mess in the Philippines left over from the Spanish-American War. President Roosevelt's management of the Philippine insurrection continued the string of tumultuous relationships between presidents and generals of which the Mexican War provides such stark examples. As in the 1840s, imperialists or expansionists served at all levels in the U.S. government, but few could be found in the military. In Roosevelt's time, this anti-imperialist movement made its political home in the Democratic Party, albeit only in small numbers, while the Republican Party now housed the expansionists, like Secretary of War Elihu Root and Senator Lodge. Roosevelt felt moderately concerned about the political effect anti-imperial sentiment could have in Congress on his grand plans for American hegemony in North and Central America, but his real opponent turned out to be the commanding general of the U.S. Army,

Nelson A. Miles. Miles, a veteran of Indian wars and of Wounded Knee fame, was the inheritor of "Ol' Fuss and Feathers" in almost every sense. His vanity and arrogance were common knowledge.[17]

Roosevelt and Miles first met during the Spanish-American War, and each man immediately disliked the other. But their aversion by the time Roosevelt became president transcended the merely personal—Miles was an ambitious Democrat with plans to unseat Roosevelt in 1904. Since someone was leaking classified information to anti-imperialists in Congress about the dismal situation in the Philippines, Roosevelt instantly suspected Miles was the culprit. Then, after General Miles issued subtly critical remarks to the press about the War Department, Roosevelt denounced him to his face at a White House party, and proceeded to censure him. This was when Roosevelt learned what Polk had discovered during his feuds with Taylor and Scott and what Harry S Truman would later come to know: in these sorts of controversies, Americans' knee-jerk response, in spite of republican rhetoric to the contrary about the inherent character flaws of professional soldiers, was to side with their generals, even if in retrospect they later changed their minds.[18]

Rumors of brutal atrocities committed by U.S. soldiers in the Philippines soon reached the American public despite War Department efforts to stifle them. Roosevelt blamed Miles for giving congressional Democrats secret reports and memoranda regarding the outrages as a means of attacking the Roosevelt administration in advance of the 1904 elections. To Roosevelt, Miles was "an intriguer" seeking "to gratify his selfish ambition, his vanity, and his spite," and therefore he was "useless as the head of the Army." This may all have been true about Miles and his motives, and he had indeed leaked sensitive information to Democrats precisely to undermine the Republican administration. But also true were the shocking acts of cruelty perpetrated by American soldiers against Filipinos, and this created a thorny situation for Roosevelt, who at first refused to believe the charges and then blamed them on the actions of a few miscreants.[19]

As the Senate prepared to hold hearings on the alleged Philippine atrocities, Secretary of War Root, to nobody's surprise, commenced efforts to reform the bureau structure established by John C. Calhoun, which had already been antiquated by the time of the Mexican War, let alone the Civil and Spanish-American Wars. Root wanted to create a more modern, centralized apparatus. In all three wars, the unwieldy bureaus had hampered communication, stranded supplies or sent the wrong ones, and been unable to prevent the misuse of War Department funds. Importantly, as far as Root was concerned, the new structure had no place for Miles's position of general in chief. Instead, in order to control completely the staff department bureaucrats who had become effectively autonomous over the years (and who had given Polk much trouble during the Mexican War), Root envisioned a German-style general staff led by a chief of staff, who would be directly under the authority of the secretary of war. Americans, predicted Root, would continue their long tradition and "insist upon civilian control of the military arm." But when Miles accused Roosevelt of aspiring to be an American Kaiser, the administration's efforts went down in defeat. Democrats cheered Miles for helping to force a rewriting of the bill that otherwise, they said, would have made the president "a military dictator." Newspapers proclaimed Miles the victor over Roosevelt.[20]

Miles was now so popular that to remove him would be imprudent, but Roosevelt had come to believe that as president he could not continue "doing great damage to the Army for the sake of avoiding trouble to myself." The question was, what to do about it? The answer came during Senate hearings on the Philippine atrocities, which revealed that orders issued by General Jacob H. Smith, commander of the army in the Philippines, and not a criminal few, were directly responsible for killing and torturing men, women, and children. The popular, moral choice for Roosevelt was clear, and General Smith immediately went before a court-martial. Concurrently, the U.S. Army finally put down the insurrection, and suddenly Roosevelt's slipping political fortunes changed course. When the court-martial merely reprimanded Smith, Roosevelt, as horrified as anyone by Smith's tactics, discharged and removed him anyway. General Miles remained popular, but now Roosevelt was more so, even among Democrats and anti-imperialists who, as historian Edmund Morris points out, "conceded that the President had outmaneuvered them at every turn."[21]

Roosevelt had only "outmaneuvered" General Miles in the sense that he recognized the debate over the Philippine Insurrection, including the atrocities, to be entirely political in nature. Miles had attached himself to the anti-imperialists and used the atrocities as ammunition against Roosevelt. After this backfired and Roosevelt triumphantly removed General Smith, Miles faded from the political scene and was not even Roosevelt's Democratic opponent in 1904. In the meantime, Roosevelt's proposed reform of the army's command structure became law, and a General Staff of around forty officers under the supervision of a chief of staff replaced Calhoun's loose, decentralized system. The bureaus remained, however.

The furor created by the American atrocities in the Philippines, the circuitous path of Root's ultimately successful reforms, and Roosevelt's failed attempt to browbeat Miles reveal the remarkable continuity in civil-military relations in the United States. Presidents have ever fought with generals and struggled against the War Department bureaucracy, and while they have won victories their successes have been mixed at best. Although the Mexican War contextually is best viewed within the Jacksonian era which gave it birth, the disputes between Polk and his leading generals form a constituent part of this long tradition. Perhaps it can be no other way in a democracy, where one of the surest paths to public acclaim and the name recognition needed to win office is military glory. Into the mid-twentieth century the majority of Americans continued to be wary of large standing armies, but the necessities of the Cold War and a peacetime draft systematically lessened this sentiment.

What has never decreased, however, is the American habit of electing war heroes to high office. The Mexican War is a good illustration of this, along with being a telling example of contingency's role in attempts to forestall such heroism. Polk weakened Taylor by ordering him to remain north of Saltillo with a small force, yet Taylor's near blunder at Buena Vista ended up a Whig political godsend. Likewise, Polk's harsh treatment of Scott via the Pillow controversy, along with his replacement of Scott with Democrat William O. Butler, did Polk no political favors. Polk may have gotten what he wanted in the form of the Mexican Cession, but despite his persistent political machinations Taylor still won the presidency in 1848. Moreover, Taylor beat a Democratic ticket that contained Butler as its vice presidential candidate.

Theodore Roosevelt expended as much popularity in his open attack on Miles as had Polk on Taylor and Scott. The difference, however, putting aside for the moment Progressive era political issues like conservation and business regulation, was that Roosevelt's cache of public esteem was superior to Polk's. Roosevelt escaped politically unscathed from his fight with Miles, due in large part to the popularity of his domestic policies and his forceful removal of General Smith. He easily won the presidential election of 1904. Polk, by contrast, lived just long enough to see Taylor become president.

WORLD WAR I

World War I featured no major civil-military clashes and no quarrel, public or private, between generals and President Woodrow Wilson, a Democrat. In part, this was because President Wilson, Theodore Roosevelt's political archenemy, did not appoint any civilians above the grade of captain, but reserved those spots for regulars only. (The fact that Roosevelt sought to lead personally a regiment in France must have had some effect on Wilson's decision.) On the declaration of war in April 1917, Wilson named General John J. Pershing to lead the American Expeditionary Force (A.E.F.) in Europe and refrained from anything resembling micromanagement of him, even though Pershing in 1915 had called the Wilson administration "a weak, chicken-hearted, white-livered lot" for not responding more forcefully to the German sinking of the *Lusitania*. Although initially ineffective and sluggish, successive chiefs of staff by 1918 managed the amazing feat of forming and supplying the A.E.F. and then transported it to Europe in time to win the war against Germany. After years of abortive reform attempts and chronic inefficiency, this achievement, largely the work of Chief of Staff James G. Harbord, according to historian Robert H. Ferrell, finally "[delivered] the War Department from its past."[22]

Unlike in past American wars, conscripts composed the bulk of the American Expeditionary Force. In 1916 Wilson had briefly toyed with the idea of forming a volunteer army in the event of war, even though that year he meanwhile was running for a second term under the slogan, "He kept us out of war." After his reelection, however, Wilson decided that only a draft could fill the allies' need for a large, modern fighting force. Soon after Congress declared war, Wilson went public with his plans for conscription, which obviously ran counter to the ethic of voluntarism in the Mexican and Spanish-American Wars, and stoked fears about a repeat of the Civil War's infamous draft riots. Wilson, however, did not ask to build a large, permanent standing army, only an "expeditionary force" capable of defeating Germany. Nor did he pack the army with Democrats as Polk had done at every opportunity. Building on this rationale, the newly created Committee on Public Information embarked on a campaign that managed to operate within the rhetorical bounds of the citizen soldier tradition in trying to convince Americans that entering World War I was just, prudent, and their patriotic duty. To a certain degree, this effort was successful, in that nearly 24 million men registered under the Selective Service Act for the draft, out of which 6.3 million were deemed fit to serve. Even so, up to 11 percent of this number evaded the draft, several percentage points higher than the desertion rate during the Mexican War. In real numbers, the statistic is more staggering: 337,649.[23]

President Wilson, openly bragging of the need for censorship, also embarked on a systematic plan to use new legislation and the Committee on Public Information to squelch opposition to the war. He revived the Alien Enemies Act of 1798 and signed new Sedition and Espionage Acts, quickly putting all three to use. Clearly, Wilson planned to operate more like John Adams and less like Polk or James Madison when it came to respecting civil liberties. In 1917 the United States had a large population of first and second generation European immigrants that other Americans, including the president, suspected might be tempted to support Germany (in the case of German-Americans) or oppose the U.S. ally, Great Britain (in the case of Irish-Americans). Deemed untrustworthy, too, were communists, pacifists, socialists, and radicals of all kinds. By war's end, the government had disemboweled the Socialist Party by deporting thousands of its members and jailing its leader, Eugene V. Debs, and had decimated using similar tactics the International Workers of the World, a group noted for employing terrorism in the name of workers. The War Department put drafted pacifists to work doing what it considered nonmilitary labor, although some religious groups still objected to assisting the army in any way. As a result, a number of conscientious objectors spent time in prison or escaped to Canada.

Just as the traditional volunteer ethic failed to counter Americans' acquiescence in the draft, the traditional guardians of liberty seemed nowhere to be found during World War I, and most Americans in the name of wartime emergency approved of the Wilson administration's tactics. Most notably, no divide developed between the two major political parties, breaking the precedent first set in the Quasi-War with France and then furthered by the War of 1812 and the Mexican War. This may have been due to even-handed conscription and Wilson's officer policy, two things which precluded the type of partisan cronyism seen in the Mexican War. The government attack on civil liberties probably lessened the likelihood of widespread dissent in Congress. The German threat, when combined with the patriotic fervor whipped up by the Committee on Public Information and the relatively short duration of the war, simply overshadowed everything else.[24]

WORLD WAR II

Partisanship also did not play a formative role in the next war, World War II, or in Franklin Delano Roosevelt's handling of it. This is a remarkable fact considering the fights between Republicans and Democrats throughout the 1930s over the plethora of government programs that formed the Democrat Roosevelt's New Deal for Americans suffering from the Great Depression. As war raged in Europe in 1940, however, Roosevelt did something of which Polk would never have dreamed: he appointed members of the opposing party, Republicans, to his cabinet. Specifically, he named Henry Stimson as secretary of war and Frank Knox as secretary of the navy, and he did so to establish a united, bipartisan front in the total war he expected to wage against Germany and Japan.[25]

Here again we see the danger in simply comparing presidents and American wars out of hand. Whigs dominated the Old Establishment of the army and its institutional supports, like West Point, during the Mexican War. Moreover, Polk encountered a party united against his strategy and territorial objectives in what it called "Mr. Polk's War." Lincoln faced a Democratic Party determined to pursue a peace that promised to sunder the Union permanently, a far more severe crisis than that posed by Whig partisanship during Polk's foreign war. But most dangerous of all was the Axis threat to the United States and its allies in World War II. Both political parties readily recognized this fact. So, too, did Roosevelt. Ideological battles did not halt between conservatives and liberals or radicals in terms of domestic policy, but the Republican and Democratic Parties, including isolationists in the former, pledged their support in defending the nation and defeating fascism.

Roosevelt's leadership and influence did not stop there. By 1943, accord-ing to James MacGregor Burns, "the foundation had been laid for a power-ful Executive Office," which along with the expanded military establishment was "to characterize the presidency for decades to come." In Burns's view, World War II transformed Roosevelt from a leader whose greatest skill was improvisation in the face of adversity to one who systematically built the efficient and organized bureaucratic machine behind the modern presidency. Indeed, Burns labels Roosevelt the first modern president, a statement any number of historians have applied to any number of presidents, and one that therefore must be qualified. More accurately, what Roosevelt did was establish in an apparently permanent way the powers past presidents, from Polk and Lincoln to Wilson, had sought or used only temporarily. Like Polk, Roosevelt accomplished this in the name of the people. Like Wilson, he did so with a direct assault on the civil liberties of citizens whom he considered dangerous. Americans of Japanese and Italian ancestry faced internment or restricted movement as a result of the Roosevelt administration's policies.[26]

In spite of a peacetime draft Roosevelt instituted in 1940 prior to the inclusion of the United States in outright hostilities, the attack on Hawaii by Japan on December 7, 1941, reinvigorated the volunteer tradition as Americans in droves joined the armed forces. World War II was to be fought by citizen soldiers after all, although these volunteers would fight as members of the extant regular army, not as members of their own companies as in the Mexican and Spanish-American Wars.

Roosevelt's most trusted advisor, General Pershing's protégé, George C. Marshall, helped the president plan strategy and to appoint and promote the right men, including Dwight D. Eisenhower. As in World War I, there would be no dangerous quarrels this time between the president and his commanders. This did not mean that Stimson and General Marshall did not have profound disagreements with or concerns about Douglas MacArthur, for example. Nor did it mean that the joint chiefs and Roosevelt always agreed on the best course of action. As Roosevelt at one point complained, "I get so many conflicting recommendations my head is splitting." But these disputes never degenerated into crass partisanship or appeared in the press as they had during the Mexican War.[27]

THE KOREAN WAR

Perhaps the most famous clash between a president and general occurred during the Korean War (1950–1953), between Democrat Harry S Truman and General MacArthur. This dispute ended more like Polk's than Theodore Roosevelt's. When all seemed lost on the Korean peninsula, MacArthur engineered an amphibious landing at Inchon that resulted in the invading North Koreans being driven out of the South. MacArthur wanted to go farther, but doing so risked China's entry into the war. When Truman asked the general to meet him face-to-face in Washington for a strategy session, MacArthur replied that he could not, because matters in Asia demanded his complete attention. So Truman, for reasons still debated by scholars, decided to meet MacArthur on Wake Island. Some historians argue that Truman's advisors wished to prevent MacArthur, a Republican, from coming to the United States and stumping for Republican candidates or otherwise using his fame to damage the administration. But Robert H. Ferrell contends that it was Truman who "was making a grandstand play before the 1950 congressional elections, giving the impression that the war was under control." Whatever the case, political connotations clouded the meeting. A president traveling thousands of miles to meet a general for one hour made the commander in chief seem the junior of the two parties. Soon after this fateful meeting, the Chinese army entered North Korea in force, and a stalemate developed along a line near the thirty-eighth parallel.[28]

The Korean War saw the culmination of the trend toward a more powerful executive in wartime that began just over 100 years earlier with Polk and had been propelled exponentially forward by Truman's immediate predecessor, Franklin D. Roosevelt. Yet, however suspicious the circumstances surrounding the outbreak of the Mexican War, at least Polk had gone to Congress to request a declaration of war. Likewise, Franklin Roosevelt steadily guided the United States down the path toward war, but it turned out to be a declared war with which few Americans could quibble. Truman, on the other hand, viewed the conflict in Korea as a "police action," did not seek a total war in any sense that Americans (including MacArthur) could understand in light of the strategy pursued in World War II, and claimed that his authority as commander in chief was Constitutionally sufficient to allow him to commit American troops under the auspices of the United Nations. This opened up Truman to political attacks from Republicans once the war went sour. More importantly, it emboldened MacArthur to make his own policy, such as offering to negotiate a peace while threatening to drop nuclear bombs on China. Mimicking Nelson A. Miles, MacArthur also sent communiqués to Republican congressmen criticizing Truman's limited strategy. In his most unpopular move as president, Truman responded to these dangerous acts of insubordination by removing MacArthur from command. The general returned to the United States a hero, complete with parades and a rousing address to Congress. Once again, a president had fought with a general and the general had won, at least in the realm of public opinion. While in later years most Americans came to support Truman's decision, at the time this was one of the greatest factors in his unpopularity.[29]

LONG-TERM TRENDS IN CIVIL-MILITARY RELATIONS

Generals or other high-ranking soldiers attempting to institute their own policy from the field has been a constant in American history. Depending on the personalities involved, this fact has consistently threatened to create an imbalance in the Constitutional relationship between the U.S. government and the U.S. Army. The advent of political parties complicated this beginning with the War of 1812. Partisanship dominated the civil-military quarrels of the Mexican War. Frémont holds the unique place in American history of having embarked on autonomous policy-making in two wars, but clearly MacArthur's behavior was the most dangerous since it occurred during the nuclear age amid the worldwide Cold War. As far as presidents go, however, none have approached their relationship to the U.S. Army when the nation was at war with the same level of attentiveness to partisan politics as Polk.

Steady growth in presidential authority over war-making has been another constant since the early 1800s. This has been the case in spite of and, in some instances, because of, the civil-military clashes detailed in this chapter. Polk set the precedent here, too, with his forceful grab for control over the War Department, his dominant role in devising strategy, and his transparent attempts to expand his (and, consequently, his party's) domination of the army's officer corps. Historian Robert W. Johannsen does not exaggerate when he writes that "Polk organized and controlled the war almost single-handedly." No similar claim can be made about any other wartime president, not even Lincoln, whose broad exercise of emergency executive power was at least explainable by the unique reality of civil war. One must realize, however, that all the powers Polk sought or gained had no institutional permanency beyond the Mexican War, only his energetic command style and the growing recognition by presidents that such things might be necessary when the nation was at war. This belief that the requirements of modern warfare, like a centralized, fast-moving command structure and well-trained, professional army, outweighed Constitutional niceties only increased as the United States industrialized, expanded its markets, established colonies, and in a variety of ways extended its reach and influence around the globe.[30]

This process culminated under President Truman, on whose watch the U.S. military budget tripled and thereafter continued to rise throughout the rest of the Cold War. The American mythologization of militia and volunteers embedded in the citizen soldier tradition, along with the long-standing republican fear of standing armies composed of career soldiers, suffocated and died beneath the weight of a peacetime draft and Cold War politics. What found new life, however, was the expansive executive that first pushed outward with Jackson, saw its limits tested by Polk, and which Lincoln used to great effect. Americans came more and more to see the president as the unique federal representative of the majority, enabling Truman, for example, to commit troops to combat in the name of an international organization but without a congressional declaration of war. Even so, the fact this act is what scholars claim made Truman so unpopular attests to the continuity not so much of American republican principles and beliefs about liberty and the separation of powers but of militancy and the demand that wars that are won be easily recognizable as victories. In a nation that had once demanded "All Mexico" and the unconditional surrender of Japan, half of Korea simply would not do. In the early 1970s Congress placed curbs like the War Powers Act on presidential war-making authority in the wake of Lyndon Johnson's abuse of the Gulf of Tonkin Resolution during the Vietnam War, but these proved only partially effective. Still, President George H. W. Bush sought and received congressional authorization before the start of the 1991 Gulf War. President George W. Bush did likewise in the Iraq War. Yet neither sought an official declaration of war from Congress, even for the war against Taliban Afghanistan following the attack on the United States on September 11, 2001.

CONCLUSION

Such are the long-term trends, traceable in varying degrees back to the Mexican War. But key questions remain about the Mexican War's short-term impact on and place within the American civil-military tradition. Did it reinforce the dearly held conviction among Americans that citizen soldiers, whether militia and volunteers, were superior warriors? Or, rather, did the war with Mexico finally shed light on the lessons from the War of 1812 Americans had so long ignored? Among these lessons were the fact that a larger army with professional officers was clearly necessary to protect the expansive, commercial nation the United States had become.

Nineteenth-century Americans collectively answered these questions with a compromise. For most Americans, the Mexican War validated West Point's value, and the Civil War only deepened American confidence in the U.S. Military Academy. Yet no one could deny that volunteers formed the bulk of the army that fought so well in Mexico. While the writings of influential Civil War veterans portrayed volunteers' off-battlefield antics in the poorest possible light, the citizen soldier tradition lived on in Theodore Roosevelt's Rough Riders.

Another point to consider in weighing the Mexican War's immediate impact on and place within the American civil-military tradition is the degree to which a strong and dominant executive is necessary to ensure victory. Most could agree that a president ought to be more forceful and dominant than Madison, who had respected civil liberties but proved an otherwise feeble commander in chief. But this is not to say that mid-nineteenth-century Americans could have foreseen just how powerful the president's war-making ability would become by the time Harry S Truman occupied the office. Polk, after all, had requested a declaration of war, even if he had maneuvered Congress into a corner in the first place by using his authority as commander in chief to put Taylor's troops in harm's way in order to provoke Mexico. To accusations that Lincoln unconscionably trampled civil liberties during the Civil War, most Americans seemed to agree after the fact with Lincoln, who appealed to explicit and implied presidential powers in the Constitution relative to national emergencies. Indeed, they sided again with the president during World War I in a nearly opposite reaction to what John Adams endured after similarly curtailing civil liberties in 1798.

Finally, why did nineteenth-century Americans not view the Mexican War as a debacle from the standpoint of military organization due to atrocities, bickering between the U.S. government and the states, malicious backbiting among generals, and an interservice rivalry that almost resulted in civil war in California? The simple answer to this question is that victory covers a multitude of sins. Because the United States won the war, so little else seemed to matter or remain long in American memory, especially once the trauma of the Civil War intervened. As with the surprising outcome of the favorable Treaty of Ghent that ended the War of 1812, the terms of the Treaty of Guadalupe Hidalgo convinced Americans that their military system was, on the whole, successful. Still, West Point stayed, and after the Civil War the regular army, not militia, entered the West and drove Indians from lands on which white Americans wished to settle. This had been the army's primary responsibility anyway, prior to the Mexican War.

American memory of the Mexican War proved different than that of the Revolutionary War and the War of 1812, although it still remained rooted in the citizen-soldier tradition and militia ethic of the early republic. In later years, Americans chided the volunteers and praised the regulars who fought in Mexico, mostly due to those same regulars' prominence in the armies that fought the Civil War. Recent historians have tried to improve the reputation of the volunteers, arguing that their bad reputation was due not so much to actual behavior and poor performance—the United States won every battle, after all, except for a skirmish near Los Angeles—but more to prejudicial regulars who even before the war despised the whole volunteer system as expensive, unwieldy, and sure to produce disaster. These biased accounts were then reproduced and spread by later historians who accepted them uncritically.

There is some truth to these accusations of prejudice, both on the part of regulars and historians, but the lack of discipline, overt disobedience, and significant number of atrocities committed by volunteers cannot be denied. Then again, a string of victories cannot easily be discounted either. One historian, in Marxian fashion, identifies Mexican War soldiers as proletarians engaged in class conflict who, as workers, exacted "the wage of Manifest Destiny" on the Mexican populace because of poor pay in the army, oppression at home, and chauvinism.[31] The fact of the matter is that these soldiers were Jacksonians in every sense, self-made men (or at least they aspired to be so) and populist democrats who believed they constituted the only race worthy of ruling the continent even as they formed "the great body of the people" who alone were fit to elect their civic representatives. In the last analysis, despite regulars' claims to the contrary, volunteers fought well in battle and many reenlisted in Mexico as regulars when their enlistment terms expired. The irony, then, is that in the one war where companies of citizen soldiers along the style of the militia actually fought well, stories of atrocities and lawlessness painted a lasting negative image of volunteers in the American mind.

What prevented Americans in the years prior to the Mexican War from concluding that a well-trained militia (or regular army, for that matter), long-term enlistment, and a professional officer corps were necessary was Andrew Jackson's militia-led victory at New Orleans in 1815. This exception to an otherwise dismal militia performance in the War of 1812 convinced Americans that their trust in the militia system was not misplaced. Unfortunately for Federalists, during the Jacksonian era the other memorable event of the war was their convention at Hartford, Connecticut. Were anyone to forget, Democrats were always willing to remind them, pointing out along the way that Whigs were the political descendants of the now defunct Federalist Party. Polk referred to his political opponents as "Federalists" and "the Federal Party," noting that such men "had from the commencement of our history been opposed to the extension of our limits."[32]

By the 1840s Americans remembered the War of 1812 with a combination of myth and reality, and the Mexican War could not but build on both of these. Along with misconceptions of what Americans had to learn from their last war against Britain, the "spoils system" mentality integral to the new politics of the Jacksonian era significantly affected the U.S. government's response to the Mexican War. President Polk and not a few congressmen seemed to understand the valuable lessons to be learned by the militia performance and clash of overlapping authorities during the War of 1812, even if they did not quite know how or have the will to translate them into workable policies.

One need only look at the outspokenness of the opposition press and vociferous abolitionist dissent to see that Polk followed Madison's policy of not using the excuse of wartime emergency to interfere with Americans' civil liberties. Like any good politician of his era, he realized he could better attack his opponents through the political system and through patronage, and so he exploited the Whigs' fear of fading into ignominy like the Federalists. Polk's failure in the lieutenant general controversy should not obscure the fact that he was following Thomas Jefferson's precedent in attempting to reform the army in order to secure a politically friendly military.

At times, the American war effort against Mexico seemed to succeed only in spite of Polk's politicking and cronyism, not to mention his undercutting of Whig generals while they were still in the field. Overall, however, it is clear that the war would have turned out far differently for the United States barring Polk's energetic and focused work as commander in chief. Besides politics, a host of other factors marred civil-military relations and threatened U.S. victory, including Jacksonian attitudes, Americans' dislike for professional armies, atrocities committed by Americans against Mexicans, disobedient officers, and inefficient military governors. The unprecedented requirements of conquest and occupation taxed the command structure of the U.S. Army and pushed the already antiquated War Department to its limits. While Polk's own political ambitions and controlling personality at times posed a threat both to troop morale and to victory, in the end his ability at crucial moments to overcome his partisan leanings, his micromanagement of war planning, and his overall strategic vision, helped avoid both an interminable occupation and the annexation of "All Mexico." The resulting American victory netted Polk's primary, geopolitical objective: the annexation of California. Any political damage done during the war to the Whig Party or to its presidential aspirants was, for Polk, merely icing on the cake.

On June 7, 1848, the Whig Party anointed Zachary Taylor its presidential candidate. Two days later Polk received news that the Mexican Congress had ratified the Treaty of Guadalupe Hidalgo. The American army was headed home. Not even one full week later Polk's cabinet opened confidential discussions with Spanish diplomats regarding the U.S. purchase of Cuba. But in this case, they told the Spanish, unless another European nation tried to wrest the island from Spain, armed conflict was out of the question. For the time being anyway, Jacksonian America had had enough of war.

Documents

JAMES K. POLK, INAUGURAL ADDRESS, 4 MARCH 1845— EXCERPT

In this excerpt from Polk's inaugural address, the president addresses traditional arguments against territorial expansion and seeks to allay American anxiety over the annexation of Texas.

The Republic of Texas has made known her desire to come into our Union, to form a part of our Confederacy and enjoy with us the blessings of liberty secured and guaranteed by our Constitution. Texas was once a part of our country—was unwisely ceded away to a foreign power—is now independent, and possesses an undoubted right to dispose of a part or the whole of her territory and to merge her sovereignty as a separate and independent state in ours. I congratulate my country that by an act of the late Congress of the United States the assent of this Government has been given to the reunion, and it only remains for the two countries to agree upon the terms to consummate an object so important to both.

I regard the question of annexation as belonging exclusively to the United States and Texas. They are independent powers competent to contract, and foreign nations have no right to interfere with them or to take exceptions to their reunion. Foreign powers do not seem to appreciate the true character of our Government. Our Union is a confederation of independent States, whose policy is peace with each other and all the world. To enlarge its limits is to extend the dominions of peace over additional territories and increasing millions. The world has nothing to fear from military ambition in our Government. While the Chief Magistrate and the popular branch of Congress are elected for short terms by the suffrages of those millions who must in their own persons bear all the burdens and miseries of war, our

Government can not be otherwise than pacific. Foreign powers should therefore look on the annexation of Texas to the United States not as the conquest of a nation seeking to extend her dominions by arms and violence, but as the peaceful acquisition of a territory once her own, by adding another member to our confederation, with the consent of that member, thereby diminishing the chances of war and opening to them new and ever-increasing markets for their products.

To Texas the reunion is important, because the strong protecting arm of our Government would be extended over her, and the vast resources of her fertile soil and genial climate would be speedily developed, while the safety of New Orleans and of our whole southwestern frontier against hostile aggression, as well as the interests of the whole Union, would be promoted by it.

In the earlier stages of our national existence the opinion prevailed with some that our system of confederated States could not operate successfully over an extended territory, and serious objections have at different times been made to the enlargement of our boundaries. These objections were earnestly urged when we acquired Louisiana. Experience has shown that they were not well founded. The title of numerous Indian tribes to vast tracts of country has been extinguished; new States have been admitted into the Union; new Territories have been created and our jurisdiction and laws extended over them. As our population has expanded, the Union has been cemented and strengthened. As our boundaries have been enlarged and our agricultural population has been spread over a large surface, our federative system has acquired additional strength and security. It may well be doubted whether it would not be in greater danger of overthrow if our present population were confined to the comparatively narrow limits of the original thirteen States than it is now that they are sparsely settled over a more expanded territory. It is confidently believed that our system may be safely extended to the utmost bounds of our territorial limits, and that as it shall be extended the bonds of our Union, so far from being weakened, will become stronger.

None can fail to see the danger to our safety and future peace if Texas remains an independent state or becomes an ally or dependency of some foreign nation more powerful than herself. Is there one among our citizens who would not prefer perpetual peace with Texas to occasional wars, which so often occur between bordering independent nations? Is there one who would not prefer free intercourse with her to high duties on all our products and manufactures which enter her ports or cross her frontiers? Is there one who would not prefer an unrestricted communication with her citizens to the frontier obstructions which must occur if she remains out of the Union? Whatever is good or evil in the local institutions of Texas will remain her own whether annexed to the United States or not. None of the present States will be responsible for them any more than they are for the local institutions of each other. They have confederated together for certain specified objects. Upon the same principle that they would refuse to form a perpetual union with Texas because of her local institutions our forefathers would have been prevented from forming our present Union. Perceiving no valid objection to the measure and many reasons for its adoption vitally affecting the peace, the safety, and the prosperity of both countries, I shall on the broad principle which formed the basis and produced the adoption of our Constitution, and not in any narrow spirit of sectional policy, endeavor by all Constitutional, honorable, and appropriate means to consummate the expressed will of the people and Government of the United States by the reannexation of Texas to our Union at the earliest practicable period.

JAMES K. POLK, MESSAGE TO CONGRESS, 11 MAY 1846

To the Senate and House of Representatives:

The existing state of the relations between the United States and Mexico renders it proper that I should bring the subject to the consideration of Congress. In my message at the commencement of your present session the state of these relations; the causes which led to the suspension of diplomatic intercourse between the two countries in March, 1845, and the long-continued and unredressed wrongs and injuries committed by the Mexican Government on citizens of the United States in their persons and property were briefly set forth.

As the facts and opinions which were then laid before you were carefully considered, I can not better express my present convictions of the condition of affairs up to that time than by referring you to that communication.

The strong desire to establish peace with Mexico on liberal and honorable terms, and the readiness of this Government to regulate and adjust our boundary and other causes of difference with that power on such fair and equitable principles as would lead to permanent relations of the most friendly nature, induced me in September last to seek the reopening of diplomatic relations between the two countries. Every measure adopted on our part had for its object the furtherance of these desired results. In communicating to Congress a succinct statement of the injuries which we had suffered from Mexico, and which have been accumulating during a period of more than twenty years, every expression that could tend to inflame the people of Mexico or defeat or delay a pacific result was carefully avoided. An envoy of the United States repaired to Mexico with full powers to adjust every existing difference. But though present on the Mexican soil by agreement between the two Governments, invested with full powers, and bearing evidence of the most friendly dispositions, his mission has been unavailing. The Mexican Government not only refused to receive him or listen to his propositions, but after a long-continued series of menaces have at last invaded our territory and shed the blood of our fellow-citizens on our own soil.

It now becomes my duty to state more in detail the origin, progress, and failure of that mission. In pursuance of the instructions given in September last, an inquiry was made on the 13th of October, 1845, in the most friendly terms, through our consul in Mexico, of the minister for foreign affairs, whether the Mexican Government would receive an envoy from the United States intrusted with full powers to adjust all the questions in dispute between the two Governments, with the assurance that should the answer be in the affirmative such an envoy would be immediately dispatched to Mexico. The Mexican minister on the 15th of October gave an affirmative answer to this inquiry, requesting at the same time that our naval force at Vera Cruz might be withdrawn, lest its continued presence might assume the appearance of menace and coercion pending the negotiations. This force was immediately withdrawn. On the 10th of November, 1845, Mr. John Slidell, of Louisiana, was commissioned by me as envoy extraordinary and minister plenipotentiary of the United States to Mexico, and was intrusted with full powers to adjust both the questions of the Texas boundary and of indemnification to our citizens. The redress of the wrongs of our citizens naturally and inseparably blended itself with the question of boundary. The settlement of the one question in any correct view of the subject involves that of the other. I could not for a moment entertain the idea that the claims of our much-injured and long-suffering citizens, many of which had existed for more than twenty years, should be postponed or separated from the settlement of the boundary question.

Mr. Slidell arrived at Vera Cruz on the 30th of November, and was courteously received by the authorities of that city. But the Government of General Herrera was then tottering to its fall. The revolutionary party had seized upon the Texas question to effect or hasten its overthrow. Its determination to restore friendly relations with the United States, and to receive our minister to negotiate for the settlement of this question, was violently assailed, and was made the great theme of denunciation against it. The Government of General Herrera, there is good reason to believe, was sincerely desirous to receive our minister; but it yielded to the storm raised by its enemies, and on the 21st of December refused to accredit Mr. Slidell upon the most frivolous pretexts. These are so fully and ably exposed in the note of Mr. Slidell of the 24th of December last to the Mexican minister of foreign relations, herewith transmitted, that I deem it unnecessary to enter into further detail on this portion of the subject.

Five days after the date of Mr. Slidell's note General Herrera yielded the Government to General Paredes without a struggle, and on the 30th of December resigned the Presidency. This revolution was accomplished solely by the army, the people having taken little part in the contest; and thus the supreme power in Mexico passed into the hands of a military leader. Determined to leave no effort untried to effect an amicable adjustment with Mexico, I directed Mr. Slidell to present his credentials to the Government of General Paredes and ask to be officially received by him. There would have been less ground for taking this step had General Paredes come into power by a regular constitutional succession. In that event his administration would have been considered but a mere constitutional continuance of the Government of General Herrera, and the refusal of the latter to receive our minister would have been deemed conclusive unless an intimation had been given by General Paredes of his desire to reverse the decision of his predecessor. But the Government of General Paredes owes its existence to a military revolution, by which the subsisting constitutional authorities had been subverted. The form of government was entirely changed, as well as all the high functionaries by whom it was administered.

Under these circumstances, Mr. Slidell, in obedience to my direction, addressed a note to the Mexican minister of foreign relations, under date of the 1st of March last, asking to be received by that Government in the diplomatic character to which he had been appointed. This minister in his reply, under date of the 12th of March, reiterated the arguments of his predecessor, and in terms that may be considered as giving just grounds of offense to the Government and people of the United States denied the application of Mr. Slidell. Nothing therefore remained for our envoy but to demand his passports and return to his own country.

Thus the Government of Mexico, though solemnly pledged by official acts in October last to receive and accredit an American envoy, violated their plighted faith and refused the offer of a peaceful adjustment of our difficulties. Not only was the offer rejected, but the indignity of its rejection was enhanced by the manifest breach of faith in refusing to admit the envoy who came because they had bound themselves to receive him. Nor can it be said that the offer was fruitless from the want of opportunity of discussing it; our envoy was present on their own soil. Nor can it be ascribed to a want of sufficient powers; our envoy had full powers to adjust every question of difference. Nor was there room for complaint that our propositions for settlement were unreasonable; permission was not even given our envoy to make any proposition whatever. Nor can it be objected that we, on our part, would not listen to any reasonable terms of their suggestion; the Mexican Government refused all negotiation, and have made no proposition of any kind. In my message at the commencement of the present session I informed you that upon the earnest appeal both of the Congress and convention of Texas I had ordered an efficient military force to take a position between the Nueces and the Del Norte. This had become necessary to meet a threatened invasion of Texas by the Mexican forces, for which extensive military preparations had been made. The invasion was threatened solely because Texas had determined, in accordance with a solemn resolution of the Congress of the United States, to annex herself to our Union, and under these circumstances it was plainly our duty to extend our protection over her citizens and soil.

This force was concentrated at Corpus Christi, and remained there until after I had received such information from Mexico as rendered it probable, if not certain, that the Mexican Government would refuse to receive our envoy. Meantime Texas, by the final action of our Congress, had become an integral part of our Union. The Congress of Texas, by its act of December 19, 1836, had declared the Rio del Norte to be the boundary of that Republic. Its jurisdiction had been extended and exercised beyond the Nueces. The country between that river and the Del Norte had been represented in the Congress and in the convention of Texas, had thus taken part in the act of annexation itself, and is now included within one of our Congressional districts. Our own Congress had, moreover, with great unanimity, by the act approved December 31, 1845, recognized the country beyond the Nueces as a part of our territory by including it within our own revenue system, and a revenue officer to reside within that district has been appointed by and with the advice and consent of the Senate. It became, therefore, of urgent necessity to provide for the defense of that portion of our country. Accordingly, on the 13th of January last instructions were issued to the general in command of these troops to occupy the left bank of the Del Norte. This river, which is the southwestern boundary of the State of Texas, is an exposed frontier.

From this quarter invasion was threatened; upon it and in its immediate vicinity, in the judgment of high military experience, are the proper stations for the protecting forces of the Government. In addition to this important consideration, several others occurred to induce this movement. Among these are the facilities afforded by the ports at Brazos Santiago and the mouth of the Del Norte for the reception of supplies by sea, the stronger and more healthful military positions, the convenience for obtaining a ready and a more abundant supply of provisions, water, fuel, and forage, and the advantages which are afforded by the Del Norte in forwarding supplies to such posts as may be established in the interior and upon the Indian frontier.

The movement of the troops to the Del Norte was made by the commanding general under positive instructions to abstain from all aggressive acts toward Mexico or Mexican citizens and to regard the relations between that Republic and the United States as peaceful unless she should declare war or commit acts of hostility indicative of a state of war. He was specially directed to protect private property and respect personal rights.

The Army moved from Corpus Christi on the 11th of March, and on the 28th of that month arrived on the left bank of the Del Norte opposite to Matamoras, where it encamped on a commanding position, which has since been strengthened by the erection of fieldworks. A depot has also been established at Point Isabel, near the Brazos Santiago, 30 miles in rear of the encampment. The selection of his position was necessarily confided to the judgment of the general in command.

The Mexican forces at Matamoras assumed a belligerent attitude, and on the 12th of April General Ampudia, then in command, notified General Taylor to break up his camp within twenty-four hours and to retire beyond the Nueces River, and in the event of his failure to comply with these demands announced that arms, and arms alone, must decide the question. But no open act of hostility was committed until the 14th of April. On that day General Arista, who had succeeded to the command of the Mexican forces, communicated to General Taylor that he considered hostilities commenced and should prosecute them. A party of dragoons of 63 men and officers were on the same day dispatched from the American camp up the Rio del Norte, on its left bank, to ascertain whether the Mexican troops had crossed or were preparing to cross the river, became engaged with a large body of these troops, and after a short affair, in which some 16 were killed and wounded, appear to have been surrounded and compelled to surrender. The grievous wrongs perpetrated by Mexico upon our citizens throughout a long period of years remain unredressed, and solemn treaties pledging her public faith for this redress have been disregarded. A government either unable or unwilling to enforce the execution of such treaties fails to perform one of its plainest duties.

Our commerce with Mexico has been almost annihilated. It was formerly highly beneficial to both nations, but our merchants have been deterred from prosecuting it by the system of outrage and extortion which the Mexican authorities have pursued against them, whilst their appeals through their own Government for indemnity have been made in vain. Our forbearance has gone to such an extreme as to be mistaken in its character. Had we acted with vigor in repelling the insults and redressing the injuries inflicted by Mexico at the commencement, we should doubtless have escaped all the difficulties in which we are now involved.

Instead of this, however, we have been exerting our best efforts to propitiate her good will. Upon the pretext that Texas, a nation as independent as herself, thought proper to unite its destinies with our own she has affected to believe that we have severed her rightful territory, and in official proclamations and manifestoes has repeatedly threatened to make war upon us for the purpose of reconquering Texas. In the meantime we have tried every effort at reconciliation. The cup of forbearance had been exhausted even before the recent information from the frontier of the Del Norte. But now, after reiterated menaces, Mexico has passed the boundary of the United States, has invaded our territory and shed American blood upon the American soil. She has proclaimed that hostilities have commenced, and that the two nations are now at war.

As war exists, and, notwithstanding all our efforts to avoid it, exists by the act of Mexico herself, we are called upon by every consideration of duty and patriotism to vindicate with decision the honor, the rights, and the interests of our country.

Anticipating the possibility of a crisis like that which has arrived, instructions were given in August last, as a precautionary measure against invasion or threatened invasion, authorizing General Taylor, if the emergency required, to accept volunteers, not from Texas only, but from the States of Louisiana, Alabama, Mississippi, Tennessee, and Kentucky, and corresponding letters were addressed to the respective governors of those States. These instructions were repeated, and in January last, soon after the incorporation of Texas into our Union of States, General Taylor was further authorized by the President to make a requisition upon the executive of that State for such of its militia force as may be needed to repel invasion or to secure the country against apprehended invasion. On the 2d day of March he was again reminded, in the event of the approach of any considerable Mexican force, promptly and efficiently to use the authority with which he was clothed to call to him such auxiliary force as he might need. War actually existing and our territory having been invaded, General Taylor, pursuant to authority vested in him by my direction, has called on the governor of Texas for four regiments of State troops, two to be mounted and two to serve on foot, and on the governor of Louisiana for four regiments of infantry to be sent to him as soon as practicable.

In further vindication of our rights and defense of our territory, I involve the prompt action of Congress to recognize the existence of the war, and to place at the disposition of the Executive the means of prosecuting the war with vigor, and thus hastening the restoration of peace. To this end I recommend that authority should be given to call into the public service a large body of volunteers to serve for not less than six or twelve months unless sooner discharged. A volunteer force is beyond question more efficient than any other description of citizen soldiers, and it is not to be doubted that a number far beyond that required would readily rush to the field upon the call of their country. I further recommend that a liberal provision be made for sustaining our entire military force and furnishing it with supplies and munitions of war.

The most energetic and prompt measures and the immediate appearance in arms of a large and overpowering force are recommended to Congress as the most certain and efficient means of bringing the existing collision with Mexico to a speedy and successful termination.

In making these recommendations I deem it proper to declare that it is my anxious desire not only to terminate hostilities speedily, but to bring all matters in dispute between this Government and Mexico to an early and amicable adjustment; and in this view I shall be prepared to renew negotiations whenever Mexico shall be ready to receive propositions or to make propositions of her own.

I transmit herewith a copy of the correspondence between our envoy to Mexico and the Mexican minister for foreign affairs, and so much of the correspondence between that envoy and the Secretary of State and between the Secretary of War and the general in command on the Del Norte as is necessary to a full understanding of the subject.

"GAINES LETTER," ZACHARY TAYLOR TO EDMUND P. GAINES, 9 NOVEMBER 1846

This controversial letter, which marked a precipitous downturn in relations between President Polk and General Taylor, appeared in newspapers around the country in early 1847. It led to a censure of Taylor and a reiteration of army regulations against the publication of private letters containing sensitive military information. Taylor's victory at the Battle of Buena Vista largely buried the controversy over the publication of the "Gaines Letter." Note the addendum at the end about the utility of short-term enlistees.

Monterey, Nov. 9th, 1846

I do not believe the authorities at Washington are at all satisfied with my conduct in regard to the terms of the capitulation entered into with the Mexican commander, which you no doubt have seen, as they have been made public through the official organ, and copied into various other newspapers....Although the terms of capitulation may be considered too liberal on our part by the President and his advisers, as well as by many others at a distance, particularly by those who do not understand the position which we occupied...yet, on due reflection, I see nothing to induce me to regret the course I pursued. The proposition on the part of General Ampudia, which had much to do in determining my course in the matter, was based on the ground that our government had proposed to settle the existing difficulties by negotiation (which I knew was the case without knowing the result), which was then under consideration by the proper authorities, and which he (General Ampudia) had no doubt would result favorably, as the whole of his people were in favor of peace. If so, I considered the further effusion of blood not only unnecessary but improper. Their force was also considerably larger than ours, and, from the size and position of the place, we could not completely invest it; so that the greater portion of their troops, if not the whole, had they been disposed to do so, could any night have abandoned the city, at once entered the mountain passes, and effected their retreat, do what we could. Had we been put to the alternative of taking the place by storm (which there is no doubt we should have succeeded in doing), we should in all probability have lost fifty or a hundred men in killed, besides the wounded, which I wished to avoid, as there appeared to be a prospect of peace, even if a distant one....Besides, they had a very large and strong fortification a short distance from the city, which, if carried with the bayonet, must have been taken at great sacrifice of life, and, with our limited train of heavy or battering artillery, it would have required twenty or twenty-five days to take it by regular approaches.

I am decidedly opposed to carrying the war beyond Saltillo in this direction, which place has been entirely abandoned by the Mexican forces, all of whom have been concentrated at San Luis Potosi; and I shall lose no time in taking possession of the former as soon as the cessation of hostilities referred to expires, which I have been notified the Mexican authorities will be the case on the 13th instant, by the direction of the President of the United States.

If we are (in the language of Mr. Polk and General Scott) under the necessity of "conquering a peace," and that by taking the capital of the country, we must go to Vera Cruz, take that place, and then march on to the city of Mexico. To do so in any other direction I consider out of the question. But, admitting that we conquer a peace by doing so—say at the end of the next twelve months—will the amount of blood and treasure which must be expended in doing so be compensated by the same? I think not, especially if the country we subdue is to be given up; and I imagine there are but few individuals in our country who think of annexing Mexico to the United States.

I do not intend to carry on my operations (as previously stated) beyond Saltillo, deeming it next to impracticable to do so. It then becomes a question as to what is best to be done. It seems to me that the most judicious course to be pursued on our part would be to take possession at once of the line we would accept by negotiation, extending from the Gulf of Mexico to the Pacific, and occupy the same, or keep what we already have possession of; and that, with Tampico (which I hope to take in the course of the next month, or as soon as I can get the means of transportation), will give us all on this side of the Sierra Madre, and as soon as I occupy Saltillo, will include six or seven states, or provinces; thus holding Tampico, Victoria, Monterey, Saltillo, Monclova, Chihuahua (which I presume General Wool has possession of by this time), Santa Fé, and the Californias, and say to Mexico, "Drive us from the country"—throwing on her the responsibility and expense of carrying on offensive war; at the same time closely blockading all her ports on the Pacific and the Gulf. A course of this kind, if persevered in for a short time, would soon bring her to her proper senses, and compel her to sue for peace, provided there is a government in the country sufficiently stable for us to treat with, which I fear will hardly be the case for many years to come. Without large reinforcements of volunteers from the

United States, say ten or fifteen thousand (those previously sent out having already been greatly reduced by sickness and other casualties), I do not believe it would be advisable to march beyond Saltillo, which is more than two hundred miles beyond our dépôts on the Rio Grande—a very long line on which to keep up supplies (over a land route, in a country like this) for a large force, and certain to be attended with an expense which will be frightful to contemplate when closely looked into.

From Saltillo to San Luis Potosi, the next place of importance on the road to the city of Mexico, is three hundred miles; one hundred and forty badly watered, where no supplies of any kind could be procured for man or horses. I have informed the War Department that 20,000 efficient men would be necessary to insure success if we move on that place (a city containing a population of 60,000, where the enemy could bring together and sustain, besides the citizens, an army of 50,000), a force which, I apprehend, will hardly be collected by us, with the train necessary to feed it, as well as to transport various other supplies, particularly ordnance and munitions of war.

In regard to the armistice, which would have expired by limitation in a few days, we lost nothing by it, as we could not move even now, had the enemy continued to occupy Saltillo; for, strange to say, the first wagon which has reached me since the declaration of war was on the 2d instant, the same day on which I received from Washington an acknowledgement of my dispatch announcing the taking of Monterey; and then I received only one hundred and thirty-five; so that I have been since May last completely crippled, and am still so, for want of transportation. After raking and scraping the country for miles around Camargo, collecting every pack mule and other means of transportation, I could bring here only 80,000 rations (fifteen days' supply), with a moderate supply of ordnance, ammunition, etc., to do which all the corps had to leave behind a portion of their camp equipage necessary for their comfort; and, in some instances among the volunteers, their personal baggage. I moved in such a way, and with such limited means, that, had I not succeeded, I should no doubt have been severely reprimanded, if nothing worse. I did so to sustain the administration.

Of the two regiments of mounted men from Tennessee and Kentucky, who left their respective states to join me in June, the latter has just reached Camargo; the former had not got to Matamoras at the latest dates from there. Admitting that they will be as long in returning as in getting here (to say nothing of the time necessary to recruit their horses), and were to be discharged in time to reach their homes, they could serve in Mexico but a very short time.

The forgoing remarks are not made with the view of finding fault with any one, but to point out the difficulties with which I have had to contend....

Source: J.F.H. Claiborne, Zachary Taylor to Edmund P. Gaines, 9 November 1846, "Gaines Letter," in *Life and Correspondence of John A. Quitman, Major-General, U.S.A., and Governor of the State of Mississippi*, (New York: Harper & Brothers, 1860), 2:256–61.

WILLIAM L. MARCY TO ZACHARY TAYLOR, 27 JANUARY 1847 — EXCERPT

> Marcy's first official letter to Taylor over the "Gaines Letter" marked the beginning of the Polk administration's response to Taylor's controversial letter. In these excerpts, Marcy lays out an argument against the letter's publication based on military exigencies, and implicitly accuses Taylor and Gaines of treason. Elsewhere in the letter, Marcy points out that the publication of the "Gaines Letter" violated military ordinances in effect since the 1820s.

I learn from General Gaines that the letter is genuine. This information, I am assured, he had previously given to others. As the letter was not marked 'confidential,' he adjudged that circumstances existed which justified the publication of some part of it, though he expresses an opinion that it was not written with such a view.

It will in a short time be in possession of our enemy; and coming, as it does, from the general to whom the conduct of the war on our part was confided; it will convey most valuable information to the Mexican commander, not only in relation to our present line of operations, but as to the new one, which alone, in your opinion, can be taken with a prospect of success, if an attempt is to be made on the city of Mexico.

The disclosure of your views as to the future operations of our forces, accompanied, as it is, with your opinion that the fruits of the war, if completely successful, will be of little worth to us, will, it is greatly to be feared, not only embarrass our subsequent movements, but disincline the enemy to enter into negotiations for peace. With particular reference to these effects, the publication is most deeply to be regretted.

Source: William L. Marcy to Zachary Taylor, 30th Congress, 1st sess., 27 January 1847, House Ex. Doc. No. 60, 391–92.

ZACHARY TAYLOR TO WILLIAM L. MARCY, 3 MARCH 1847 — EXCERPTS

> This is Taylor's response to Marcy's letter of 27 January 1847, regarding the "Gaines Letter." In these excerpts, Taylor points out that the letter was meant to be private, but stands by his criticisms of the war and of Polk's strategy.

Although your letter does not convey the direct censure of the department or the President, yet...I am not permitted to doubt that I have become the subject of executive disapprobation. To any expression of it, coming with the authority of the President, I am bound by my duty, and by my respect for his high office, patiently to submit; but, lest my silence be construed into a tacit admission to the grounds and conclusions set forth in your communication, I deem it a duty which I owe to myself, to submit a few remarks in reply. I shall be pardoned for speaking plainly.

In the first place, the published letter bears upon its face the most conclusive evidence that it was intended only for private perusal, and not at all for publication. It was published without my knowledge, and contrary to my wishes....The letter was a familiar one, written to an old military friend.... That he should think it proper, under any circumstances, to publish it, could not have been foreseen by me.

...I have carefully examined the letter in question, and I do not admit that it is obnoxious to the objections urged by your communication. I see nothing in it which, under the same circumstances I would not write again. To suppose that it will give the enemy valuable information touching our past or prospective line of operation, is to know very little of the Mexican sources of information, or of their extraordinary sagacity and facilities in keeping constantly apprised of our movements. As to my particular views in regard to the general policy to be pursued towards Mexico, I perceive, from the public journals, that they are shared by many distinguished statesmen, and also, in part, by a conspicuous officer of the navy, the publication of whose opinions is not perhaps obstructed by any regulations of his department.

...I have sought faithfully to serve the country by carrying out the wishes and instructions of the Executive. But it cannot be concealed that, since the capitulation at Monterey, the confidence of the department, and I too much fear, of the President, has been gradually withdrawn, and my consideration and usefulness correspondingly diminished. The apparent determination of the department to place me in an attitude antagonistical to the government, has an apt illustration in the well known fable of Æsop. While entrusted with the command in this quarter, I shall continue to devote all my energies to the public good, looking for my reward to the consciousness of pure motives, and to the final verdict of impartial history.

Source: Zachary Taylor to William L. Marcy, 30th Congress, 1st sess., 3 March 1847, House Ex. Doc. No. 60, 809–10.

"LEONIDAS LETTER," 16 SEPTEMBER 1847—EXCERPTS

James K. Polk's confidant, Gideon J. Pillow, participated in the publication of this letter, which effusively praises his military exploits and demeans those of Winfield Scott. The letter's publication resulted in a major civil-military clash, which Polk used as an opportunity to undermine Scott. According to the *Daily Picayune*, "the passages in italics are those which are understood to have been suppressed in the original publication of the letter" in the *New Orleans Delta*.

Mixcoaca, Mexico, August 27, 1847, Three Miles from the Capital

Gentlemen: I beg leave to hand you the annexed account of our engagement with the enemy, which commenced on the 19th inst., at a strongly fortified position, about four miles west of San Agustin.

...Late in the evening Gen. Scott came upon the field, and brought with him Gen. Shields's brigade of volunteers, whom he advanced to the support of the forces then under Gen. Cadwalader, but it was so late they did not get into position until in the night....

Having achieved this signal and brilliant victory, Gen. Pillow immediately resolved to pursue the retreating forces of the enemy, and while his troops were flushed with victory, give battle to a large force, said still to be in San Angel, which he did, and drove them before him. He then sent an officer of his staff back to Gen. Scott to say to him, if he would cause Gen. Worth to cooperate with him, he would sweep around the valley, and assault the strong works of San Antonio in the reverse, and carry that place, so as to open the direct route to the capital for the advance of his siege train, upon the other battery on that road. Gen. Scott replied that Worth should cooperate with him. Gen. Pillow then moved rapidly around the valley at the head of his victorious forces...While waiting for this purpose, Gen. Scott overtook the army...Gen. Scott, who now assumed command for the first time...ordered Gen. Pillow to lead Cadwalader's brigade and assault the enemy upon the left, and in front of the main work at the bridge or causeway....Pillow's division, in the effort to get to the battle ground, were compelled to wade waist deep in mud and water; the general dismounting from his horse and plunging through, called upon his column to follow him, which they did with great ardor. He advanced rapidly with it, in front of the enemy's main work, and finding it would be cut down by the terrible fire of grape and cannister which swept down the road, he turned it into the field on the right, to attack the main battery on its left flank. Here his forces and Worth's were joined, and went forward and gallantly carried this work.

During this great battle, which lasted two days, Gen. Pillow was in command of all the forces engaged, except Gen. Worth's division, and this was not engaged, except in taking the last work. (Gen. Scott gave but one order, and that was to reinforce Gen. Cadwalader's brigade.) The position the enemy's battery occupied was a height commanding the only road passing through a wide plain covered with lava stone, which was rent into deep chasms and fissures, so as to be almost impassable even for infantry. It was entirely so for all other purposes. In this position the enemy had entrenched twenty-nine pieces of heavy artillery, which swept the approach in every direction. The enemy's reinforcements increased their force to 16,000—about 5000 of which were cavalry. A stronger position could not have been selected, and a more powerful battery was perhaps never so successfully assailed.

The necessity of attacking this work and carrying it had become manifest....It was to open this road, and to drive the enemy and carry this battery, strong as it was known to be, that Gen. Pillow was ordered out by Gen. Scott. The general's [Pillow's] plan of battle, and the disposition of his forces, were most judicious and successful. *He evinced on this, as he has done on other occasions, that masterly military genius and profound knowledge of the science of war, which has astonished so much the mere martinets of the profession. His plan was very similar to that by which Napoleon effected the reduction of the Fortress of Ulm, and Gen. Scott was so perfectly well pleased with it that he could not interfere with any part of it, but left it to the gallant projector to carry it into glorious and successful execution....*The victory was most brilliant and complete. Nothing could have been better planned than this battle. *I must relate an interesting and exciting incident that occurred during the rage of the battle. A Mexican officer being seen by one of Gen. Pillow's aids to leave the enemy's lines, and to advance several yards nearer our position, the general, as soon as he heard of the impudent rashness of the Mexican, put spurs to his charger and galloped at full speed towards him. As soon as he got near to the Mexican, the general called out in Spanish...let the honor and prowess of our respective countries be determined by the issue of this combat. Straight-way the Mexican drew his sword with one hand and balanced his lance in the other, and rushed towards our general, who, with a revolver in one hand and his sabre in the other, waited the onset of the Mexican. The combat was a long and severe one. The Mexican was a large, muscular man, and handled his arms with great vigor and skill, but our general was his superior in dexterity and coolness. At last the Mexican made one terrible charge at our general with his lance, which the latter evaded with great promptitude and avidity, using his sword, tossed the weapon* *of the Mexican high into the air, and then quietly blew his brains out with a revolver. Both the American and Mexican armies witnessed this splendid effort.*

The forgoing account of this unparalleled victory I was myself an eye-witness to, and will vouch for its correctness, and nothing but an order from the commander-in-chief prevented the occupancy of the city by our troops upon the evening of the second day of attack. I cannot refrain on the present occasion from expressing a wish that Congress may do something for our gallant band, who have, under such adverse circumstances and disparity of forces, carried, at the point of the bayonet, the enemy's outposts, and so nobly upheld and maintained the honor of the American nation....

I am, very truly, yours,

LEONIDAS.

Source: "Leonidas Letter," in *New Orleans Daily Picayune*, 16 September 1847.

THOMAS HART BENTON, "VINDICATION OF THE PRESIDENT" SPEECH, 25 JANUARY 1847—EXCERPTS

Under the guise of vindicating President's Polk's motives for seeking to revive the rank of lieutenant general, Senator Benton, in these excerpts, tries to defend his own role in the controversy. In so doing, he calls for the Democratization of the military and implies that Whigs Zachary Taylor and Winfield Scott cannot be trusted to execute the wishes of the commander in chief.

———————

I feel myself called upon by the remarks of the Senator from North Carolina [Mr. Badger] to vindicate the President from the unconstitutional and dangerous design which the hypothetical observations of that Senator would attribute to him; and shall do so in the simplest form of narrative, repeating to the Senate all that has taken place between the President and myself in relation to this appointment, and thereby enabling the Senate and the people to judge of the justice of the accusation.

It was at the beginning of the month of September last, and in the moment that I was about setting out to the West, that the President sent for me, and informed me that he had done so for the purpose of offering me a high appointment. He named it. It was the mission to France...I declined the appointment....

Immediately after refusing the mission to France I went off to the West.... I returned to this city in November....The day after my arrival I called upon the President; and here we approach the dangerous ground! For, in that first interview, he actually asked me my opinion about the future mode of conducting the Mexican war.... This request did not strike me as being anything strange or unreasonable.... He asked me for my opinion as to the future mode of conducting the war. I gave it to him, first in speech, face to face, and afterwards in writing. And here it is! [holding up a roll of paper] for I chose to retain the original for myself, while sending a copy to him. Here it is! and at the proper time the public shall see it, but not now....

The President approved the plan: and it so happened that the nature of the plan required a head to the army...to unite and combine the whole into one harmonious and consistent movement. It so happened, also, that enough was known of the ideas of the two highest in rank of the officers of the army to know that their plans were different; and it is a maxim of fundamental observance in war, that no general is to be required to execute a plan which he disapproves. A new commander became indispensable; and as any new major general would be subordinate to all now in commission, the solution of the difficulty lay in the creation of a new rank, superior to that of major general and inferior to the constitutional commander-in-chief.... This rank appeared to be the natural and regular derivation from the President's own political and military character, and the proper connecting link between him and the army. As President, he was both the civil head of the Government and the military head of the army and navy, and of the militia or volunteers when in service. They were all then in service, and in a foreign country....

The President was bound to command: he could not go to Mexico to command in person; and he could not command from Washington.... This was the view of the *office* of lieutenant general: as to the proposed *officer*, there was no breach of military rule, law, etiquette, or propriety, in the proposed appointment. The office was original, and belonged to no person. The President had a right to nominate, and the Senate to confirm, whom they pleased.

Source: Thomas Hart Benton, "Vindication of the President" speech, *Congressional Globe*, 29th Congress, 2nd sess., 25 January 1847, 246–47.

WINFIELD SCOTT, "PROCLAMATION TO THE GOOD PEOPLE OF MEXICO," 11 APRIL 1847—EXCERPT

Winfield Scott's proclamations to the Mexican people mirror those of Taylor and other American commanders during the Mexican War. These proclamations, of which Scott's is excerpted below, executed Polk's conciliation policy and expressed his desire to avoid civil unrest in Mexico.

Mexicans! At the head of a powerful army, soon to be doubled, a part of which is advancing on your capital, and with another army under Major General Taylor, in march from Saltillo towards San Luis de Potosi, I think myself called upon to address you.

Mexicans! Americans are not your enemies, but the enemies, for a time, of the men who, a year ago, misgoverned you, and brought about this unnatural war between two great republics. We are the friends of the peaceful inhabitants of the country we occupy, and the friends of your holy religion, its hierarchy, and its priesthood.

For the church of Mexico, the unoffending inhabitants of the country, and their property, I have, from the first, done everything in my power to place them under the safe guard of *martial law*, against the few bad men in this army.

My orders to that effect, known to all, are precise and rigorous. Under them, several Americans have already been punished, by fine, for the benefit of Mexicans, besides imprisonment; and one, for a rape, has been hung by the neck.

Is this not a proof of good faith and energetic discipline? Other proofs shall be given as often as injuries to Mexicans may be detected.

Source: Winfield Scott, "Proclamation to the Good People of Mexico," 30th Congress, 1st sess., 11 April 1847, House Ex. Doc. No. 60, 937.

WINFIELD SCOTT, "PROCLAMATION TO THE GOOD PEOPLE OF MEXICO," 11 MAY 1847 — EXCERPTS

Not all of Scott's proclamations were as conciliatory as the one of 11 April 1847, as excerpts from this one, promulgated one month later, show.

I desire, in conclusion, to say to you, with equal frankness, that, were it necessary, an army of one hundred thousand Americans would soon be among you; and that the United States, if forced to terminate, by arms, their differences with you, would not do it in an uncertain or precarious, or still less in a dishonorable manner....

The system of forming guerilla parties to annoy us, will, I assure you, produce only evils to this country, and none to our army, which knows how to protect itself, and how to proceed against such cut-throats; and if, so far from calming resentments and passions, you try to irritate, you will but force upon us the hard necessity of retaliation. In that event, you cannot blame us for the consequences which will fall upon yourselves.

...We desire peace, friendship, and union; it is for you to choose whether you prefer continued hostilities. In either case, be assured I will keep my word.

Source: Winfield Scott, "Proclamation to the Good People of Mexico," 30th Congress, 1st sess., 11 May 1847, House Ex. Doc. No. 60, 971–74.

STEPHEN W. KEARNY, "PROCLAMATION TO THE CITIZENS OF NEW MEXICO, BY COLONEL KEARNY, COMMANDING THE UNITED STATES FORCES," 31 JULY 1846

The undersigned enters New Mexico with a large military force, for the purpose of seeking union with and ameliorating the condition of its inhabitants. This he does under instructions from his government, and with the assurance that he will be amply sustained in the accomplishment of this object. It is enjoined on the citizens of New Mexico to remain quietly at their homes, and to pursue their peaceful avocations. So long as they continue in such pursuits, they will not be interfered with by the American army but will be respected and protected in their rights, both civil and religious.

Source: Stephen W. Kearny, "Proclamation to the citizens of New Mexico, by Colonel Kearny, commanding the United States forces," 30th Congress, 1st sess., 31 July 1846, House Ex. Doc. No. 60, 168.

STEPHEN W. KEARNY, "PROCLAMATION TO THE INHABITANTS OF NEW MEXICO BY BRIGADIER GENERAL S.W. KEARNY, COMMANDING THE TROOPS OF THE UNITED STATES IN THE SAME," 22 AUGUST 1846—EXCERPTS

Before leaving for California, Kearny established a legal code and government in New Mexico, which he claimed for the United States by right of conquest. This move was controversial among Americans opposed to the war and those concerned about military subordination to civil authority. Note that even prior to a peace treaty or formal annexation Kearny refers to Mexican resisters in conquered New Mexico as "traitors."

As by the act of the republic of Mexico, a state of war exists between that government and the United States; and as the undersigned, at the head of his troops, on the 18th instant, took possession of Santa Fé, the capital of the department of New Mexico, he now announces his attention to hold the department, with its original boundaries, (on both sides of the Del Norte,) as a part of the United States, and under the name of "the territory of New Mexico."

The undersigned has instructions from his government to respect the religious institutions of New Mexico—to protect the property of the church—to cause the worship of those belonging to it to be undisturbed, and their religious rights in the amplest manner preserved to them....And he requires of those who have left their homes and taken up arms against the troops of the United States, to return *forthwith* to them, or else they will be considered as enemies and traitors, subjecting their persons to punishment and their property to seizure and confiscation....

It is the wish and intention of the United States to provide for New Mexico a free government, with the least possible delay, similar to those in the United States; and the people of New Mexico will then be called on to exercise the rights of freemen in electing their own representatives to the territorial legislature. But until this can be done, the laws hitherto in existence will be continued until changed or modified by competent authority; and those persons holding office will continue in the same for the present, provided they will consider themselves good citizens and are willing to take the oath of allegiance to the United States.

The United States hereby absolves all persons residing within the boundaries of New Mexico from any further allegiance to the republic of Mexico, and hereby claims them as citizens of the United States....those who are found in arms, or instigating others against the United States, will be considered as traitors, and treated accordingly.

Don Manuel Armijo, the late governor of this department, has fled from it: the undersigned has taken possession of it without firing a gun, or spilling a single drop of blood, in which he most truly rejoices, and for the present will be considered as governor of the territory.

Source: Stephen W. Kearny, "Proclamation to the inhabitants of New Mexico by Brigadier General S. W. Kearny, commanding the troops of the United States in the same," 30th Congress, 1st sess., 22 August 1846, House Ex. Doc. No. 60, 170–71.

JOHN D. SLOAT, "PROCLAMATION TO THE INHABITANTS OF CALIFORNIA," 7 JULY 1846—EXCERPTS

Commodore John D. Sloat, unwilling to conquer California until he possessed unequivocal proof that war existed between Mexico and the United States, issued this proclamation once the actions of John C. Frémont and the Bear Flaggers convinced him that war had begun.

I declare to the inhabitants of California that, although I come in arms with a powerful force, I do not come among them as an enemy to California: on the contrary, I come as their best friend, as henceforward California will be a portion of the United States, and its peaceful inhabitants will enjoy the same rights and privileges they now enjoy...and the same protection will be extended to them as to any other State in the Union. They will also enjoy a permanent government....Under the flag of the United States, California will...rapidly advance and improve both in agriculture and commerce, as, of course, the revenue laws will be the same in California as in all other parts of the United States....

Such of the inhabitants of California, whether native or foreigners, as may not be disposed to accept the high privileges of citizenship, and to live peaceably under the government of the United States, will be allowed time to dispose of their property, and to remove out of the country, if they choose, without any restriction; or remain in it, observing strict neutrality.

Source: John D. Sloat, "Proclamation to the inhabitants of California," 30th Cong., 1st sess., 7 July 1846, House Ex. Doc. No. 60, 261–62.

ROBERT F. STOCKTON, "PROCLAMATION TO THE PEOPLE OF CALIFORNIA," 17 AUGUST 1846—EXCERPTS

John D. Sloat felt relieved to be replaced by Robert F. Stockton, and quickly left California. Note how much less forgiving of non-neutral *Californios* Commodore Stockton was, compared to Sloat.

———————

The Territory of California now belongs to the United States, and will be governed, as soon as circumstances will permit, by officers and laws similar to those by which the other Territories of the United States are regulated and protected.

But, until the governor, the secretary, and council are appointed, and the various civil departments of the government are arranged, military law will prevail, and the commander-in-chief will be the governor and protector of the Territory....

No persons will be permitted to remain in the Territory who do not agree to support the existing government; and all military men who desire to remain are required to take an oath that they will not take up arms against it, or do or say anything to disturb the peace.

Source: Robert F. Stockton, "Proclamation to the people of California," 30th Cong., 1st sess., 17 August 1846, House Ex. Doc. No. 60, 266–70.

ROBERT F. STOCKTON, "PROCLAMATION TO THE PEOPLE OF CALIFORNIA," UNDATED—EXCERPT

Commodore Stockton's second proclamation is more forceful still, and reiterates the permanent status of California as belonging to the United States, despite the fact that no peace treaty had yet been signed or ratified, and Congress had not approved annexation.

I, Robert F. Stockton, commander-in-chief of the United States forces in the Pacific ocean, and governor of the Territory of California, and commander-in-chief of the army of the same, do hereby make known to all men that, having by right of conquest taken possession of that Territory, known by the name of Upper and Lower California, do now declare it to be a Territory of the United States, under the name of the Territory of California.

Source: Robert F. Stockton, "Proclamation to the people of California," 30th Cong., 1st sess., undated, House Ex. Doc. No. 60, 268–70.

ROBERT F. STOCKTON TO GEORGE BANCROFT, 28 AUGUST 1846—EXCERPTS

In this letter to Secretary of the Navy George Bancroft, Commodore Stockton takes for granted the new status of California, due to his successful conquest of it.

I have now the honor to inform you that the flag of the United States is flying from every commanding position in the Territory of California, and that this rich and beautiful country belongs to the United States, and is forever free of Mexican dominion.

...In less than a month after I assumed the command of the United States force in California, we have chased the Mexican army more than three hundred miles along the coast; pursued them thirty miles in the interior of their own country; routed and dispersed them, and secured the Territory to the United States; ended the war; restored peace and harmony among the people; and put a civil government into successful operation....

When I leave the Territory, I will appoint Major Frémont to be governor....

Source: Robert F. Stockton to George Bancroft, 30th Cong., 1st sess., 28 August 1846, Ex. Doc. No. 60, 265–66.

ABRAHAM LINCOLN TO WILLIAM H. HERNDON, 15 FEBRUARY 1848

This private letter of Abraham Lincoln illustrates some of the core arguments Whigs and John C. Calhoun leveled against the Mexican War, namely, that President James K. Polk had usurped Congress's war-making authority, thereby threatening the Constitutional balance between the executive and legislative branch, setting a dangerous precedent.

Dear William:

Your letter of the 29th January was received last night. Being exclusively a constitutional argument, I wish to submit some reflections upon it in the same spirit of kindness that I know actuates you. Let me first state what I understand to be your position. It is that if it shall become necessary to repel invasion, the President may, without violation of the Constitution, cross the line and invade the territory of another country, and that whether such necessity exists in any given case the President is the sole judge.

Before going further consider well whether this is or is not your position. If it is, it is a position that neither the President himself, nor any friend of his, so far as I know, has ever taken. Their only positions are—first, that the soil was ours when the hostilities commenced; and second, that whether it was rightfully ours or not, Congress had annexed it, and the President for that reason was bound to defend it; both of which are as clearly proved to be false in fact as you can prove that your house is mine. The soil was not ours, and Congress did not annex or attempt to annex it. But to return to your position. Allow the President to invade a neighboring nation whenever he shall deem it necessary to repel an invasion, and you allow him to do so whenever he may choose to say he deems it necessary for such purpose, and you allow him to make war at pleasure. Study to see if you can fix any limit to his power in this respect, after having given him so much as you propose. If today he should choose to say he thinks it necessary to invade Canada to prevent the British from invading us, how could you stop him? You may say to him,—"I see no probability of the British invading us"; but he will say to you, "Be silent: I see it, if you don't."

The provision of the Constitution giving the war making power to Congress was dictated, as I understand it, by the following reasons: kings had always been involving and impoverishing their people in wars, pretending generally, if not always, that the good of the people was the object. This our convention understood to be the most oppressive of all kingly oppressions, and they resolved to so frame the Constitution that no one man should hold the power of bringing this oppression upon us. But your view destroys

the whole matter, and places our President where kings have always stood.
Write soon again.
Yours truly,
A. Lincoln.

Source: Abraham Lincoln to William H. Herndon, 15 February 1848, in *The Writings of Abraham Lincoln*, ed. Arthur Brooks Lapsley, 8 vols., (New York: The Lamb Publishing Company, c. 1905–06), 2:19.

Notes

INTRODUCTION

1. Alexis de Tocqueville, *Democracy in America,* trans. Arthur Goldhammer (1835–40; New York: Penguin Books, 2004), 192–93.

2. Ibid., 763.

3. Sean Wilentz, *The Rise of American Democracy: Jefferson to Lincoln* (New York and London: W. W. Norton & Company, 2005), 562–63; Thomas R. Hietala, *Manifest Design: American Exceptionalism and Empire,* Revised Edition (Ithaca: Cornell University Press, 1985), 215. See also Frederick Merk, *Manifest Destiny and Mission in American History: A Reinterpretation* (New York: Alfred K. Knopf, 1963). For the interplay between Manifest Destiny sentiment and other elements prevalent in American thought during the 1840s, like anti-Catholicism and Anglo-Saxonism, see Reginald Horsman, *Race and Manifest Destiny: The Origins of American Racial Anglo-Saxonism* (Cambridge: Harvard University Press, 1981) and John C. Pinheiro, "'Extending the Light and Blessings of Our Purer Faith': Anti-Catholic Sentiment among American Soldiers in the U.S.–Mexican War," *Journal of Popular Culture* (Fall 2001):129–52.

4. Justin H. Smith, *The War with Mexico* (2 vols., Gloucester: The Macmillan Company, 1919; reprint, The American Missionary Association, 1963), 2:268–93; Otis A. Singletary, *The Mexican War* (Chicago and London: The University of Chicago Press, 1960), 102–27; John S.D. Eisenhower, "Polk and His Generals," in Douglas W. Richmond, ed., *Essays on the Mexican War* (College Station: Texas A&M University Press, 1986), 34–35, 63.

5. Paul Foos, *A Short, Offhand, Killing Affair: Soldiers and Social Conflict during the Mexican War* (Chapel Hill: University of North Carolina Press, 2002), 13–17.

6. Richard Bruce Winders, *Mr. Polk's Army: The American Military Experience in the Mexican War* (College Station: Texas A&M University Press, 1997), 3, 12–14.

CHAPTER 1

1. George Washington to Robert Dinwiddie, 9 November 1756, in John C. Fitzpatrick, ed., *The Writings of George Washington from the Original Manuscript*

Sources, 1775–1799 (39 vols., Washington, D.C., 1931–44), 1:492–93; Washington to a Continental Congress Camp Committee, 29 January 1778, in Edward G. Lengel, ed., *The Papers of George Washington: Revolutionary War Series* (15 vols. to date, Charlottesville and London: University of Virginia Press, 2003), 13:377.

2. *Journals of Each Provincial Congress in Massachusetts in 1774 and 1775* (Boston, 1838), 121; Charles Royster, *A Revolutionary People at War* (Chapel Hill: University of North Carolina Press, 1979), 188.

3. Robert Middlekauff, *The Glorious Cause: The American Revolution, 1763–1789* (New York and Oxford: Oxford University Press, 1982), 300–301; Washington to the President of Congress, 20 August 1780, in Fitzpatrick, ed., *Writings of George Washington,* 19:408–9.

4. Glenn A. Phelps, "The Republican General," in Don Higginbotham, *George Washington: Reconsidered* (Charlottesville and London: University of Virginia Press, 2001), 186–87; Marie-Joseph-Paul-Yves-Roch-Gilbert du Motier, marquis de Lafayette to George Washington, 30 December 1777, Washington to Lafayette, 31 December 1777, in Lengel, ed., *The Papers of George Washington: Revolutionary War Series,* 13:68, 83.

5. Royster, *A Revolutionary People at War,* 368.

6. C. Edward Skeen, *Citizen Soldiers in the War of 1812* (Lexington: University Press of Kentucky, 1999), 7–9.

7. Marshall Smelser, *The Democratic Republic, 1801–1815* (New York: Harper & Row, 1968), 227.

8. Russell Kirk, *The Politics of Prudence* (Bryn Mawr, Penn.: Intercollegiate Studies Institute, 1993), 6.

9. Theodore J. Crackel, *Mr. Jefferson's Army: Political and Social Reform of the Military Establishment, 1801–1809* (New York and London: New York University Press, 1987), 13.

10. Ibid., 180–81.

11. Ibid., 160–63, 181.

12. Ibid., 163–64.

13. Skeen, *Citizen Soldiers,* 39–40.

14. Ibid., 174.

15. Ibid., 13.

16. Robert S. Quimby, *The U.S. Army in the War of 1812: An Operational and Command Study* (East Lansing: Michigan State University Press, 1997), 1:173–79, 2:953–54; Skeen, *Citizen Soldiers,* 174–75.

17. Skeen, *Citizen Soldiers,* 175.

18. Smelser, *Democratic Republic,* 282.

19. Skeen, *Citizen Soldiers,* 21, 141–56.

20. Gordon S. Wood, *Revolutionary Characters: What Made the Founders Different* (New York: The Penguin Press, 2006), 170–72.

21. Quimby, *The U.S. Army in the War of 1812,* 1:173–79, 2:953–54.

22. For the social, religious, and attitudinal changes wrought by the market revolution, and its role in the birth of Jacksonian democracy, see Charles Sellers, *The Market Revolution: Jacksonian America, 1815–1846* (New York: Oxford University Press, 1991).

23. Tocqueville, *Democracy in America,* 684, 690.

24. John William Ward, *Andrew Jackson: Symbol for an Age* (New York: Oxford University Press, 1955).

25. Winfield Scott, *Memoirs of Lieut.-General Scott, LL.D.* (2 vols., New York: Sheldon and Conway, 1864), 2:390. For Jackson's fight against the Second B.U.S., see Robert V. Remini, *Andrew Jackson and the Bank War: A Study in the Growth of Presidential Power* (New York, 1967).

26. For the market revolution's part in the creation of the Second Party System, see Harry L. Watson, *Liberty and Power: The Politics of Jacksonian America* (New York: The Noonday Press, 1990).

27. Wilentz, *The Rise of American Democracy*, 572.

28. Skeen, *Citizen Soldiers*, 181–84; Foos, *A Short, Offhand, Killing Affair*, 31–43.

29. Michael C. Meyer and William H. Beezley, eds., *The Oxford History of Mexico* (Oxford: Oxford University Press, 2000), 277–317.

30. Henry Clay to Joel Poinsett, 25 March 1825, *American State Papers: Foreign Relations*, 5:908.

31. "Treaty of Limits with the United Mexican States," ibid., 6:946–47; "Treaty of Amity, Commerce, and Navigation between the United States of America and the United Mexican States," ibid., 952–57; Smith, *The War with Mexico*, 1:58–62.

32. Constituent Congress of Mexico, National Colonization Law, 18 August 1824; State of Coahuila and Texas, Colonization Law, 24 March 1825.

33. James K. Polk, Inaugural Address, 4 March 1845.

34. *United States Magazine and Democratic Review* (July 1845):9.

35. John Slidell to Polk, 29 December 1845, in Wayne Cutler, ed., *The Correspondence of James K. Polk* (Knoxville: University of Tennessee Press, 2004), 10:449.

36. *Journal of the House of Representatives*, 41:785.

37. Joel H. Silbey, *Martin Van Buren and the Emergence of American Popular Politics* (Lanham, Boulder, New York: Rowan & Littlefield Publishers, Inc., 2002), 145–46.

38. Allan Nevins, ed., *Polk: The Diary of a President, 1845–1849* (London and New York: Longmans, Green, and Co., 1929), 106.

39. Zachary Taylor to Dr. Wood, 21, 30 June 1846, in Zachary Taylor, *Letters of Zachary Taylor, from the Battle-Fields of the Mexican War* (Rochester: The Genesee Press, 1908), 14, 20.

40. Taylor to Wood, 23 August 1846, in ibid., 48; John S.D. Eisenhower, *Agent of Destiny: The Life and Times of Winfield Scott* (Norman: University of Oklahoma Press, 1997), 225; Scott, *Memoirs*, 2:385.

41. Winfield Scott to William L. Marcy, 21 May 1846, *Congressional Globe*, 29th Cong., 2d sess., appendix, 650.

CHAPTER 2

1. Nevins, *Polk: The Diary of a President*, 81–82.

2. *Nashville Republican Banner*, 19 May 1847; *National Intelligencer*, 3 June 1847.

3. *New York Herald*, 21 May 1846; Smith, *The War with Mexico*, 1:195.

4. *New York Tribune*, 1 June 1846.

5. James M. McCaffrey, *Army of Manifest Destiny: The American Soldier in the Mexican War, 1846–1848* (New York and London: New York University Press, 1992), 15–17.

6. Paul H. Bergeron, *The Presidency of James K. Polk* (Lawrence: University Press of Kansas, 1987), 11–16.

7. Nevins, *Polk: The Diary of a President*, 93–94.

8. Ibid.

9. Winders, *Mr. Polk's Army*, 10–11; Smith, *The War with Mexico*, 1:183; *Statutes at Large*, 29th Cong., 1 sess., 11–14.

10. *Congressional Globe*, 29th Cong., 1st sess., appendix, 641–45; *Congressional Globe*, 29th Cong., 1st sess., 789, 805.

11. *Statutes at Large*, 29th Cong., 1 sess., 11–14; *Congressional Globe*, 29th Cong., 1st sess., 153.

12. *Congressional Globe*, 29th Cong., 1st sess., 818, 826–28.

13. Smith, *The War with Mexico*, 1:190; *Statutes at Large*, 29th Cong., 1st sess., 9.

14. Smith, *The War with Mexico*, 1:182; *Statutes at Large*, 29th Cong., 1st sess., 9.

15. McCaffrey, *Army of Manifest Destiny*, 17.

16. Foos, *A Short, Offhand, Killing Affair*, 31–43.

17. Skeen, *Citizen Soldiers*, 184.

18. Winders, *Mr. Polk's Army*, 12.

19. *Fayetteville Journal*, 30 July 1846; Winders, *Mr. Polk's Army*, 12.

20. Mary Ellen Rowe, *Bulwark of the Republic: The American Militia in the Antebellum West* (Wesport: Praeger, 2003), 120.

21. Ibid., 120–21.

22. Henry Clay to Octavia W. Levert, 6 November 1846, to Octavia Walton LeVert, 25 June 1846, in Melba Porter Hay, ed., *The Papers of Henry Clay* (10 vols., Lexington: The University Press of Kentucky, 1991), 10:274–75, 284–85.

23. Foos, *A Short, Offhand, Killing Affair*, 45–48.

24. *Washington Daily Union*, 12 August 1847.

25. Nevins, *Polk: The Diary of a President*, 195–96.

26. *Congressional Globe*, 29th Cong., 1st sess., 796–97.

27. Nathaniel Cheairs Hughes, Jr., and Timothy D. Johnson, eds. *A Fighter from Way Back: The Mexican War Diary of Lt. Daniel Harvey Hill, 4th Artillery, USA* (Kent and London: Kent State University Press, 2002), 169; *Washington Daily Union*, 12 August 1847.

28. Smith, *The War with Mexico*, 2:74.

29. *Congressional Globe*, 29th Cong., 2d sess., 123, 140, 146, 347. The concern over patronage even worked its way into a concurrent debate over whether to appoint chaplains to army regiments. See ibid., 222.

30. *Congressional Globe*, 29th Cong., 2d sess., 111.

31. *Congressional Globe*, 29th Cong., 2d sess., 110–11.

32. Ibid., 154.

33. Ibid., 271, 276–78.

34. Ibid., 279.

35. Ibid., 300–302.

36. Ibid., 348–49, 375–77.

37. Nevins, *Polk: The Diary of a President*, 195–97.

38. Smith, *The War with Mexico*, 2:24, 76, 363–64.

CHAPTER 3

1. Nevins, *Polk: The Diary of a President*, 150.

2. Ibid., 144–45.

3. Zachary Taylor to Robert C. Wood, 10 November 1846, 9 February 1847, in Zachary Taylor, *Letters of Zachary Taylor, from the Battle-Fields of the Mexican War* (Rochester: The Genesee Press, 1908), 67, 85.

4. K. Jack Bauer, *Zachary Taylor: Soldier, Planter, Statesman of the Old Southwest* (Baton Rouge and London: Louisiana State University Press, 1985), 185.

5. Taylor to Wood, 9 February 1847, in Taylor, *Letters*, 86.

6. Taylor to Wood, 27 September 1847, in ibid., 136.

7. Henry Clay to John M. Clayton, 16 April 1847, in Melba Porter Hay, ed., *The Papers of Henry Clay* (10 vols., Lexington: The University Press of Kentucky, 1991), 10:323; Taylor to Wood, 21 June 1846, 30 May, 23 June, 20 July 1847, in Taylor, *Letters*, 14, 103, 108, 118.

8. Taylor to Wood, 12, 21, 30 June, 23 August 1846, in Taylor, *Letters*, 9, 14, 20–21, 48.

9. Smith, *The War with Mexico*, 1:346, 507. A fuller story of Gaines's unauthorized requisition of troops is told in Chapter 5.

10. Nevins, *Polk: The Diary of a President*, 191–93.

11. Taylor to Wood, 9 February, 20 March, 4 April, 20 July, 27 September 1847 in Taylor, *Letters*, 85–86, 90–91, 95, 118, 136.

12. Taylor to Wood, 9 February, 20 March, 4 April 1847, in ibid., 87, 90, 94.

13. Nevins, *Polk: The Diary of a President*, 99–100; Scott, *Memoirs*, 2:399.

14. Glyndon G. Van Deusen, *The Jacksonian Era, 1828–1848* (New York: Harper and Brothers, 1959), 40–41, 86–89, 179, 184–86, 192.

15. Nevins, *Polk: The Diary of a President*, 86–87.

16. Ibid., 163–65.

17. Ibid., 165, 169–71.

18. Smith, *The War with Mexico*, 2:75.

19. *Congressional Globe*, 29th Cong., 2d sess., 104–105, 156–58, 175–76, 184–87; *Speech of Mr. Milton Brown, of Tenn., on the Causes of the Mexican War* (n.p., n.d.), 13.

20. *Congressional Globe*, 29th Cong., 2d sess., 246.

21. Ibid., 247.

22. Nevins, *Polk: The Diary of a President*, 190–91.

23. Scott, *Memoirs*, 399–400.

24. Ibid., 401.

25. *Nashville Republican Banner*, May 16, 20, 25, 29, 3, June 6, 1846; *Nashville Whig*, May 19, 28, June 2, 4, 1846; *Tri-Weekly Nashville Union*, May 28, June 4, 1846; *Goodspeed's History of Tennessee from the Earliest Times to the Present* (1887; Greenville, SC: Southern Historical Press, 1978), 474.

26. William B. Campbell to David Campbell, 4 June 1846, in "Mexican War Letters of Colonel William Bowen Campbell, of Tennessee, Written to Governor David Campbell, of Virginia, 1846," *Tennessee Historical Magazine* 1 (June 1915):

134–36; John Blout Robertson, *Reminiscences of a Campaign in Mexico; by a Member of "the Bloody First"* (Nashville: John York and Co., 1849), 63–64; *Lincoln County Journal,* September 17, 1846.

27. Eisenhower, *Agent of Destiny,* 256.

28. Scott, *Memoirs,* 416.

29. Gideon Pillow to Mary Pillow, 28 September 1847, Huntington Library, Pasadena, California.

30. Scott, *Memoirs,* 2:416.

31. Worth's troubled governance of Puebla is explored at length in Chapter 4.

32. Scott, *Memoirs,* 2:583–84.

33. Scott to Marcy, 9 February 1848, in ibid., 573.

34. Eisenhower, *Agent of Destiny,* 315, 310–20.

35. Ibid., 320.

36. Smith, *The War with Mexico,* 2:186.

37. Scott, *Memoirs,* 2:583–84.

38. Ibid., 416.

39. Ibid., 380, 383.

40. Joseph E. Chance, ed., *Mexico Under Fire: Being the Diary of Samuel Ryan Curtis, 3rd Ohio Volunteer Regiment, During the American Military Occupation of Mexico, 1846–48* (Fort Worth: Texas Christian University Press, 1994), 129; *Daily Picayune,* November 7, 1847; Robert Ryal Miller, ed., *The Mexican War Journal and Letters of Ralph W. Kirkham* (College Station: Texas A&M University Press, 1991), 102.

41. Nevins, *Polk: The Diary of a President,* 100.

CHAPTER 4

1. Albert Lombard, *The "High Private," with a Full and Exciting History of the New York Volunteers* (New York: privately printed, 1848), 8.

2. *National Intelligencer,* September 10, 1846.

3. T.E. Dansbee to Brother and Sister, 14 October 1846, T.E. Dansbee Letter, Tennessee Historical Society, Tennessee State Library and Archives, Nashville; *Daily Picayune,* November 3, 1846.

4. Joseph E. Chance, ed., *The Mexican War Journal of Captain Franklin Smith* (Jackson: University of Mississippi Press, 1991), 203.

5. Singletary, *The Mexican War,* 144–46; Maurice Garland Fulton, ed., *Diary and Letters of Josiah Gregg* (2 vols., Norman: University of Oklahoma Press, 1941, 1944), 2:59.

6. T.E. Dansbee Letter, Tennessee Historical Society, Tennessee State Library and Archives, Nashville; Frank S. Edwards, *A Campaign in New Mexico with Colonel Doniphan* (Philadelphia: Carey and Hart, 1847), 69–74; John R. Kenly, *Memoirs of a Maryland Volunteer* (Philadelphia: J.B. Lippincott and Co., 1873), 335.

7. "Diary of Philip Gooch Ferguson, 1847–1848," in Ralph P. Bieber, ed., *Marching with the Army of the West, 1846–1848* (Glendale, Calif.: The Arthur H. Clark Company, 1936), 333.

8. George W. Hughes, Order, 15 December 1847, Jalapa, Huntington Library, Pasadena.

9. John F. Meginness Journal, John F. Meginness Papers, University of Texas at Arlington, Special Collections.

10. George Winston Smith and Charles Judah, *Chronicle of the Gringos: The U.S. Army in the Mexican War, 1846–1848* (Albuquerque: University of New Mexico Press, 1968), 57–58; Henry S. Lane to Samuel Stone, 5 November 1846, typescript, Miscellaneous Papers of Henry Smith Lane, Filson Historical Society, Louisville, Kentucky.

11. *United States Magazine and Democratic Review* (July 1845):5.

12. William McCarty, ed., *National Songs, Ballads, and Other Patriotic Poetry, Chiefly Relating to the War of 1846* (Philadelphia: William McCarty, 1846), 89, 95, 104.

13. Samuel Chamberlain, *My Confession* (New York: Harper and Brothers, 1956), 88; *Liberator*, April 16, 1847.

14. *General Taylor and His Staff: Comprising Memoirs of Generals Taylor, Worth, Wool, and Butler, Interspersed with Numerous Anecdotes of the Mexican War* (New York: Leavitt, Trow and Co., 1848), 157; Robert H. Ferrell, ed., *Monterrey is Ours!: The Mexican War Letters of Lieutenant Dana, 1845–1847* (Lexington: University Press of Kentucky, 1990), 152–53.

15. [Luther Giddings], *Sketches of the Campaign in Northern Mexico. In Eighteen Hundred Forty-Six and Seven. By an Officer of the First Regiment of Ohio Volunteers* (New York: George P. Putnam and Co., 1853), 221; *Daily Picayune*, May 5, 1846, February 4, July 23, 1847; *Washington Daily Union*, May 5, 1846.

16. Robert F. Stockton to James K. Polk, 26 August 1846, James K. Polk Papers, Library of Congress; *Boston Daily Advertiser,* September 2, 1845, August 5, 1847; *New York Tribune*, January 4, 1848; *Presbyterian*, January 8, 1848.

17. Smith and Judah, *Chronicle of the Gringos*, 423–24.

18. For details on Polk's Catholic conciliation policy, accusations of a Polk-Papal intrigue, and the two priests sent to Mexico, see John C. Pinheiro, "'On Their Knees to Jesuits': Nativist Conspiracy Theories and the Mexican War" in W. Todd Groce and Stephen V. Ash, eds., *Nineteenth-Century America: Essays in Honor of Paul H. Bergeron* (Knoxville: University of Tennessee Press, 2005), 35–53.

19. Robert Ryal Miller, *Shamrock and Sword: The Saint Patrick Battalion in the U.S.–Mexican War* (Norman: University of Oklahoma Press, 1989), 23.

20. K. Jack Bauer, *The Mexican War, 1846–1848* (New York: Macmillan Publishing Co., Inc., 1974), 327.

21. Scott, *Memoirs,* 2:396.

22. Singletary, *The Mexican War,* 76.

23. Smith, *The War with Mexico,* 2:70–71.

24. Raphael Semmes, *Afloat and Ashore during the Mexican War* (Cincinnati: Wm. H. Moore & Co., 1851), 318.

25. Smith, *The War with Mexico,* 2:72, 361.

26. *New York Herald,* May 30, 1847.

27. Bauer, *The Mexican War,* 326.

28. J.A. Quitman and Leandro Estrada, "Office of the Civil and Military Governor/Secretaria del Gobernador Civil y Militar," October 6, 1847, Broadside, Special Collections Library, University of Texas at Arlington.

29. Madison Mills Diary, October 12–13, 1847, Filson Historical Society, Louisville, Kentucky; Smith, *The War with Mexico,* 2:459.

30. Taylor to Adjutant General, June 16, 1847, 30th Cong., 1st sess., Ex. Doc. No. 60, 1178; General Orders No. 146, No. 149, in ibid., 512–13.

31. Ferrell, *Monterrey is Ours!*, 152.

32. Ibid., 152.

33. Emma Jerome Blackwood, ed., *To Mexico with Scott: Letters of Captain E. Kirby Smith to his Wife* (Cambridge: Harvard University Press, 1917), 151–52.

34. Bauer, *Zachary Taylor*, 211–13.

35. Winfield Scott to David Conner, 16 March 1847, Huntington Library, Pasadena.

36. Winfield Scott to Henry J. Wilson, 13 October 1847, Huntington Library, Pasadena.

37. Winfield Scott, General Order 17, 11 January 1848; William Walton Morris to G.M. Henry, 13 January 1848, Huntington Library, Pasadena.

38. William Orlando Butler, General Order 9, 6 February 1848, Huntington Library, Pasadena.

39. Lewis G. DeRussy, Semi-Monthly Field Report from Tampico, 15 April 1848, Huntington Library, Pasadena.

40. Pinheiro, "'Extending the Light and Blessings of Our Purer Faith,'" 131–36.

41. Smith, *The War with Mexico*, 2:459; *Liberator*, October 15, 1847.

42. Singletary, *The Mexican War*, 144–46.

43. Smith and Judah, *Chronicles of the Gringos*, 133.

CHAPTER 5

1. Bauer, *Zachary Taylor*, 199–220.

2. Bauer, *The Mexican War*, 19–20.

3. Ibid., 57–58.

4. William Marcy to Zachary Taylor, 23 May 1846, 30th Cong., 1st sess., Ex. Doc. No. 60, 281.

5. Marcy to Taylor, 28 May 1846, 30 May 1846, in ibid., 281–83; Taylor to Robert C. Wood, 25 July 1846, in Zachary Taylor, *Letters of Zachary Taylor, from the Battle-Fields of the Mexican War* (Rochester: The Genesee Press, 1908), 30.

6. Zachary Taylor to William Marcy, 20 May 1846, 30th Cong., 1st sess., Ex. Doc. No. 60, 298.

7. Isaac Johnson to William Marcy, 12 June 1846, in ibid., 309–10.

8. William Marcy to Isaac Johnson, 25 June 1846, in ibid., 311–15.

9. Ibid.

10. William Marcy to Zachary Taylor, 3 August 1846, in ibid., 316–17.

11. Zachary Taylor to Robert C. Wood, 30 June 1846, in Taylor, *Letters of Zachary Taylor*, 21.

12. Nevins, *Polk: The Diary of a President*, 139.

13. Ibid., 140.

14. Singletary, *The Mexican War*, 113.

15. Nevins, *Polk: The Diary of a President*, 155.

16. Ibid., 156.

17. Dwight L. Clarke, *Stephen Watts Kearny: Soldier of the West* (Norman: University of Oklahoma Press, 1961), 11.

18. William Marcy to Stephen Watts Kearny, 3 June 1846, 30th Cong., 1st sess., Ex. Doc. No. 60, 153–54.

19. Ibid., 155–56.

20. Stephen W. Kearny, "Proclamation of 31st July," and "Proclamation of 22nd August," in ibid., 168, 170–71.

21. Bauer, *The Mexican War,* 135.

22. *United States Magazine and Democratic Review* (April 1847):297.

23. Nevins, *Polk: The Diary of a President*, 153.

24. George Bancroft to John D. Sloat, 24 June 1845, 30th Cong., 1st sess., Ex. Doc. No. 60, 231.

25. Bancroft to Sloat, 13, 15 May, 8 June, 12 July, 30th Cong., 1st sess., Ex. Doc. No. 60, 233–39; John C. Frémont, *Memoirs of My Life* (Chicago: Belford, Clark & Co., 1887; reprint, New York: Cooper Square Press, 2001), 536–37.

26. John D. Sloat, "Proclamation to the Inhabitants of California," 7 July 1846, in Steven R. Butler, ed., *A Documentary History of the Mexican War* (Richardson, Texas: Descendants of Mexican War Veterans, 1995), 146.

27. Bauer, *The Mexican War,* 172.

28. Frémont, *Memoirs,* 534–35.

29. Stockton, Proclamations and Circulars, and Stockton to Bancroft, 28 August 1846, 30th Cong., 1st sess., Ex. Doc. No. 60, 265–70; *New York Tribune,* January 4, 1848.

30. Bauer, *The Mexican War,* 193–94; Singletary, *The Mexican War,* 69.

31. Clarke, *Stephen Watts Kearny,* 88–89.

32. Tom Chaffin, *Pathfinder: John C. Frémont and the Course of American Empire* (New York: Hill and Wang, 2002), 369–70; *Defence of Lieut. Col. J. C. Frémont, Before the Military Court Martial* (Washington, January, 1848), 2.

33. Chaffin, *Pathfinder,* 369–70; Chaffin, *Defence of Frémont,* 2.

34. Chaffin, *Pathfinder,* 371–72.

35. Nevins, *Polk: The Diary of a President,* 264.

36. Ibid., 252, 256.

37. Chaffin, *Defence of Frémont,* 78.

38. Ibid., 31.

39. Ibid., 78.

40. Ibid., 339.

41. Nevins, *Polk: The Diary of a President,* 301; *Defence of Frémont,* 340–41. Despite Polk's grant of clemency, Frémont chose to resign from the army, rather than admit guilt.

42. Zachary Taylor to Adjutant General, 7 February 1847, 30th Cong., 1st sess., Ex. Doc. No. 60, 1110.

43. Smith, *The War with Mexico,* 2:438.

44. *National Intelligencer,* July 20, 1847.

CHAPTER 6

1. Winders, *Mr. Polk's Army,* 34.

2. Ibid., 64; Singletary, *The Mexican War,* 24.

3. Michael F. Holt, *The Rise and Fall of the Whig Party: Jacksonian Politics and the Onset of the Civil War* (New York: Oxford University Press, 1999), 234.

4. *Washington Daily Union,* April 11, 18 ,1847.

5. Russell F. Weigley, *History of the United States Army* (Bloomington: Indiana University Press, 1967), 176.

6. Nevins, *Polk: The Diary of a President,* 93.

7. Ibid., 93–106; Pinheiro, "'On Their Knees to Jesuits,'" 38–43.

8. Nevins, *Polk: The Diary of a President,* 93–94.

9. Paul H. Bergeron, *The Presidency of James K. Polk* (Lawrence: University Press of Kansas, 1987), 150–56.

10. Winders, *Mr. Polk's Army,* 16–19. For an in-depth look at the U.S. Army's organization and the inner workings of the War Department during the Mexican War, see Winders, *Mr. Polk's Army,* 15–23.

11. Nevins, *Polk: The Diary of a President,* 100; Weigley, *History,* 176.

12. Weigley, *History,* 176; Winders, *Mr. Polk's Army,* 17; Bergeron, *Presidency of Polk,* 43.

13. Bergeron, *Presidency of Polk,* 30–31.

14. Nevins, *Polk: The Diary of a President,* 69.

15. Ibid., 33–34, 47.

16. Ibid., 64.

17. *Congressional Globe,* 29th Cong., 2d sess., appendix, 218–23, 395–403; *Congressional Globe,* 29th Cong., 2d sess., Proceedings, 494.

18. *Congressional Globe,* 29th Cong., 2d sess., appendix, 274–78, 433–35.

19. Ibid., 222.

20. *Congressional Globe,* 29th Cong., 2d sess., Proceedings, 546–47.

21. *Congressional Globe,* 29th Cong., 2d sess., appendix, 296–305.

22. *Congressional Globe,* 29th Cong., 2d sess., Proceedings, 259, 541–43; *Congressional Globe,* 29th Cong., 2d sess., appendix, 556.

23. *Congressional Globe,* 29th Cong., 2d sess., Proceedings, 515.

24. George Putnam, *God and Our Country: A Discourse Delivered in the First Congregational Church of Roxbury* (Boston: William Crosby and H.P. Nichols, 1847), 6–20; Andrew Peabody, *The Triumphs of War: A Sermon Preached on the Day of the Annual Fast, April 15, 1847* (Portsmouth: John W. Foster, 1847), 5–6; Theodore Parker, *A Sermon on War, Preached at the Melodeon, on Sunday, June 7, 1846* (Boston: I.R. Butts, 1846), 25–26; Theodore Parker, *A Sermon on the Mexican War, Preached at the Melodeon, on Sunday, June 25h, 1848* (Boston: Coolidge and Wiley, 1848), 50–54; Orville Dewey, *An Address Delivered before the American Peace Society, Boston, May, 1848* (Boston: American Peace Society, 1848), 12–16.

25. John H. Schroeder, *Mr. Polk's War: American Opposition and Dissent, 1846–1848* (Madison: University of Wisconsin Press, 1973), 92.

26. John Blout Robinson, *Reminiscences of a Campaign in Mexico; by a Member of "The Bloody First"* (Nashville: John York and Co., 1849), 101–2; [Luther Giddings], *Sketches of the Campaign in Northern Mexico. In Eighteen Hundred Forty-Six and Seven. By an Officer of the First Regiment of Ohio Volunteers* (New York: George P. Putnam and Co., 1853), 53–54.

27. Nevins, *Polk: The Diary of a President,* 286–89.

28. *Congressional Globe,* 30th Cong., 1 sess., appendix, 50–52.

29. Bergeron, *Presidency of Polk,* 104–10; Nevins, *Polk: The Diary of a President,* 261.

30. Nevins, *Polk: The Diary of a President,* 290–91.

31. Frederick Merk, *Manifest Destiny and Mission in American History: A Reinterpretation* (New York: Alfred K. Knopf, 1963). For the variety of sentiments included under the broader term, "Manifest Destiny," see Horsman, *Race and Manifest Destiny*; Thomas R. Hietala, *Manifest Design: Anxious Aggrandizement in Late Jacksonian America* (Ithaca: Cornell University Press, 1985); and Pinheiro, "'Extending the Light,'" 129–52.

32. Hietala, *Manifest Design,* 173–216. On precisely for whom liberty ought to be extended and secured, see Albert K. Weinberg, *Manifest Destiny: A Study of Nationalist Expansionism in American History* (Baltimore: The Johns Hopkins Press, 1935).

33. Norman Graebner, *Empire on the Pacific: A Study in American Continental Expansion* (New York: The Ronald Press Company, 1955), 226.

34. Nevins, *Polk: The Diary of a President,* 19.

CHAPTER 7

1. Ulysses S. Grant, *Personal Memoirs of U.S. Grant* (2 vols., New York: Charles L. Webster & Company, 1885), 1:53, 56; Ulysses S. Grant to Julia Grant, 28 July 1846, in John Y. Simon, ed., *The Papers of Ulysses S. Grant* (24 vols. to date, Carbondale and Edwardsville: Southern Illinois University Press, 1967–), 1:99.

2. Grant, *Personal Memoirs,* 1:53.

3. T. Harry Williams, *Lincoln and his Generals* (New York: Vintage Books, 1952), 3.

4. James M. McPherson, *Battle Cry of Freedom: The Civil War Era* (New York: Oxford University Press, 1988), 274–75.

5. Ibid., 294.

6. Ibid., 276, 290–93.

7. Williams, *Lincoln and his Generals,* 3–4; Nevins, *Polk: The Diary of a President,* 100; Smith, *The War with Mexico,* 2:418.

8. McPherson, *Battle Cry of Freedom,* 296.

9. Williams, *Lincoln and his Generals,* 35–39.

10. Ibid., 178.

11. McPherson, *Battle Cry of Freedom,* 772.

12. Ibid., 328–29; Williams, *Lincoln and His Generals,* 210–211.

13. Timothy D. Johnson, *Winfield Scott: The Quest for Military Glory* (Lawrence: University Press of Kansas, 1998), 230–33.

14. David Herbert Donald, *Lincoln* (New York: Simon and Schuster, 1995), 438–40, 444–45.

15. McPherson, *Battle Cry of Freedom,* 326–27.

16. Ibid., 327–30.

17. Edmund Morris, *Theodore Rex* (New York: Random House, 2001), 24.

18. Ibid., 78–79.

19. Ibid., 97.

20. Ibid., 98–99.

21. Ibid., 100–104, 110, 127.

22. Robert H. Ferrell, *Woodrow Wilson and World War I, 1917–1921* (New York: Harper and Row, Publishers, 1985), 24–30, 48–50.

23. Ibid., 16–18.

24. Ibid., 206–218.

25. For two contrasting interpretations of how politics and ideology impacted Franklin Delano Roosevelt's leadership during WWII, see James MacGregor Burns, *Roosevelt: The Soldier of Freedom, 1940–1945* (New York: Harcourt Brace Jovanovich Inc., 1970) and Thomas Fleming, *The New Dealers' War: F.D.R. and the War within World War II* (New York: Basic Books, 2001).

26. Burns, *Roosevelt,* 343.

27. Ibid.

28. Robert H. Ferrell, *Harry S. Truman and the Modern American Presidency* (New York: HarperCollins Publishers, 1983), 120–21.

29. Ibid., 124–28.

30. Robert W. Johannsen, *To the Halls of the Montezumas: The Mexican War in the American Imagination* (New York: Oxford University Press, 1985), 15.

31. Foos, *A Short, Offhand, Killing Affair,* 113–14.

32. Nevins, *Polk: The Diary of a President,* 356–57.

Selected Bibliography

PRIMARY SOURCES

MANUSCRIPTS AND UNPUBLISHED SOURCES

Filson Historical Society, Louisville Kentucky
  Miscellaneous Papers of Henry Smith Lane
Huntington Library, Pasadena California
  Bird-Johnston Collection
  Letter from Gideon Johnson Pillow
Library of Congress
  James K. Polk Papers
Tennessee Historical Society, Tennessee State Library and Archives, Nashville
  T.E. Dansbee Letter
  Madison Mills Diary
Texas A&M University Digital Library
  Sons of DeWitt Colony Texas
University of Texas at Arlington, Special Collections
  John F. Meginness Papers
  Quitman, J.A. and Leandro Estrada, "Office of the Civil and Military Governor/
    Secretaria del Gobernador Civil y Militar," 6 October 1847, Broadside.

PUBLISHED SOURCES

American State Papers: Foreign Relations
Bieber, Ralph P., ed. *Marching with the Army of the West, 1846–1848.* Glendale,
    Calif.: The Arthur H. Clark and Company, 1936.
Blackwood, Emma Jerome, ed. *To Mexico with Scott: Letters of Captain E. Kirby
    Smith to his Wife.* Cambridge: Harvard University Press, 1917.
Butler, Steven R., ed. *A Documentary History of the Mexican War.* Richardson,
    Texas: Descendants of Mexican War Veterans, 1995.
Chamberlain, Samuel. *My Confession.* New York: Harper and Brothers, 1956.

Chance, Joseph E., ed. *The Mexican War Journal of Captain Franklin Smith*. Jackson: University of Mississippi Press, 1991.

Chase, Philander, ed. *The Papers of George Washington: Revolutionary War Series*. Vol. 13, Edward G. Lengel. ed., Charlottesville and London: University of Virginia Press, 2003.

Congressional Globe. 1836–50. Washington, DC, 1834–73.

Cutler, Wayne, ed. *The Correspondence of James K. Polk*. 11 vols. to date. Knoxville: University of Tennessee Press, 1969–.

Defence of Lieut. Col. J. C. Frémont, Before the Military Court Martial. Washington: n.p., 1848.

Dewey, Orville. *An Address Delivered before the American Peace Society, Boston, May, 1848*. Boston: American Peace Society, 1848.

Edwards, Frank S. *A Campaign in New Mexico with Colonel Doniphan*. Philadelphia: Carey and Hart, 1847.

Ferrell, Robert H., ed. *Monterrey is Ours!: The Mexican War Letters of Lieutenant Dana, 1845–1847*. Lexington: University Press of Kentucky, 1990.

Fitzpatrick, John C., ed. *The Writings of George Washington from the Original Manuscript Sources, 1775–1799*. 39 vols. Washington, DC, 1931–44.

Frémont, John C. *Memoirs of My Life*. Chicago: Belford, Clark & Co., 1887; reprint, New York: Cooper Square Press, 2001.

Fulton, Maurice Garland, ed. *Diary and Letters of Josiah Gregg*. 2 vols. Norman: University of Oklahoma Press, 1941, 1944.

General Taylor and His Staff: Comprising Memoirs of Generals Taylor, Worth, Wool, and Butler, Interspersed with Numerous Anecdotes of the Mexican War. New York: Leavitt, Trow and Co., 1848.

[Giddings, Luther]. *Sketches of the Campaign in Northern Mexico. In Eighteen Hundred Forty-Six and Seven. By an Officer of the First Regiment of Ohio Volunteers*. New York: George P. Putnam and Co., 1853.

Grant, Ulysses S. *Personal Memoirs of U.S. Grant*. 2 vols. New York: Charles L. Webster & Company, 1885.

Hay, Melba Porter, ed. *The Papers of Henry Clay*. 10 vols. Lexington: The University Press of Kentucky, 1959–92.

Hughes, Nathaniel Cheairs, Jr., and Timothy D. Johnson, eds. *A Fighter from Way Back: The Mexican War Diary of Lt. Daniel Harvey Hill, 4th Artillery, USA*. Kent and London: Kent State University Press, 2002.

Journals of Each Provincial Congress in Massachusetts in 1774 and 1775. Boston: n.p., 1838.

Kenly, John R. *Memoirs of a Maryland Volunteer*. Philadelphia: J.B. Lippincott and Co., 1873.

Lombard, Albert. *The "High Private," with a Full and Exciting History of the New York Volunteers*. New York: privately printed, 1848.

McCarty, William, ed. *National Songs, Ballads, and Other Patriotic Poetry, Chiefly Relating to the War of 1846*. Philadelphia: William McCarty, 1846.

"Mexican War Letters of Colonel William Bowen Campbell, of Tennessee, Written to Governor David Campbell, of Virginia, 1846." *Tennessee Historical Magazine* (June 1915): 134–36.

Nevins, Allan, ed. *Polk: The Diary of a President, 1845–1849.* London and New York: Longmans, Green, and Co., 1929.

Parker, Theodore. *A Sermon on the Mexican War, Preached at the Melodeon, on Sunday, June 25th, 1848.* Boston: Coolidge and Wiley, 1848.

Parker, Theodore. *A Sermon on War, Preached at the Melodeon, on Sunday, June 7, 1846.* Boston: I.R. Butts, 1846.

Peabody, Andrew. *The Triumphs of War: A Sermon Preached on the Day of the Annual Fast, April 15, 1847.* Portsmouth: John W. Foster, 1847.

Putnam, George. *God and Our Country: A Discourse Delivered in the First Congregational Church of Roxbury.* Boston: William Crosby and H.P. Nichols, 1847.

Robertson, John Blout. *Reminiscences of a Campaign in Mexico; by a Member of "the Bloody First."* Nashville: John York and Co., 1849.

Scott, Winfield. *Memoirs of Lieut.-General Scott, LL.D.* 2 vols. New York: Sheldon and Conway, 1864.

Semmes, Raphael. *Afloat and Ashore during the Mexican War.* Cincinnati: Wm. H. Moore & Co., 1851.

Simon, John Y., ed. *The Papers of Ulysses S. Grant.* 24 vols. to date. Carbondale and Edwardsville: Southern Illinois University Press, 1967–.

Sketches of the Campaign in Northern Mexico...By an Officer of the First Regiment of Ohio Volunteers. New York: George P. Putnam and Co., 1853.

Smith, George Winston, and Charles Judah, eds. *Chronicle of the Gringos: The U.S. Army in the Mexican War, 1846–1848.* Albuquerque: University of New Mexico Press, 1968.

Speech of Mr. Milton Brown, of Tenn., on the Causes of the Mexican War. n.p., n.d. At Tennessee State Library and Archives.

Statues at Large of the United States of America, 1789–1873. 17 vols. Washington, DC: 1850–73.

Taylor, Zachary. *Letters of Zachary Taylor, from the Battle-Fields of the Mexican War.* Rochester: The Genesee Press, 1908.

Tocqueville, Alexis de. *Democracy in America.* Translated by Arthur Goldhammer. New York: Penguin Books, 2004.

U.S. Congress. H.R. Exec. Doc. No. 60, 30th Cong., 1st sess. (1848).

U.S. Congress. *Journal of the House of Representatives.* 29th Congress.

NEWSPAPERS

Boston Daily Advertiser
Fayetteville Journal
Liberator
Lincoln County Journal
Nashville Republican Banner
Nashville Whig
National Intelligencer. Washington, DC
New Orleans Daily Picayune
New York Herald
New York Tribune
Presbyterian

Tri-Weekly Nashville Union
United States Magazine and Democratic Review. New York.
Washington Daily Union

SECONDARY SOURCES

Bauer, K. Jack. *The Mexican War, 1846–1848.* New York: Macmillan Publishing Co., Inc., 1974.

Bauer, K. Jack. *Zachary Taylor: Soldier, Planter, Statesman of the Old Southwest.* Baton Rouge and London: Louisiana State University Press, 1985.

Bergeron, Paul H. *The Presidency of James K. Polk.* Lawrence: University Press of Kansas, 1987.

Burns, James MacGregor. *Roosevelt: The Soldier of Freedom, 1940–1945.* New York: Harcourt Brace Jovanovich Inc., 1970.

Chaffin, Tom Chaffin. *Pathfinder: John C. Frémont and the Course of American Empire.* New York: Hill and Wang, 2002.

Clarke, Dwight L. *Stephen Watts Kearny: Soldier of the West.* Norman: University of Oklahoma Press, 1961.

Crackel, Theodore J. *Mr. Jefferson's Army: Political and Social Reform of the Military Establishment, 1801–1809.* New York and London: New York University Press, 1987.

Donald, David Herbert. *Lincoln.* New York: Simon and Schuster, 1995.

Eisenhower, John S.D. *Agent of Destiny: The Life and Times of Winfield Scott.* Norman: University of Oklahoma Press, 1997.

Ferrell, Robert H. *Harry S. Truman and the Modern American Presidency.* New York: HarperCollins Publishers, 1983.

Ferrell, Robert H. *Woodrow Wilson and World War I, 1917–1921.* New York: Harper and Row, Publishers, 1985.

Fleming, Thomas. *The New Dealers' War: F.D.R. and the War within World War II.* New York: Basic Books, 2001.

Foos, Paul. *A Short, Offhand, Killing Affair: Soldiers and Social Conflict during the Mexican War.* Chapel Hill: University of North Carolina Press, 2002.

Hietala, Thomas R. *Manifest Design: American Exceptionalism and Empire.* Revised Edition. Ithaca: Cornell University Press, 1985.

Horsman, Reginald. *Race and Manifest Destiny: The Origins of American Racial Anglo-Saxonism.* Cambridge: Harvard University Press, 1981.

Goodspeed's History of Tennessee from the Earliest Times to the Present. Originally published 1887; reprint, Greenville, SC: Southern Historical Press, 1978.

Graebner, Norman. *Empire on the Pacific: A Study in American Continental Expansion.* New York: The Ronald Press Company, 1955.

Groce, W. Todd, and Stephen V. Ash, eds.. *Nineteenth-Century America: Essays in Honor of Paul H. Bergeron.* Knoxville: University of Tennessee Press, 2005.

Higginbotham, Don, ed. *George Washington: Reconsidered.* Charlottesville and London: University of Virginia Press, 2001.

Holt, Michael F. *The Rise and Fall of the Whig Party: Jacksonian Politics and the Onset of the Civil War.* New York: Oxford University Press, 1999.

Johannsen, Robert W. *To the Halls of the Montezumas: The Mexican War in the American Imagination.* New York: Oxford University Press, 1985.

Johnson, Timothy D. *Winfield Scott: The Quest for Military Glory*. Lawrence: University Press of Kansas, 1998.

Kirk, Russell. *The Politics of Prudence*. Bryn Mawr, Penn.: Intercollegiate Studies Institute, 1993.

McCaffrey, James M. *Army of Manifest Destiny: The American Soldier in the Mexican War, 1846–1848*. New York and London: New York University Press, 1992.

McPherson, James M. *Battle Cry of Freedom: The Civil War Era*. New York: Oxford University Press, 1988.

Merk, Frederick. *Manifest Destiny and Mission in American History: A Reinterpretation*. New York: Alfred K. Knopf, 1963.

Meyer, Michael C., and William H. Beezley, eds. *The Oxford History of Mexico*. Oxford: Oxford University Press, 2000.

Middlekauff, Robert. *The Glorious Cause: The American Revolution, 1763-1789*. New York and Oxford: Oxford University Press, 1982.

Miller, Robert Ryal. *Shamrock and Sword: The Saint Patrick Battalion in the U.S.– Mexican War*. Norman: University of Oklahoma Press, 1989.

Morris, Edmund. *Theodore Rex*. New York: Random House, 2001.

Pinheiro, John C. "'Extending the Light and Blessings of Our Purer Faith': Anti-Catholic Sentiment among American Soldiers in the U.S.–Mexican War." *Journal of Popular Culture* (Fall 2001): 129–52.

Quimby, Robert S. *The U.S. Army in the War of 1812: An Operational and Command Study*. 2 vols. East Lansing: Michigan State University Press, 1997.

Remini, Robert V. *Andrew Jackson and the Bank War: A Study in the Growth of Presidential Power*. New York: W.W. Norton and Company, 1967.

Richmond, Douglas W., ed. *Essays on the Mexican War*. College Station: Texas A&M University Press, 1986.

Rowe, Mary Ellen. *Bulwark of the Republic: The American Militia in the Antebellum West*. Wesport: Praeger, 2003.

Royster, Charles. *A Revolutionary People at War*. Chapel Hill: University of North Carolina Press, 1979.

Schroeder, John H. *Mr. Polk's War: American Opposition and Dissent, 1846–1848*. Madison: University of Wisconsin Press, 1973.

Sellers, Charles. *The Market Revolution: Jacksonian America, 1815–1846*. New York: Oxford University Press, 1991.

Silbey, Joel H. *Martin Van Buren and the Emergence of American Popular Politics*. Lanham, Boulder, New York: Rowan & Littlefield Publishers, Inc., 2002.

Singletary, Otis A. *The Mexican War*. Chicago and London: The University of Chicago Press, 1960.

Skeen, C. Edward. *Citizen Soldiers in the War of 1812*. Lexington: University Press of Kentucky, 1999.

Smelser, Marshall. *The Democratic Republic, 1801–1815*. New York: Harper & Row, 1968.

Smith, Justin H. *The War with Mexico*. 2 vols. Gloucester: The Macmillan Company, 1919; reprint, The American Missionary Association, 1963.

Van Deusen, Glyndon G. *The Jacksonian Era, 1828–1848*. New York: Harper and Brothers, 1959.

Ward, John William. *Andrew Jackson: Symbol for an Age.* New York: Oxford University Press, 1953.

Watson, Harry L. *Liberty and Power: The Politics of Jacksonian America.* New York: The Noonday Press, 1990.

Weigley, Russell F. *History of the United States Army.* Bloomington: Indiana University Press, 1967.

Weinberg, Albert K. *Manifest Destiny: A Study of Nationalist Expansionism in American History.* Baltimore: The Johns Hopkins Press, 1935.

Wilentz, Sean. *The Rise of American Democracy: Jefferson to Lincoln.* New York and London: W.W. Norton & Company, 2005.

Williams, T. Harry. *Lincoln and His Generals.* New York: Vintage Books, 1952.

Winders, Richard Bruce. *Mr. Polk's Army: The American Military Experience in the Mexican War.* College Station: Texas A&M University Press, 1997.

Wood, Gordon S. *Revolutionary Characters: What Made the Founders Different.* New York: The Penguin Press, 2006.

Index

About the Author

JOHN C. PINHEIRO is Assistant Professor of History at Aquinas College in Grand Rapids, Michigan. Co-editor of Volume 12 of the Presidential Series of the *Papers of George Washington,* his articles on the Mexican War have appeared in the *Journal of the Early Republic,* the *Journal of Popular Culture,* and in the anthology, *Nineteenth-Century America* (2005).